A COMMENTARY ON THE

DOCTRINE

— AND —

COVENANTS

VOLUME THREE

Stephen E. Robinson
H. Dean Garrett

DESERET BOOK COMPANY
SALT LAKE CITY, UTAH

Library of Congress Cataloging-in-Publication Data

Robinson, Stephen Edward.
   A commentary on the Doctrine and Covenants / Stephen E. Robinson and H. Dean Garrett.
     p.   cm.
   Includes bibliographical references.
   ISBN 1-57345-784-1 (v. 1)
   ISBN 1-57345-851-1 (v. 2)
   ISBN 1-57345-852-X (v. 3)
   ISBN 1-57345-853-8 (v. 4)
   1. Doctrine and Covenants—Commentaries.   I. Garrett, H. Dean.
II. Title
   BX8628 .R65   2000
   289.3'2—dc21

                          00-040441

Printed in the United States of America   72076
Publishers Printing, Salt Lake City, Utah

10 9 8 7 6 5 4 3 2 1

CONTENTS

CONTENTS

DOCTRINE AND COVENANTS

81

BACKGROUND

Doctrine and Covenants 81 is the last of four revelations Joseph Smith mentioned receiving before 20 March 1832 and for which he gave no other background information.[1] The Kirtland Revelation Book records that Doctrine and Covenants 81 was received in Hiram, Ohio, on 15 March 1832.[2]

Originally, Doctrine and Covenants 81 was directed to a man named Jesse Gause, who had been selected and ordained a counselor in the Presidency of the High Priesthood on 8 March 1832.[3] Brother Gause left the Church before the end of the year, however, and was excommunicated 3 December 1832. He was replaced as a counselor to Joseph Smith by Frederick G. Williams after a revelation was received by the Prophet on 5 January 1833; that revelation is not included in the Doctrine and Covenants.[4] Formal organization of the First Presidency of the Church (as distinct from the Presidency of the High Priesthood) took place on 18 March 1833, a year after Doctrine and Covenants 81 was received.[5] For these reasons, when section 81 was first published in the 1835 Doctrine and Covenants, the name of the functioning counselor to Joseph Smith, Frederick G. Williams, was substituted for that of the departed Jesse Gause. This substitution created no difficulty, because the duties of a counselor to the Prophet and the promises and blessings contained in Doctrine and Covenants 81 applied as much to President Williams at that time as they had earlier to Jesse Gause.

COMMENTARY

1. Frederick G. Williams. Frederick G. Williams joined the Church after being taught by the Lamanite missionaries as they passed through Kirtland on their way to Missouri in the fall of 1830.[6] He volunteered to leave his family and travel with the missionaries to Missouri, and his 144-acre farm in Kirtland was given over to the use of the Church. Members of his family, Ezra Thayre, the Prophet's parents, and other Church members occupied it during his absence.[7] In the fall of 1832, Williams returned to Kirtland and was ordained a high priest. On 20 July 1832, he began serving as Joseph Smith's scribe. He became a member of the First Presidency before 8 March 1833 (see D&C 90:6), being formally ordained with Sidney Rigdon on 18 March 1833. Williams served as a member of the First Presidency until 1837.

The original recipient of this revelation, Jesse Gause, had been a member of the Shaker community in North Union, Ohio. He had arrived there with his family in October 1831, about seven months after Latter-day Saint missionaries visited that community (see D&C 49). He must have come into contact with the Church soon afterward, for he was called as a counselor to Joseph Smith on 8 March 1832, less than five months later, during which time he had been converted and baptized. His contact with the Church and subsequent conversion may have been delayed results of the mission to the Shakers.[8]

Gause was about twenty years older than Joseph Smith and ten years older than Sidney Rigdon. He accompanied the Prophet to Missouri in April and appears to have served faithfully until August 1832, when, on a mission with Zebedee Coltrin, he visited his estranged wife in a proselyting effort among the Shakers at North Union. For health reasons, Coltrin returned to Kirtland on

19 August; Gause, unable to reconcile with his wife, "continued east and walked right out of the history of the Church, never again to return."[9] Gause was excommunicated on 3 December 1832, for reasons unknown, although the *Far West Record* notes that he "denied the faith," and it is possible that his wife had something to do with the matter.[10]

1. A counselor unto my servant Joseph. The specific calling of Jesse Gause in 1832 was as a counselor to Joseph Smith in the Presidency of the High Priesthood (see v. 2). This calling is not exactly equivalent to being a counselor in the First Presidency of the Church, because the First Presidency as such was not organized until a year later, on 18 March 1833 (see D&C 90). The distinction between the two is small, if there is a functional difference at all, because the Presidency of the High Priesthood presided over the whole Church and not just over the high priests (see D&C 107:78–82, received 11 Nov. 1831).[11]

2. Unto whom. That is, unto Joseph Smith alone. The President of the Church himself is the only individual who exercises by right all the keys of the kingdom at one time. These keys are always extended through the President to his counselors in the presidency by virtue of their association with him in that quorum. When he dies, however, his counselors' authority to exercise those keys ends, and the presidency is dissolved. At the death of the President, the counselors in the First Presidency resume their places in the other quorums of the Church, and the President of the Quorum of the Twelve automatically becomes the presiding officer of the Church. Because the Twelve as a quorum hold all the keys collectively (see D&C 107:24), they also have the authority, collectively, to reorganize the First Presidency and designate the new President. He then becomes the only individual who exercises by right all the keys of the kingdom at one time, as stated in Doctrine and Covenants 132:7: "There is never but one on the earth at a time on whom this power and the keys of this priesthood are conferred."

2. Keys of the kingdom. Keys are the power to direct,

control, and authorize or forbid the exercise of priesthood power.[12] Any valid priesthood ordinance must be performed by one who holds the required priesthood, and it must be authorized by one who holds the keys of that particular work or ordinance. Where there are organized units of the Church, this is usually the presiding authority over that area, that is, the bishop or stake president. Thus, any priest in a ward has the authority to bless the sacrament or to baptize, but only the priests directed by the bishop of that ward (who holds the keys) may actually do so and then only in the prescribed manner, time, and place.

2. Presidency of the High Priesthood. The Presidency of the High Priesthood is a priesthood office. The First Presidency as we know it today was not organized for another year (18 March 1832). Today the prophet and his counselors in the First Presidency are simultaneously the Presidency of the Church (with all its members and auxiliaries) and also the Presidency of the High Priesthood.

3. I acknowledge him and will bless him. That is, the Prophet Joseph Smith.

3–5. And also thee, inasmuch as thou art faithful. Jesse Gause (or his successor in the Presidency, Frederick G. Williams) will be blessed to the extent that he is faithful in his subordinate position to the Prophet Joseph. His duties as a counselor to the Prophet and member of the presidency are enumerated. First, he is to be "faithful in counsel" (v. 3). The Lord, in his wisdom, provides leaders with counselors, not just to share the workload but to share insights, knowledge, and wisdom. In other words, even the prophet can benefit from the advice of others. Counselors are not to be "yes men," but neither are they to be inflexible when their president decides against their views. The Lord governs his kingdom by councils. One individual (in this case, the President of the High Priesthood) has the keys and authority to have the final word, but even the prophet is to consider the wisdom and inspiration of his counselors.

Second, he is to pray always (see v. 3). It is important for every leader to seek counsel from him whose kingdom this is. Therefore, faithful and wise leaders will always pray for inspiration and revelation in their policies and deliberations.

Third, he is to proclaim the gospel (see v. 3). Every calling in the Church has with it the responsibility of proclaiming the gospel in one way or another, and preaching and praying are the two activities that will do the most good upon this earth (see v. 4).

Fourth, he is to "succor the weak, lift up the hands which hang down, and strengthen the feeble knees" (v. 5). This duty has a dual application. First, the counselors in the First Presidency are to care for the poor, the weak, and the afflicted members of the Church by implementing the law of the gospel. Second, they are to assist the President in the event of his weakness or incapacity. President Harold B. Lee, when serving as counselor to the aging President Joseph Fielding Smith, gave this insight into his responsibility:

"As I thought of the role of President Tanner and myself as his counselors, I thought of a circumstance in the life of Moses. . . . As Moses sat upon a hill and raised the rod of his authority, or the keys of his priesthood, Israel prevailed over their enemies; but as the day wore on, his hands became heavy and began to droop at his side. And so [his counselors] held up his hands so they would not be weakened and the rod would not be lowered. He would be sustained so that the enemies of the church would not prevail over the saints of the Most High God. (See Exod. 17:8–12.)

"I think that is the role that President Tanner and I have to fulfill. The hands of President Smith may grow weary. They may tend to droop at times because of his heavy responsibilities; but as we uphold his hands, and as we lead under his directions, by his side, the gates of hell will not prevail against you and against Israel."[13]

7. Alpha and Omega. See Commentary on Doctrine and Covenants 19:1.

---

1. See Smith, *History of the Church,* 1:255; Background to D&C 78.
2. See Kirtland Revelation Book, 17.

3. See Kirtland Revelation Book, 10–11.
4. See Woodward, "Jesse Gause," 362–64; Cook, *Revelations of the Prophet Joseph Smith,* 172, 362.
5. See Smith, *History of the Church,* 1:334; see also Background to D&C 90; Commentary on 90:6.
6. See Background to D&C 32.
7. See Background to D&C 56.
8. See Background to D&C 49.
9. Woodward, "Jesse Gause," 364.
10. Cannon and Cook, *Far West Record,* 47–48.
11. See Cannon and Cook, *Far West Record,* 51.
12. See Commentary on D&C 65:2.
13. Lee, in Conference Report, Oct. 1970, 153.

BACKGROUND

O n 1 March 1832, Joseph Smith, Sidney Rigdon, and Newel K. Whitney had been commanded to travel to Independence, Missouri, to counsel with the Saints in Zion (see D&C 78:9). Over the next three weeks, the Prophet received several more revelations, began establishing the united firm in Kirtland, and organized the Presidency of the High Priesthood. As Joseph then prepared for the commanded journey to Missouri, several unpleasant events took place.

The Prophet mentioned a confrontation sometime in March with a son of John Johnson, in whose home he and Emma were then living with their adopted twins.[1] Olmsted Johnson, the young man, rejected the gospel and left home in a bad spirit, and Joseph prophesied that "he would never return or see his father again."[2] Another of the Johnson sons, John Jr., had already apostatized, so it seems that the Johnsons were experiencing domestic troubles at this time.

By the fourth week of March, the Smiths' adopted ten-month-old twins and the Rigdon children who lived nearby were suffering from measles. On 24 March, Joseph stayed up with the little boy, who was the sicker of the two babies, to let Emma get some much-needed sleep. During the night, a mob led by the apostate Symonds Ryder dragged Joseph Smith and Sidney Rigdon from their homes and beat, tarred, feathered, and otherwise abused them.[3] After the attack, Joseph was awake all night while friends and relatives scraped the tar from his body. Nonetheless, in the morning he preached his usual Sunday sermon to a congregation that included some of his attackers.

The following Thursday, 29 March, Emma and Joseph's baby son died, possibly on account of the additional stress and exposure caused by the mobbing. Three days later, on Sunday, 1 April, Joseph Smith, Sidney Rigdon, and Newel K. Whitney began their journey to Missouri in obedience to the commandment of the Lord. With them went Jesse Gause, the newly appointed counselor in the Presidency of the High Priesthood.

Joseph and his party arrived in Independence on 24 April 1832, and, according to his own account, "on the 26th, I called a general council of the Church, and was acknowledged as the President of the High Priesthood, according to a previous ordination at a conference of High Priests, Elders and members, held at Amherst, Ohio, on the 25th of January, 1832. The right hand of fellowship was given to me by the Bishop, Edward Partridge, in behalf of the Church. The scene was solemn, impressive and delightful. During the intermission, a difficulty or hardness which had existed between Bishop Partridge and Elder Rigdon, was amicably settled, and when we came together in the afternoon, all hearts seemed to rejoice and I received the following [D&C 82]."[4]

The minutes of this Missouri conference, during which Doctrine and Covenants 82 was received, indicate that "Br. Sidney Rigdon then stated the items embraced in a Revelation received in Ohio [D&C 78] & the reason why we were commanded to come to this land & sit in council with the High priests here." In the afternoon session, it was recorded, "all differences [had been] settled & the hearts of all run together in love. A Revelation [was] received through him whom the Church has appointed respecting organization."[5] This revelation was section 82, which was first published in the 1835 Doctrine and Covenants.[6]

COMMENTARY

1. You have forgiven one another your trespasses. This statement refers to the hard feelings between Bishop Edward Partridge and Sidney Rigdon, mentioned in Joseph Smith's account and the minutes of the meeting. Others had been drawn to take sides in the affair. Apparently, Sidney had previously made a lengthy complaint against Bishop Partridge for a number of infractions, among them improper distribution of funds, failure to follow Church policy, and speaking against Joseph Smith. On 10 March, a conference of elders in Missouri considered the complaint and replied to Elder Rigdon that most of the infractions had already been corrected and that Bishop Partridge was repentant for any wrongdoing. This conference of Missouri brethren also chided Sidney about "whether he was not actuated by his own hasty feelings rather than the Spirit of Christ" in pursuing the matter.[7] In addition, there seem to have been hard feelings by some brethren in Missouri against the Prophet himself, a matter which the Lord would mention again in the future (see D&C 84:76).[8]

These personal tensions between the brethren of Zion and the brethren of Kirtland were resolved amicably between the morning and afternoon sessions of the Missouri conference, at least for the time being. Once hard feelings had been dispelled and the spirit of love and harmony restored, the Lord blessed the conference in the afternoon session with the revelation known as Doctrine and Covenants 82. It is worthy of note that *first* the Saints forgave one another; *then* the Lord forgave and blessed them. Moreover, the spirit of revelation operates best when the Saints are united.

2. All of you have sinned. One of the basic claims of the Christian gospel is that all human beings past the age of accountability, except Jesus Christ alone, are sinners (see D&C 82:6; Romans 3:10, 23; 1 Nephi 10:6; Mosiah 2:21). The range of human behaviors rightly described by the term *sin* is so broad, however, that misunderstandings are common when the scriptures use this term. For example, all human beings have committed at least one sin, and therefore all human beings (except Jesus Christ and children under eight years of age) are sinners in some degree. It follows, then, that the terms *sin* and *sinner* can refer in this sense even to the most faithful Saint, on the one hand, or to the vilest child of hell, on the other.

All human beings sin, but not all love to sin. All human beings sin, but some commit sins of omission or of momentary weakness, whereas others commit sins of open rebellion and opposition to God. Therefore, the terms *sin* and *sinner* must always be understood in their proper context in order to differentiate between the meaning of *imperfect* at one end of the spectrum (see D&C 82:2, 6; Romans 3:23) and *wilfully wicked* at the other (see D&C 82:7; 1 John 3:8–9).

3. Unto whom much is given much is required. When human beings sin, the degree of their guilt, or culpability, depends upon the extent of their knowledge and blessings. Two different persons may commit exactly the same sin and yet be held accountable in vastly different degrees, depending on their individual knowledge and background. Elder George Albert Smith declared: "We will not be judged as our brothers and sisters of the world are judged, but according to the greater opportunities placed in our keeping. We will be among those who have received the word of the Lord, who have heard His sayings, and if we do them it will be to us eternal life, but if we fail condemnation will result."[9]

Moreover, for those who have accepted the fulness of the gospel by covenant, it is not that the Lord *expects* much of us but that he *requires* it. Having been given the means of obtaining exaltation, we are required to use those means toward that end. Once blessed by God's gracious gifts and obligated by our own covenant promises, should we then choose wickedness or sloth, we do so to our own greater condemnation.

5. Darkness reigneth. The ruler of this world—not of the earth, but of Babylon, the world—is Satan.[10] The ruler of the *next* world, the millennial world, and of its heirs who must for now live in Babylon, is Christ. As we approach the end of this world, Satan's power is growing and spreading. Even as the Saints watch and wait for the end of this world and the coming of the next, they will see darkness grow, and they themselves will become more isolated, marginalized, and persecuted until the coming of their Savior.

6. None doeth good. The whole world lies in the ignorance resulting from apostasy, and all have gone astray from the full truth of the gospel, hence the need for Joseph Smith and the Restoration.[11]

7. Will not lay any sin to your charge. See Romans 4:8. Because all humans sin in some degree and "none doeth good [perfectly]" (v. 6), being found innocent at the Judgment cannot lie in our perfect performance (that is, salvation by law or by works; see 2 Nephi 2:5) but rather in our sins not being charged against us on that day (that is, salvation through grace; see D&C 20:30; 2 Nephi 2:6–8; 3 Nephi 27:16). That is the great gift of the Atonement and the fruit of faithful repentance, which belong to those who make and keep the gospel covenant. As we reject Satan and commit ourselves to the lordship of Christ and to righteousness, our sins and mistakes past, present, and forevermore are not charged against us, having been remitted through the atoning blood, suffering, and death of Jesus Christ.[12] Thus, "all that we could do," Ammon says, is *"to repent sufficiently before God that he would take away our stain"* (Alma 24:11; emphasis added; see also 2 Nephi 25:23). We bring faith and repentance to the covenant union; our Savior provides the innocence and perfect righteousness we seek.

7. Sin no more. Considered by itself (without the law of mercy), the law of justice requires perfect performance. In addition, a Christlike moral perfection is our ultimate and eternal goal. Yet this kind of perfection is not possible in our present fallen and mortal state. On a practical level, total perfection in all things is simply beyond us right now, so in the meantime the law of mercy allows us to repent, to be forgiven, and to be declared innocent even when we are not perfectly obedient. Thus, "sin no more" can mean "become morally perfect" as an eternal goal, but it can also mean "cease to serve Satan and seek to serve Christ" while we are here in mortality. Both are correct goals, but only the latter is achievable in this life. That is one reason why Christ is the only way to salvation for mortals.[13]

7. Unto that soul who sinneth shall the former sins return. When those who have sinned repent and are baptized, or, if already baptized, repent and renew their covenants by partaking of the sacrament, then their sins are forgiven them through the atonement of Christ. Even though a particular sin through weakness or other circumstances may recur, it is forgiven again upon further repentance. In the context of the gospel covenant, the Lord will continue to forgive and cleanse us as long as we sincerely repent (see Mosiah 26:30). The Atonement is a shield from all our guilt as long as we continue to repent and remain in the covenant.[14]

Nevertheless, should we choose to break the covenant and refuse to repent, should we shift our loyalty and commitment from Christ to our sins, then the atonement of Christ can no longer shield us, and we become once again accountable for *all* our own sins. In the context of this verse, *sinneth* does not mean failing to be perfect; rather, it means to switch our loyalties, to break our covenants with Christ by choosing to serve sin (and, therefore, to serve Satan; see Romans 6:16). Doctrine and Covenants 82:7 must be understood against the backdrop of Mosiah 26:30: "Yea, and as often as my people repent will I forgive them their trespasses against me." Faithful Saints need not fear that their occasional weaknesses will put them outside the covenant and the power of the Atonement. On the other hand, those whose loyalty is to their sins first and to Christ second, third, or not at all, need not expect to be shielded from justice in any degree for all they may have done in this life. If we sin, we must repent. If we sin often, we must repent often. But we must never let go of the rod, never shift our commitment from Christ to our sins. Finally, should we repudiate our covenants, thus losing the shield of the Atonement, not only will our former sins return but they will bring with them a disposition to evil even greater than before (see Matthew 12:43–45).[15]

8. A new commandment. The new commandment (see vv. 12–13, 15) is specifically to organize the united order (or united firm) and a bishops' storehouse in Independence, Missouri, as well as in Kirtland, Ohio. Although the term *united order* is the more familiar term and is also the term by which the order is known in the Doctrine and Covenants, many contemporary historical sources use the term *united firm* for the same entity. Both terms mean the same thing.

9. I give unto you directions. We sometimes view God's commandments as restrictive and demanding. Yet in verses 8 and 9 God reminds us that his commandments are actually informative and enabling. Whatever God commands is aimed at bringing us greater freedom, joy, and glory (see Moses 1:39). His commandments are like the directions on a treasure map— instructions and directions for getting to the celestial kingdom.

10. I, the Lord, am bound. How can an infinite and omnipotent God be bound by anything? We certainly do not bind God; it is arrogance even to think we could. God may be bound but only by himself, by his own choice, by his own word, and by his own promises. We bind ourselves to truths, which God honors. All covenants, including gospel covenants, are binding on both parties. And though humans sometimes break their promises and violate their covenants, God never does. This truth is an indication of his power, not of his weakness.

11. To be bound together by a bond and covenant. The members of the united order will be bound by covenant to each other in a business partnership. This covenant partnership included only the leaders in Kirtland and Zion and was called the united firm, or united order, or the order of Enoch.[16]

11. That cannot be broken by transgression, except . . . Of course this covenant can be broken, but it cannot be broken without immediate and painful consequences.

13. I have consecrated Kirtland . . . for a stake to Zion. It was important for the Saints to keep the proper perspective. Zion was the center place, and Missouri, therefore, was to increase and be enlarged (v. 14). But God had consecrated Kirtland for a holy purpose (construction of the Kirtland Temple) and to be a support in other ways (hence, a tent-*stake* to Zion, Zion being the center post). The metaphor of the "stakes of Zion" portray Zion as a large tent, like the portable tabernacle of God that traveled with Moses and the children of Israel in the wilderness. This holy structure was pitched in the center of the camp of Israel, and like most tents it was supported by ropes, or cords, attached to many stakes driven into the ground outside the tent itself (see, for example, Isaiah 54:2). In the modern Church, the units called stakes support the central goal of Zion, which endowed members of the Church are bound by covenant to establish and to build up.

14. For Zion must increase. On the one hand, the establishment of a physical Zion in Missouri was ultimately the goal of the Church and its members. Kirtland was important and had its purposes, but its importance was temporary. Building a physical Zion with its center in Independence, Missouri, was the immediate goal of the Saints. On the other hand, the spiritual Zion, which consists of the pure in heart wherever they may dwell, must also increase. The increase in numbers of Church members who are pure in heart enlarges the borders of spiritual Zion, regardless of where the members may live. The several metaphors here depict Zion or Jerusalem as a bride being adorned for her marriage to the coming Bridegroom (see Isaiah 62:4–5; Matthew 25:6; John 3:29; Revelation 19:7–9).

14. Her borders must be enlarged. Significantly, this verse recalls the closing words of Moroni in the Book of Mormon (see Moroni 10:31). Moroni may, in turn, have been citing Isaiah (see 52:2); if so, his text is different from that of the King James Version, and Doctrine and Covenants 82:14 more closely follows Moroni's wording.

14. Zion must arise and put on her beautiful garments. In

14

the Book of Mormon (see Moroni 10:30–33), these activities are equated with coming to Christ and making and keeping the gospel covenants in order that God might bless and adorn Zion (that is, Jerusalem, both old and new). This understanding is supported by the Prophet's interpretation of Isaiah 52:1, found in Doctrine and Covenants 113:7–8, in which "put[ting] on her strength" is equated with receiving again the priesthood that Zion had lost. Again, the metaphor depicts Zion as a bride putting on her wedding adornments.

15. Bind yourselves by this covenant. Although the law of consecration is a law for the whole Church, this specific application of it was only for those Church leaders who, acting as a business corporation, were called to consecrate their property in the united order to establish a bishops' storehouse and to meet other financial needs.[17] The same principle of consecration that applies to members individually was applied to the united order collectively.[18]

17. You are to be equal. A similar injunction for equality was issued to the members of the Church's other consecrated order, the literary firm (see D&C 70:14).[19]

18. For the benefit of the church. The popular wisdom of the world is that competitive self-interest is the only consistently successful motivation for personal or professional achievement. That may often seem true in a society where celestial, terrestrial, and telestial beings mingle, with the latter two classes predominating, but it is clearly false in a Zion society. Truly celestial individuals can be consistently motivated to achieve and to excel by the needs of others and by love for God and his Church. Countless individuals in the Church today magnify their callings as nursery leaders, Scoutmasters, teachers, Young Women and Young Men presidencies, bishoprics, and general authorities for exactly these unselfish reasons. Thousands upon thousands of the Saints have consecrated their time, talents, and financial resources not for their own benefit but "for the benefit of the church," and they will continue to do so forever in the glorious celestial kingdom of God.

18. Improve upon his talent. This phrase is an allusion to the parable of the talents, in which those who increased in wealth did so not for their own enrichment but for their Master (see Matthew 25:14–30).

19. Every man seeking the interest of his neighbor. In a Zion society every person is concerned about the interests and well-being of his or her neighbors. The success and the happiness of our brothers and sisters in Zion is at least as important to us as our own. President Spencer W. Kimball taught: "First, we must eliminate the individual tendency to selfishness. . . . Second, we must cooperate completely and work in harmony one with the other. . . . Third, we must lay on the altar and sacrifice whatever is required by the Lord."[20]

19. With an eye single. See Commentary on Doctrine and Covenants 4:5.

20. An everlasting order . . . inasmuch as you sin not. The united firm (united order) was disbanded two years later, on 23 April 1834, due to the transgressions of some of its members (see D&C 104:52–53).

21. The soul that sins against this covenant. He who violates his agreement as a member of the united order.

21. According to the laws of my church. The laws of the Church are stated in Doctrine and Covenants 42 and deal with denying fellowship, excommunication, and, in some cases, turning offenders over to civil authorities.

21. The buffetings of Satan. See Commentary on Doctrine and Covenants 78:12.

22. Make . . . friends with the mammon of unrighteousness. According to Elder Joseph Fielding Smith: "It is not intended that in making friends of the 'mammon of unrighteousness' [Luke 16:9] that the brethren were to partake with them in their sins; to receive them to their bosoms, intermarry with them and otherwise come down to their level. They were to so live that peace with their enemies might be assured. They were to treat them kindly, be friendly with them as far as correct and virtuous principles would permit, but never to swear with them or drink and carouse with them. If they could allay prejudice and show a willingness to trade with and show a kindly spirit, it might help to turn them away from their bitterness. Judgment was to be left with the Lord."[21]

Moreover, a righteous individual can learn how wealth and the world operate and then work with the system for righteous purposes. When that is sincerely the motive, such action is not collaboration with Babylon but a way of building Zion.

24. The kingdom is yours. Once again we learn that the faithful possess the kingdom of God even now, and they will possess it as long as they endure. It is theirs to keep, or theirs to throw away—but it is already theirs.

1. See Commentary on D&C 52:3.
2. Smith, *History of the Church*, 1:260.
3. Smith, *History of the Church*, 1:261–65.
4. Smith, *History of the Church*, 1:267.
5. Cannon and Cook, *Far West Record*, 45.
6. For a discussion of unusual names once associated with this revelation, see Commentary on D&C 78:1.
7. Cannon and Cook, *Far West Record*, 40–42, 45.
8. See Jessee, *Personal Writings*, 270–74.
9. Smith, in Conference Report, Oct. 1906, 47.
10. See Commentary on D&C 1:13, 16; 19:3.
11. See Commentary on D&C 82:2; 35:12.
12. See Commentary on D&C 82:2; 35:12.
13. See Commentary on D&C 82:2.
14. See Commentary on D&C 82:2.
15. See Ballard, *New Era*, May 1991, 50.
16. See Background to D&C 78 and Commentary on D&C 78:4–9.
17. See Background to D&C 78.
18. See Commentary on D&C 82:8, 11.
19. See Commentary on D&C 51:3; 70:14; 78:5–7.
20. Kimball, in Conference Report, Apr. 1978, 123.
21. Smith, *Church History and Modern Revelation*, 1:323.

DOCTRINE AND COVENANTS

83

BACKGROUND

After traveling from Ohio to Independence, Missouri, in April 1832, Joseph Smith and his companions remained in Missouri for two weeks, conducting Church business and "sitting in council with the Saints," according to the commandment they had received in Doctrine and Covenants 78:9. Joseph arrived in Independence on 24 April. He held conference on 26 April, and, after reconciling some hard feelings between the Missouri and Ohio brethren, received Doctrine and Covenants 82. The conference continued on 27 April, and Joseph noted that the Saints in Missouri "were settling among a ferocious set of mobbers, like lambs among wolves."[1]

Joseph then visited the Colesville Saints in Kaw Township, west of Independence, on 28 and 29 April and returned to Independence the following day for meetings of the literary firm and the newly organized united order (united firm). At this meeting of the literary firm, it was agreed to print only three thousand copies of the Book of Commandments rather than the ten thousand originally planned.[2] A subsequent meeting of the united order appointed Sidney Gilbert and Newel K. Whitney as agents for the two branches of that order in Missouri and Ohio, respectively. It was also agreed that the united order should take out a loan for fifteen thousand dollars, probably for startup costs for the bishops' storehouses.[3]

Sometime on 30 April 1832 (perhaps in connection with the meeting of the literary firm or united firm, although their minutes do not mention it), Joseph received Doctrine and Covenants 83. He recorded the event as follows: "On the 30th [of April], I returned to Independence, and again sat in council with the brethren, and received the following: [D&C 83]."[4]

COMMENTARY

1. In addition to the laws of the church. The revelation recorded in Doctrine and Covenants 83 was an addendum to the law of the Church on matters found in Doctrine and Covenants 42:30–34, which discussed the rights and obligations of stewards but did not address the rights of dependents, particularly if the steward died.

2. Women have claim on their husbands. The primary responsibility for the support of married women in the Church lies not with the Church but with their husbands. In the context of the law of consecration, faithful wives have the right to claim support from their husbands as part of their covenant relationship. This was a very liberal idea in frontier America in the nineteenth century. President Ezra Taft Benson declared: "This is the divine right of a wife and mother. She cares for and nourishes her children at home. Her husband earns the living for the family, which makes this nourishing possible. With that claim on their husbands for their financial support, the counsel of the Church has always been for mothers to spend their full time in the home in rearing and caring for their children."[5]

Certainly there are exceptions to this policy in practice. Not every female Church member has a husband; not every married sister has a worthy husband; some sisters have husbands who are disabled or otherwise unable to work. Financial realities may be different from the ideal, and in such cases adjustments can be made in righteousness. Nonetheless, the general policy remains, and it applies to the vast majority of cases: the husband bears primary responsibility for the support of his wife and family as long as he lives (see 1 Timothy 5:8).

3. And if they are not faithful. Some might claim that an unfaithful widow has no right to the Lord's resources entrusted to her faithful husband, but the Church is not to turn an unfaithful widow out of her home. Such a widow might be refused fellowship according to the same law of the Church that applies to all members, but faithful or unfaithful, a widow is to retain possession of her husband's legally deeded stewardships.

3. According to the laws of the land. Most states and countries have laws governing inheritance and the rights of surviving dependents. In all cases, the policy and practice of the Church are to be in harmony with civil statutes.

4. All children have claim upon their parents. The primary responsibility for the support of dependent children lies with the parents. In the rearing and support of children, the wife shares responsibility with her husband. Just as the wife has claim upon her husband for her maintenance (see v. 2), so also children have claim upon their parents until they are of age.

5. After that. After children become of age.

5. They have claim upon the church. The context of this revelation is families living under the law of consecration. When children of such families are of an age to support themselves and start families of their own, they may receive a portion of their parents' stewardship to start out but only if the parents' resources are great enough to be divided. If the stewardship of the parents cannot sustain such division, the Church is to provide stewardships, or inheritances, for the new family out of the resources of the bishops' storehouse.

6. The storehouse shall be kept by the consecrations of the church. The resources from which the bishops' storehouse will operate will come from the united order and from the surpluses of all the stewards in the Church who are also living under the law of consecration (even though they might not be members of the united order).

6. Widows and orphans. All faithful widows, orphans, and poor persons in the Church without other means of support have a claim upon the bishops' storehouse, and even unfaithful widows retain possession of their deceased husband's stewardships (v. 3). The poor who are unfaithful to their covenants have no claim upon the resources of the Church, beyond the simple necessity of saving their lives, if it comes to that (see Mosiah 4:16). The Church has no obligation for continuing, daily support of those who do not keep the faith.

According to President Joseph F. Smith: "It is intended that the widows shall be looked after when they are in need, and that the fatherless and the orphans shall be provided for from the funds of the Church; that they shall be clothed and fed, and shall have opportunity for education, the same as other children who have parents to look after them. When a child is fatherless and motherless the Church becomes the parent of that child, and it is obligatory upon the Church to take care of it, and to see that it has opportunities equal with the other children in the Church. This is a great responsibility. Have we ever seen the day since the Church was organized when we could carry out this purpose of the Lord fully, and to our heart's content? We have not, because we never have had the means to do it with. But if men will obey the laws of God so that there shall be abundance in the storehouse of the Lord, we will have wherewith to feed and clothe the poor and the orphan and to look after those who are in need in the Church."[6]

---

1. Smith, *History of the Church,* 1:269.
2. See Cannon and Cook, *Far West Record,* 46; see also Background to D&C 1.
3. See Smith, *History of the Church,* 1:270; Cannon and Cook, *Far West Record,* 47–48.
4. Smith, *History of the Church,* 1:269.
5. Benson, *Teachings of Ezra Taft Benson,* 547.
6. Smith, in Conference Report, Oct. 1899, 39–40.

DOCTRINE AND COVENANTS
84

BACKGROUND

After spending two weeks in Missouri "sitting in council with the Saints," organizing the Missouri branch of the united firm,[1] and providing for the establishment of bishops' storehouses in Independence and Kirtland as commanded by the Lord, Joseph Smith and his companions, except for Jesse Gause (who remained in Missouri at least until June), returned to Ohio. On the return journey, Bishop Newel K. Whitney's leg and foot were broken in a coach accident, and Joseph stayed with him in Greenville, Indiana, until the bishop could travel. After staying at an inn for nearly a month, Joseph was poisoned one night at dinner but recovered through a priesthood blessing. He and Bishop Whitney left the inn promptly the following day, arriving in Kirtland in late June. They had been away from their families for almost three months.[2]

In September 1832, the Prophet moved from the Johnson home in Hiram, Ohio, into quarters above Bishop Whitney's store in Kirtland, with a kitchen downstairs. During the time Joseph had been in Missouri, Emma, pregnant again and still grieving for the death of her adopted son, Joseph, had been required to live with three different families in Kirtland under cramped and difficult circumstances.[3]

During 1832 certain difficulties involving Sidney Rigdon

began. Sidney had suffered from depression from time to time but for the most part had been able to keep it under control. During the mobbing of 24 March 1832, Sidney was also dragged by his heels along the ground, so that his head suffered severe blows. Following this physical abuse, in addition to his emotional trauma, his depression apparently worsened. After returning to Kirtland from Missouri, Sidney claimed on 5 July 1832 to have had a revelation and "was telling the people that the kingdom was rent from them, and they might as well all go home for they were rejected."[4] Reportedly, he also bemoaned that "it was useless to pray or do anything."[5] His emotional distress is particularly apparent in this last statement.

In response to Sidney's claims, Joseph went immediately from Hiram to Kirtland and relieved Sidney of his priesthood calling and of his license to preach, but three weeks later a repentant Sidney Rigdon was reinstated in the Presidency of the High Priesthood. Joseph Smith, ever kindhearted, explained these events in a letter to W. W. Phelps: "When Brother Sidney learned the feelings of the Brethren [in Missouri] in whom he had placed so much confidence, for whom he had endured so much fatigue and suffering, and whom he loved with so much love, his heart was grieved, his spirits failed, and for a moment he became frantic, and the adversary taking the advantage, he spake unadvisedly with his lips. . . . [B]ut [he] has since repented like Peter of old, and after a little suffering by the buffeting of Satan, has been restored to his high standing in the church of God."[6] Nevertheless, President Rigdon was never quite the same man after the mobbing and beating in March 1832 and the difficult journey to Missouri immediately thereafter.[7] Sidney had already moved from Hiram, so when Joseph returned with Bishop Whitney in late June, he spent the rest of that summer in Hiram working on the Joseph Smith Translation of the Bible with Frederick G. Williams as scribe rather than Sidney. In August 1832, Joseph received Doctrine and Covenants 99 at Hiram.[8]

Several months before, in January 1832, the Lord had called

at least twenty-four elders on missions, mostly to the eastern states (D&C 75). By September 1832, these missionaries began returning to Ohio with accounts of their many successes. Joseph Smith, by then relocated in Kirtland, recorded this joyful news as follows: "The Elders during the month of September began to return from their missions to the Eastern States, and present the histories of their several stewardships in the Lord's vineyard; and while together in these seasons of joy, I inquired of the Lord, and received on the 22nd and 23rd of September, the following revelation on Priesthood [D&C 84]."⁹

COMMENTARY

1. And six elders. Joseph Smith indicated that Doctrine and Covenants 84 was received over a two-day period. There is good evidence that verses 1–41 were received on 22 September and verses 42–120 on 23 September. The two earliest manuscripts of Doctrine and Covenants 84, both in the handwriting of Frederick G. Williams, who was serving as the Prophet's scribe at that time, agree that six elders were present to receive verse 1 and following verses (presumably on 22 September). Both manuscripts note that verse 42 and following verses were received by ten elders on 23 September.¹⁰

2. His church. This verse explains a dual purpose for establishing the Church in the last days. First, the Church was established to restore the house of Israel, the chosen people of the Lord. This will be done by searching out both the literal descendants of Israel and those who will be adopted into the house of Israel from among the Gentiles, teaching and baptizing them, thereby restoring or adopting them into the covenant. Second, the Church has been organized to gather the Saints of God to establish Zion in preparation for the second coming of Christ. The establishment of Zion refers to both the spiritual Zion, which exists wherever the pure in heart dwell (see D&C 97:21), and also the physical Zion, which is the New Jerusalem, whose center will be at Independence, Missouri.

2. Mount Zion. "Mount Zion" is synonymous with Jerusalem or, more specifically, with the Temple Mount in Jerusalem. However, in scripture, the term sometimes refers to Old Jerusalem (see Psalm 78:68–69; Isaiah 10:12), but more usually to New Jerusalem, the Zion to be built upon the American continent (see for example, Isaiah 24:23; Obadiah 1:21; Micah 4:7; Articles of Faith 1:10). Mount Zion is the dwelling place of God (see Isaiah 4:5), and thus the term refers specifically to the temple and by extension to the land and society centered around the temple, which have become sanctified like the temple itself.[11]

The Mount Zion referred to here is the New Jerusalem which, by the time this revelation was received, the Saints had been commanded to build in Independence, Missouri (se D&C 57:1–3). Joseph Smith once observed: "I shall say with brevity, that there is a New Jerusalem to be established on this continent, and also Jerusalem shall be rebuilt on the eastern continent."[12]

3. Beginning at the temple lot. The temple lot is described in Doctrine and Covenants 57:3, and it had been dedicated a year earlier, on 3 August 1831. When the enemies of the Church prevented the establishment of Zion and the construction of its temple in Jackson County, this commandment was revoked (see D&C 124:49–51). Nonetheless, Zion will be built, and it will be built beginning with the construction of a temple in Independence, Missouri. It seems likely, but may not be necessary (given D&C 124:49–51), that this temple will be constructed on the lot dedicated for that purpose by the Prophet Joseph Smith (see Background to D&C 58; Commentary on D&C 58:1, 57). This property is now owned by the Church of Christ, Temple Lot; this group is commonly known as the Hedrickites, after an early leader, Granville Hedrick.

3. By the hand of Joseph Smith. Likely another occurrence of the biblical idiom described in the commentary on verse 12.[13]

3. The Lord was well pleased. Note the past tense. Although the individuals who dedicated the location of Zion and its temple were approved of the Lord when they performed that labor, Ezra Booth had since left the Church and some others had weakened in their commitment by the time Doctrine and Covenants 84 was received.

4. Built by the gathering of the saints. The purpose for gathering to Independence, Missouri, both in the past and in the future, is to build the city and temple of God and establish the center place of Zion. In the future gathering for this purpose, however, it will not be necessary to call all the Saints to Missouri, for "My cities . . . shall yet be spread abroad" (Zechariah 1:17; see also D&C 97:18). Those who are called to build up the center place of Zion will be called by the priesthood leaders of the Church at that time and will labor under their direction, but there will not be a worldwide gathering of all the Saints to Missouri, for Missouri could not hold them all. Elder Bruce R. McConkie taught: "The place of gathering for the Mexican Saints is in Mexico . . . and so it goes throughout the length and breadth of the whole earth. Japan is for the Japanese; Korea is for the Koreans; Australia is for the Australians; every nation is the gathering place for its own people."[14]

4. Which temple shall be reared in this generation. For "generation," see Commentary on Doctrine and Covenants 45:21. This passage can be understood to constitute a *commandment* rather than a *prophecy*, as indicated in Doctrine and Covenants 124:51. Even though the Lord said, "Thou shalt not commit adultery," it does not make God incorrect every time someone commits this sin, because that statement also is a commandment rather than a prophecy. When God says "thou shalt," and then we fail to obey, the contradiction is to the commandment, not to the omniscience of God (see D&C 124:49–51). In the case of the temple in Zion, the failure to obey the commandment to build a temple in Zion appears to be due in part to the opposition of enemies as well as to collective unfaithfulness of the Saints (see D&C 101:2, 6–8; 124:49–51).

5. For verily, this generation shall not pass away. If any part of verses 3–5 were to be understood prophetically, it would be this verse, which does not specify the location of the temple being described here. One way or another, at Independence or somewhere else, a temple for receiving God's choicest blessings was going to be built by that generation of Saints. The temples in Nauvoo, St. George, Manti, Logan, and Salt Lake—and perhaps others, depending on the definition of *generation*—would all fulfill the specifics of verse 5, if it were understood as a prophecy.[15] On the other hand, if verse 5, like verse 4, is understood as a commandment rather than a prophecy, then the commentary on verse 4 also applies to verse 5. Either way, neither the Lord nor his prophet misstated himself.

5. A cloud shall rest upon it. This description in this passage is reminiscent of Old Testament references to the Lord's house (see, for example, 1 Kings 8:10–11; 2 Chronicles 5:13–14), particularly to the tabernacle in the wilderness when the glory of the Lord descended in a pillar of cloud by day and fire by night and filled the tabernacle. "The Lord manifested Himself in ancient Israel in a cloud, shaped as a pillar, which became luminous at night. It guided the people on the journey to Canaan. It stood at the entrance to the Sanctuary, and in it God spoke to Moses. It rested on the Sanctuary and filled it, when that sacred tent was set up. It was the visible sign of God's guiding and protecting care over his people. This glory of the Lord is known as the *Shekinah*. When the first temple was dedicated, it filled the house (II. Chron. 7:1–3), and the people bowed down and worshiped. The *Shekinah* departed when the Temple was profaned (Ez. 10:19; 11:22), but Ezekiel, in his vision of the Temple in the latter days, saw the glory of the Lord returning (Ez. 43:2–3). The presence of the Lord will be manifested in this Temple of the Latter-day Zion."[16]

6. Sons of Moses. The biblical idiom "son of" or "children of" can mean either biological offspring or someone who is in a certain category or belongs to a certain group (see, for example, Luke 5:34; Ephesians 2:3). In this passage, the phrase "according to the

Holy Priesthood" makes it clear that these are Moses' sons in the latter sense. As in Doctrine and Covenants 84, the "sons of Moses" here are all those who, like Moses, receive the Melchizedek Priesthood. The subject of "the sons of Moses" is followed by a long, extremely important parenthetical explanation of how the two priesthoods, the Melchizedek and the Aaronic, came to be held by Moses and Aaron. The Lord returns to the subject of "the sons of Moses" once again in verse 31.

6. His father-in-law, Jethro. When Moses fled alone from Egypt, he traveled to the land of Midian, where he married Zipporah, the daughter of Jethro the Midianite (see Exodus 2:15–4:20). The Midianites, who lived in the western part of what is now Saudi Arabia, were descendants of Abraham by his wife Keturah and were therefore distant cousins of the Israelites. From his Midianite in-laws, Moses learned the gospel and received the Melchizedek Priesthood, which had been passed down among the Midianites from the time of Abraham to Jethro through the lineage indicated in verses 6 through 14. The priesthood lineage of Jethro (and Moses) back to Adam is traced in verses 14 through 17.

12. Esaias received it under the hand of God. The prophet Esaias is someone other than the prophet Isaiah, although Isaiah's name is uniformly rendered Esaias in the King James Version of the New Testament. The prophet referred to here and in Doctrine and Covenants 76:100 lived in the days of Abraham and is otherwise unknown to us.

The Hebrew phrase "by the hand of" or "under the hand of" (*beyad* or *tachat yad*) means "under authority, control, or direction of," as well as literally "by the hand of." It is unlikely that verse 12 intends to convey the idea of ordination directly under God's hands, because the God of Abraham, Isaac, and Jacob (Jesus Christ) did not yet have a physical body and because heavenly beings are not sent when there are righteous priests available in the flesh to perform ordinances *under God's direction [or hand]*.[17] It may have been in this sense that Joseph Smith said, "All the prophets had the Melchizedek Priesthood and were ordained by

God himself."[18] Besides, if Esaias had somehow received his priesthood literally at the hands of God, then the priesthood lineage given in verses 6–16 would be disrupted, any priests before Esaias would be links in a different chain of authority back to God, and their inclusion in Moses' priesthood lineage would be pointless.

13. Esaias . . . was blessed of [Abraham]. It is probable that Esaias received the priesthood from Abraham at the Lord's direction and that this ordination was the larger part of Abraham's "blessing" of Esaias. In just the same way, the Bible states that Melchizedek blessed Abraham (see Genesis 14:19); we know from Doctrine and Covenants 84 and other sources that this blessing included ordination to the Melchizedek Priesthood.[19] It is odd that though the Midianites were descended from Abraham through Midian, Midian himself is not mentioned in the priesthood lineage between Abraham and Jethro. Perhaps Midian, which is actually a place name, was a title or some other alternative designation for Esaias, just as the scriptures refer to Jethro as Reuel (see Exodus 2:18), Raguel (see Numbers 10:29), or Hobab (see Judges 4:11).

14. Melchizedek. Melchizedek, a contemporary of Abraham, was a non-Israelite who held the keys of the high priesthood and who ordained the patriarch Abraham. Melchizedek was an ancient king of Shiloam or Salem (ancient Jerusalem, according to the Bible Dictionary) who succeeded in calling his wicked people to repentance and establishing peace by preaching the gospel to them (see Alma 13:14–19; JST Genesis 14:25–40).[20]

14. Through the lineage of his fathers, even till Noah. The language in this passage clearly assumes more than one generation between Melchizedek and Noah. Moreover, Alma 13:19–20 states that Melchizedek reigned in Salem "under his father" and that there were "many before him," which gives the similar impression that there were generations between Melchizedek and Noah, or at least that Noah was not the father of Melchizedek. Though it is a belief of some in the Church that Melchizedek is Shem, the son of Noah, this identification cannot be confirmed from the scriptures or from modern revelation. The reference in Doctrine and Covenants 138:41 to "Shem, the great high priest" is not sufficient to establish this connection, especially in light of Doctrine and Covenants 84:14 and Alma 13:19–20. Some early Church leaders did express the opinion that Shem was Melchizedek,[21] but this information likely came from their reading in Jewish rabbinic literature.[22] In the fourth century after Christ, Saint Jerome had also heard the same stories.[23] Ironically, the rabbis' purpose in identifying Melchizedek with Shem, beginning about the fourth or fifth century, was to combat Christian arguments for the existence of a "Melchizedek" priesthood outside the lineage of Aaron (see Hebrews 7:1–21).[24]

16. Adam, who was the first man. The First Presidency wrote in 1909: "It is held by some that Adam was not the first man upon this earth, and that the original human being was a development from lower orders of the animal creation. These, however, are the theories of men. The word of the Lord declares that Adam was 'The first man of all men' [Moses 1:34], and we are therefore in duty bound to regard him as the primal parent of our race. It was shown to the brother of Jared that all men were created in the *beginning* after the image of God [Ether 3:15]; and whether we take this to mean the spirit or the body, or both, it commits us to the same conclusion: Man began life as a human being, in the likeness of our heavenly Father."[25]

17. Which priesthood continueth. Whenever the true Church has been upon the earth, it has been governed by the same authority and keys of the Melchizedek Priesthood. No credible claim to being *the* true church can be made in any time or place without possession of the keys of the Melchizedek Priesthood.

17. Without beginning of days or end of years. This allusion and the Joseph Smith Translation clear up a misunderstanding about Melchizedek from the text of Hebrews 7:3, in which Melchizedek is said to be "without father, without mother, without descent, having neither beginning of days, nor end of life."

The Joseph Smith Translation and Doctrine and Covenants 84 clarify that it is the priesthood of Melchizedek, not the man himself, that was so described. According to Joseph Smith, "The Priesthood is an everlasting principle, and existed with God from eternity, and will to eternity, without beginning of days or end of years. The keys have to be brought from heaven whenever the Gospel is sent."[26]

18. Confirmed a priesthood upon Aaron. Besides the priesthood after the order of Melchizedek, there is another order of priesthood that is also eternal. It is called the order of Aaron, or the Aaronic Priesthood. This is a lesser priesthood, which does not require the same level of knowledge or have all the authority of the priesthood after the order of Melchizedek (see v. 26). According to Joseph Smith, "All Priesthood is Melchizedek, but there are different portions or degrees of it."[27] In other words, all priesthood is the authority of God; however, that priesthood authority can be conferred in at least two different orders, each with its own privileges or limitations. These two different orders of priesthood power are the order of Aaron, the lesser priesthood, and the order of Melchizedek, the holiest order of all.

19. And this greater priesthood. The order of Melchizedek.

19. Administereth the gospel. It is not possible to have the fulness of the gospel without the Melchizedek Priesthood to administer its higher ordinances. For example, John the Baptist, who held the Aaronic Priesthood and who knew the gospel, could baptize, but only Jesus and his disciples who held the Melchizedek Priesthood could bestow the gift of the Holy Ghost, administer the Church of Christ, and exercise the keys of the kingdom of heaven (see Matthew 3:11; 16:18–19).

19. The key of the mysteries of the kingdom. See Commentary on Doctrine and Covenants 6:7; 8:11; 36:2.

19. The key of the knowledge of God. According to John, the specific gift of the power of knowing God is ultimately equated with eternal life itself (see John 17:3). We cannot really know someone until we are able to see things from their perspective and feel what they feel. Therefore, the power of knowing God logically depends upon the power of becoming like God—the power of godliness.

20. In the ordinances thereof. Through the ordinances of the Melchizedek Priesthood alone the power of actually becoming like God is conferred upon his children, in order that they may come to know God by becoming as he is. By truly knowing God in this way, by "walking in his ways," one ultimately receives the gift of eternal life (Mosiah 23:14; see also John 17:3). Therefore, the blessing of eternal life cannot be separated from the exercise of the ordinances of the Melchizedek Priesthood or the possibility of becoming like God, which they bestow.

20. The power of godliness. Godliness is God-like-ness. The power of godliness is the power of becoming like God. Among the ordinances that allow us, his children, to become like him are baptism (to become clean as he is clean), receiving the gift of the Holy Ghost (to become holy as he is holy and to know his mind), eternal marriage (to become one as our heavenly parents are one and to create as they create), and making temple covenants (to learn to behave as they behave).

Kindliness is the state of being kind; loneliness is the state of being alone; holiness is the state of being holy; saintliness is the state of being saintly; yet the world refuses to understand that the scriptural word "godliness" means being like God. Because the power of becoming like God is in the ordinances of the holy priesthood, Doctrine and Covenants 84 continues to teach the Saints the ancient Christian doctrine of deification. This doctrine, first alluded to in modern revelation (see D&C 76:58), is that through the grace of God his children can become as he is (see 2 Peter 1:3–4).[28]

22. Without this no man can see the face of God. "This" does not mean without holding the priesthood. Here, "this" refers to the power of godliness. Without the power of godliness no one can see the face of God and live, and godliness can be permanently, individually attained only through the ordinances of the holy priesthood. Nevertheless, "godliness" or being like God can be attained temporarily in another way—by transfiguration. If the Holy Ghost enters into our physical bodies, so that for a moment we become one with the Spirit, then having been thus "transfigured" to godliness, we are able to see the face of God and live (see D&C 67:11; Moses 1:9, 11, 15). Possibly that was how Joseph Smith was able to see God before receiving the ordinances of the Melchizedek Priesthood and still live. Many Saints have also been privileged to see the Savior without ordination to the Melchizedek Priesthood.

23. This Moses plainly taught to the children of Israel. When Moses taught the Israelites, he held the Melchizedek Priesthood. He taught them the gospel of Jesus Christ and that they needed the ordinances of the holy priesthood to see God and become as he is. It was Moses' intention, in taking the children of Israel to Mount Sinai, to give them these ordinances, including the ordinances of the temple (hence, the tabernacle) and to introduce them into the presence of God ("that they might behold the face of God").

23. Sought diligently to sanctify his people. To sanctify is to make holy. Moses sought to make his people holy, or Saints, in the only way people *can* be sanctified or be made Saints—through the first principles and ordinances of the gospel of Jesus Christ (faith in Christ, repentance, baptism, and receiving the Holy Ghost).

While Moses was in Midian, he learned the gospel of Jesus Christ (see Moses 1:17), received the Melchizedek Priesthood from his father-in-law (see v. 6), and experienced the vision of the burning bush, which called him to minister to the children of Israel still captive in Egypt (see Exodus 3:1–4:17). It was the intention of Moses and the will of God that the children of Israel should also be taught the gospel of Jesus Christ, be sanctified by the Holy Spirit, ordained, endowed, and brought into the presence of God at Mount Sinai. For this reason, they were brought to the mount (see Exodus 19:3–13). Initially, the children of Israel collectively accepted the Lord's proposals (see Exodus 19:7–8; 24:3–8), and many of them received the ordinances, made the covenants, and were consequently brought into the very presence of God (see Exodus 24:9–11).

24. But they hardened their hearts. Despite Moses' intentions, however, the children of Israel weakened in their resolve and collectively refused to receive the covenants of the gospel. They did not fully repent, and they did not really want to know God or enter into his presence. Those who had already received the ordinances and made the covenants violated them. "God cursed the children of Israel because they would not receive the last law [the gospel] from Moses. . . . The Israelites prayed that God would speak to Moses and not to them [Exodus 20:19; Deuteronomy 5:23–27]; in consequence of which he cursed them with a carnal law [the law of Moses]."[29]

Beyond rejecting the opportunity to receive the fulness of the gospel, the children of Israel then brazenly sinned against even the lesser law (and those who had seen God broke their holy covenants by making and worshiping the golden calf; see Exodus 32:7–9). While Moses was on the mountain receiving a dispensation of the higher laws of the gospel, Aaron and the people below "corrupted themselves" with idolatry (Exodus 32:7). In consequence, they became unworthy of the higher law, and God in his anger revoked the promises made in the gospel covenant.

24. They should not enter into his rest. The conditional promises God had made to Israel were revoked because the conditions for them had not been met. The privileges of the gospel covenants and the ordinances of the Melchizedek Priesthood which alone can bring us into the rest, or presence, of God were denied to Israel collectively from this time forward until the mortal ministry of Jesus Christ among them.[30]

25. He took Moses . . . and the Holy Priesthood also. This doctrine is crucial to an understanding of the Old Testament scriptures. Why is the fulness of the gospel of Jesus Christ not clearly found in the writings of Moses and the other Old Testament prophets? Is it because these originally "Christian" texts have become corrupted and the references to the gospel have been removed? No, not usually (but see Moses 1:41). The fulness of the gospel cannot be found in the Old Testament writings because most of it was never put there. According to this verse in Doctrine and Covenants 84, God took the fulness of the gospel away from Israel as a nation at Sinai. Individual prophets and some others associated with them, such as the kings David and Solomon, did receive the fulness of the gospel and its covenants in Old Testament times (see D&C 132:39), but the gospel and its covenants were withheld from Israel collectively by divine decree because of Israel's rejection of these blessings at Sinai. Joseph Smith wrote: "Was the Priesthood of Melchizedek taken away when Moses died? . . . That portion which brought Moses to speak with God face to face [the Melchizedek] was taken away; but that which brought the ministry of angels [the Aaronic] remained."[31]

The public writings of Moses preserved in the Old Testament (Genesis, Exodus, Leviticus, Numbers, and Deuteronomy) are documents specifically adapted to a people living a lesser law under the lesser priesthood. Because the knowledge of the fulness of the gospel, along with the higher priesthood and its ordinances, was removed from ancient Israel by command of the Lord (see Moses 1:23), a restoration of the Melchizedek Priesthood in the latter days also called for a revision of the Old Testament scriptures, restoring them from their post-Sinai to their pre-Sinai point of view. The Joseph Smith Translation and the books of Moses and Abraham in the Pearl of Great Price fulfill this need by putting the events of Genesis and other Old Testament passages in their proper setting of the fulness of the gospel. As presently constituted, the biblical books of Moses are preparatory documents, perhaps corresponding to the Aaronic Priesthood (see Galatians 3:19, 24), whereas the Creation accounts and the Patriarchal narratives recorded by Joseph Smith in the Pearl of Great Price and the Joseph Smith Translation represent the restoration of the fulness, corresponding to the Melchizedek Priesthood.

26. The lesser priesthood continued. When Israel sinned by its idolatry, Moses broke the stone tablets that God had made for Israel (see Exodus 32:19). This set of tablets contained upon them the new and everlasting covenant of the gospel. After Israel had been punished and the wicked and unrepentant killed, Moses returned to the mount and received another law based on the same principles as the original but formulated as a law of carnal commandments (a list of do's and don'ts) with the fulness of the gospel and the higher priesthood removed from it (see vv. 25–27). This lesser law was not the gospel of Jesus Christ, but the law of Moses, named not after the divine Christ but after the man Moses, its lesser mediator (see JST Exodus 34:1–2; Galatians 3:19; JST Galatians 3:19; D&C 42:18; 76:69).[32] When the knowledge and powers of the Melchizedek Priesthood were taken away from Israel, the Aaronic Priesthood was allowed to continue, but from that time on the people were forbidden entrance into the temple itself. "High priests" in Israel were Aaronic priests who administered only ordinances of the Aaronic Priesthood, and the only "temple" ordinances available to the people were animal sacrifices performed outside the building itself in the courtyard.

26. The key of the ministering of angels. *To minister* means "to serve," just as *ministry* means "service." The Aaronic Priesthood holds the keys that entitle one to be visited and aided when necessary by angels sent from the presence of God.[33] Nevertheless, the Melchizedek Priesthood and the power of godliness manifested in its ordinances are necessary for one to enter into the presence of God himself (see vv. 19–22).

26–27. The preparatory gospel . . . and the law of carnal commandments. The lesser law of Moses is not the gospel of Jesus Christ. It does not contain full knowledge of Jesus as Savior, of the gift of the Holy Ghost (the conferring of which is a Melchizedek Priesthood ordinance), or of justification through grace (see D&C 20:30), for these all pertain to the fulness of the gospel.³⁴ The law of Moses is a preparatory gospel of obedience, repentance, and baptism for the remission of sins. The law of Moses with its carnal commandments prepares human beings for the fulness of the gospel by raising them from a level of disobedience and wickedness associated with the telestial kingdom to a level of obedience and relative righteousness associated with the terrestrial kingdom. In this condition, having learned obedience by following rules, they are prepared to receive the celestial principles of the gospel and to become perfected and sanctified through the atonement of Jesus Christ.³⁵

Carnal commandments are rules, sometimes even seemingly arbitrary rules. Rules require less understanding than do principles, and rules are therefore better suited to the spiritually immature than are principles. Rules are usually black and white—do this; don't do that. A law of carnal commandments is essentially a collection of rules that require little thought, wisdom, or spiritual experience and sensitivity from those who live them. Rules require *obedience,* not understanding. If one is obedient, one can live the law of carnal commandments, even if one has no idea why some behaviors are demanded and others are forbidden. Once one has learned to obey (through the observance of rules or carnal commandments), then, and only then, is one equipped and prepared to be instructed in the higher principles upon which the rules are based. Thus, observing rules develops the commitment of obedience, which then prepares us to receive principles. The succession of kingdoms (telestial, terrestrial, and celestial) is loosely paralleled by a succession of obedience (wickedness through disobedience, righteousness through rules, and perfection through gospel principles).

27. The Lord in his wrath. The law of Moses with its carnal commandments was not a blessing to ancient Israel at Sinai; it was a curse (see Galatians 3:10, 13).³⁶ Those to whom God had offered the fulness of the celestial gospel at Sinai were cursed by having the fulness of the gospel withdrawn from them and by being given only a preparatory gospel in its place. Moreover, the lesser law itself pronounces a curse upon all who disobey even one of its tiniest rules (see Deuteronomy 27:26), and because all humans sin, all Israel falls under the curse of the law. On the other hand, to later generations of Israel the law of Moses was both a curse and a blessing—a curse for these same reasons but also a blessing because it provided a divine law that reminded them of their duties and responsibilities to the God of their fathers.

27. Until John. The preparatory nature of the law of Moses is exemplified by the ministry of John the Baptist, who held the Aaronic Priesthood, and who affirmed that the kingdom of God was approaching, and preached repentance and baptism for the remission of sins (see Matthew 3:1–6). He did these things to prepare Israel for the One who was coming to "baptize you with the Holy Ghost, and with fire" (Matthew 3:11; see also v. 28). John did not himself publicly preach the fulness of the gospel of Christ, however; that was a ministry for Jesus' apostles. John prepared the way by readying Israel to be worthy to hear the fulness of the gospel and to receive its ordinances.[37] The preparatory gospel was truly a gospel because its administrator, John, held authority from God and because its principles and ordinances were faith, repentance, baptism in water, and the remission of sins—the first, second, and third principles of the gospel (see Articles of Faith 1:4). Nevertheless, it was only a preparatory gospel because it did not contain the fourth principle of the gospel: baptism by fire and the Holy Ghost. Also missing was the Melchizedek Priesthood with its other ordinances.

27. Filled with the Holy Ghost from his mother's womb. The Holy Ghost had come upon John even before his birth (see Luke 1:15, 41), and John had the companionship and influence of the Spirit with him throughout his life. Although we do not know where, when, or how John received the ordinance of the laying on of hands, he surely did, for the ordinances of the gospel are ever the same. Just as Jesus received baptism, though he had no sins, so John accepted the laying on of hands, though he already enjoyed the companionship of the Holy Ghost.

The Holy Spirit may, at God's discretion, come upon anyone, to any degree, and for any length of time, even if an individual is not yet a confirmed member of the Church. This was the case, for example, with Elizabeth, Zacharias, Simeon, Cornelius, and the young Joseph Smith (see Luke 1:41, 67; 2:25; Acts 10:47; Joseph Smith–History 1:73). In all such cases, however, these persons must subsequently receive the laying on of hands to receive the gift of the Holy Ghost by the power of the Melchizedek Priesthood.[38]

28. Baptized while he was yet in his childhood. John was baptized as a child, but not before the age of accountability, which is eight years of age. In the Judaism of John's day, one was considered a child until the age of twelve, so John would probably have been baptized sometime between his eighth and twelfth birthdays and perhaps sooner rather than later. We have no record of who may have performed this baptism.

28. Ordained by the angel . . . unto this power. The word *ordain* has a broader range of meanings than we may sometimes recognize. According to Elder Bruce R. McConkie, the ministration described here was not an ordination to the priesthood but was what might now be more technically called a "setting apart" for a specific mission and receiving all the rights and powers pertaining to that mission. "Naming of children and circumcision of male members of the house of Israel took place on [the eighth] day. In the case of John, he 'was ordained by the angel of God at the time he was eight days old'—not to the Aaronic Priesthood, for such would come later, after his baptism and other preparation but—'unto this power, to overthrow the kingdom of the Jews, and to make straight the way of the Lord before the face of his people, to prepare them for the coming of the Lord, in whose hand is given all power' (D&C 84:28). That is, at this solemn eighth day ceremony, an angel, presumably Gabriel, gave the Lord's Elias the divine commission to serve as the greatest forerunner of all the ages."[39]

28. To overthrow the kingdom of the Jews. The kingdom

of the Jews was neither the kingdom of Israel nor the kingdom of heaven. At the time of John, it was merely one of the fallen kingdoms of mortal men, a suburb of Babylon, governed by an Edomite usurper, King Herod, and led spiritually by apostate priests who did not hold the keys necessary to their office. The rightful successor to the priesthood of the house of Aaron and he who held the keys of the Aaronic Priesthood by right of succession at the time of John's birth was Zacharias, John's own father. According to Joseph Smith, "John was a priest after his father, and held the keys of the Aaronic Priesthood, and was called of God to preach the Gospel of the kingdom of God. The Jews, as a nation, having departed from the law of God and the Gospel of the Lord, prepared the way for transferring it to the Gentiles."[40] In other words, the preaching of John overthrew the corrupt kingdom of the Jews, because their rejection of the gospel and John's testimony of Christ led to the gospel being taken from them and given to the Gentiles. Joseph Smith went on to say that "John, at that time, was the only legal administrator in the affairs of the kingdom there was then on the earth, and holding the keys of power. The Jews had to obey his instructions or be damned, by their own law. . . . The son of Zacharias wrested the keys, the kingdom, the power, the glory from the Jews, by the holy anointing and decree of heaven."[41]

29. The offices of elder and bishop. These offices are subcategories, or "necessary appendages," within the Melchizedek Priesthood. Elders hold the authority of Melchizedek but not necessarily the keys of that priesthood or the right to preside, as do high priests set apart to their offices. Bishops are here assumed to be bishops by right of ordination as high priests in the Melchizedek Priesthood rather than by right of Aaronic lineage. Technically, literal descendants who are the firstborn of the sons of Aaron have the legal right to the office of presiding bishop, but even such a descendant must be found worthy and appointed by those in authority holding the keys of the Melchizedek Priesthood (see D&C 68:15–20). In the Church today, presiding bishops who are not literal descendants of Aaron preside over the Aaronic Priesthood by virtue of their Melchizedek Priesthood, which allows them to "officiate in all the lesser offices" (D&C 68:19), so long as they are appointed by those in authority who also hold the Melchizedek Priesthood.[42]

30. The offices of teacher and deacon. These offices are sub-categories, or "necessary appendages" (v. 29), within the Aaronic Priesthood.

31. Therefore, as I said concerning the sons of Moses. Here the Lord returns to his original topic, after a parenthetical diversion of twenty-five verses. Verse 31 does not refer to the literal offspring of Moses and Aaron but rather to those who, like Moses and Aaron, have entered into the covenants of the Melchizedek and Aaronic Priesthoods, respectively.[43]

31. Shall offer an acceptable offering and sacrifice. See Commentary on Doctrine and Covenants 13:1.

31. Which house shall be built unto the Lord in this generation. See Commentary on verses 3–4.

32. Upon Mount Zion in the Lord's house. See Commentary on verse 2.

32. Whose sons ye are. Joseph Smith and the elders with him who had accepted calls and served missions and had otherwise been faithful to their priesthood covenants, by virtue of righteously holding the Melchizedek Priesthood (and the Aaronic, which it embraces), are "sons" of Moses and of Aaron. "Son of" here does not mean that one's lineage is now literally reckoned differently (through Levi) but rather that one is now heir to the same priesthood blessings once received by Moses and Aaron.

33. Obtaining these two priesthoods. This phrase means more than just being ordained. It means actually *obtaining,* coming to have in one's own possession, the powers of heaven. That can be done only "upon the principles of righteousness" (D&C 121:36). Many who are ordained to the priesthood fail to obtain or keep its powers because they do not exercise those powers in righteousness.

33. Magnifying their calling. The Book of Mormon prophet Jacob offered an excellent scriptural definition for this term: "And we did magnify our office unto the Lord, taking upon us the responsibility, answering the sins of the people upon our own heads if we did not teach them the word of God with all diligence" (Jacob 1:19). To magnify our office or calling is to accept the responsibility to perform the duties of that office fully and completely. To magnify our office is to "make it great," that is, to make it greatly effective, so that no one whom we are called to serve can shift responsibility for their sins from their own choices to our negligence. Conversely, failing to magnify our calling is to neglect our duty, so that blame for the sins of others is due in part to our own negligence. In this case, Jacob said, "Their blood would come upon our garments, and we would not be found spotless at the last day" (Jacob 1:19; see also Jacob 2:2; Romans 11:13; 24:3–9).

33. Sanctified by the Spirit unto the renewing of their bodies. To be sanctified is to be made holy. We are reminded here that the agent by which we are sanctified and made holy (or made Saints) is the Holy Spirit (see Alma 5:54; 13:12; 3 Nephi 27:20). But the power of the Spirit does not sanctify only our spirits; it also sanctifies our physical bodies. The sacrament bread is blessed to sanctify the souls (both spirits and bodies; see D&C 88:15) of those who partake of it (see Moroni 4:3; 20:77). Moreover, this power of the Spirit to sanctify our bodies while we are still in the flesh is experienced to different degrees by different individuals. In the most sublime cases, bodies can be sanctified to the point of reversing the effects of the Fall almost completely. According to Mormon, this was true of the Three Nephites: "I knew not whether they were cleansed from mortality to immortality—but behold . . . there was a change wrought upon them, insomuch that Satan could have no power over them, that he could not tempt them; and they were sanctified in the flesh, that they were holy, and that the powers of the earth could not hold them" (3 Nephi 28:36–39). This would seem to be what the scriptures call transfiguration, or, rather, that long-term or extended transfiguration called "being translated." In other cases, the power of the Spirit to sanctify the flesh has been experienced in varying degrees, but it seems always directed toward assisting faithful individuals to further magnify their callings.

President Hugh B. Brown once testified that President David O. McKay had "been sanctified by the Spirit unto the renewing of his body" and added that "some of the rest of us are better off today than we were many years ago so far as physical health is concerned—and we attribute that fact to [the Lord's] blessing."[44] Elder Carlos E. Asay reported: "Many of us have felt the influence of this 'renewal promise.' Without it, scores of our assignments might have gone unfinished."[45]

34. They become. To whatever degree the sanctification of the Spirit is experienced, those who obtain the two priesthoods and magnify their callings are really, personally, changed in some degree by doing so.

34. The seed of Abraham. When this term is used in a singular sense, it refers to Jesus Christ (see Galatians 3:16). In a collective sense, however, it refers to all who, like Abraham, have faith in Christ (see Galatians 3:7). Just as those who follow Moses and Aaron in obtaining the priesthood become the children (sons) of Moses and Aaron, so all those who follow Abraham by having faith in Christ become the children, or seed, of Abraham. They are adopted into the house of Israel, and they are heirs of all the blessings promised to Abraham (see Galatians 3:27–29; Abraham 2:10).

35. All they who receive this priesthood receive me. "Receive" may have a double meaning here.[46] It is true that males "receive the priesthood" by receiving ordination, but in another sense, all humans "receive the priesthood" by accepting and obeying the authority of ordained servants of Christ. In the former sense, "the priesthood" refers to the authority of God; in the latter sense, "the priesthood" refers collectively to God's servants who hold that authority. Anyone, male or female, may "receive the priesthood" in the latter sense. Understanding the phrase "receive this priesthood" in that sense causes verse 35 to lead naturally and logically to verse 36 and also makes these verses more meaningful for those who cannot receive the priesthood by ordination.

36–38. The promises of God to the faithful are linked together here in a marvelous progression: whoever receives the servants of God (the priesthood) receives also their Master, the Son; whoever receives the Son receives also the Father who sent him; whoever receives the Father receives all that the Father has. Verses 33 through 38 are promises that God makes to all those who "receive the priesthood" in either sense of that phrase and thus includes both male and female members of the Church. Elder Marion G. Romney declared: "This statement is worth emphasizing. 'He that receiveth my servants receiveth me.' Who are his servants? They are his representatives in the offices of the Priesthood—the General, Stake, Priesthood Quorum, and Ward officers. It behooves us to keep this in mind when we are tempted to disregard our presiding authorities, bishops, quorum and stake presidents, etc., when, within the jurisdiction of their callings, they give us counsel and advice."[47]

38. All that my father hath shall be given unto him. This is the promise of exaltation in the celestial kingdom of God. It is the promise of becoming like God, of becoming gods. Once again, the doctrine of deification was beginning to be taught to the Saints (see John 17:21–23; Romans 8:14–17; 1 Corinthians 3:21–23; 2 Corinthians 3:18; Galatians 4:7; 1 John 3:2; Revelation 3:21; 21:7).[48] Those who receive the priesthood and magnify their offices or callings will, as joint-heirs with Christ, receive all that the Father now possesses, just as Christ has received it. They will receive all the power, comprehension, and knowledge of God the Father. They will share his celestial glory and will live his type of celestial life.

39–40. According to the oath and covenant. One difficulty in dealing with the subject of the "oath and covenant" of the priesthood is that the principles involved have more than one legitimate context or application, depending on the understanding, experience, and progress of the individuals involved. For example, for a missionary elder, the logical application or understanding of the oath and covenant of the priesthood might be something like this: An elder may receive the blessings enumerated in verses 33–38 by keeping the covenant contained in these same verses. A covenant, of course, is a two-sided agreement. Each party in a covenant relationship has obligations to the other. Because God proposes this covenant of the priesthood, its form is essentially this: "If you (the elder) will do ABC, then I (God) will do XYZ." The obligation of the elder under this covenant is to follow or receive God's servants, to obtain the two priesthoods, and to magnify his calling therein (see v. 33). The obligation of God under the same covenant is then to sanctify the elder (see v. 33), to make him a son of Moses and Aaron and of the seed of Abraham (see v. 34), to make him an elect member of the church and kingdom of God (see v. 34), and ultimately to give the elder all that God himself possesses (see v. 38).

Additionally, the terms of this priesthood covenant are guaranteed by an unbreakable oath, but it is not the elder who swears this oath. It is God himself who swears and who thereby binds himself eternally to keep his covenant promises when the elder's covenant obligations have been met (see D&C 124:47; Psalm 105:6–7; Luke 1:73–75). Thus, the elder may know of a certainty, by God's own oath, that if he is faithful in meeting his obligation, the terms of the covenant will be kept, and he will be exalted in the celestial kingdom of God (see D&C 40).

In another context, however, a married couple might understand the covenant in "oath and covenant of the priesthood" to be the new and everlasting covenant of the gospel, including marriage for eternity. Those who receive these ordinances and make these covenants, the fulness of the new and everlasting covenant (see D&C 131), become heirs of all the promises which God made first to Adam and Eve, and then to Abraham, Isaac, and Jacob with their wives. The terms of this covenant, received fully only in the temple, might be paraphrased something like this: "If you (the elder and his wife) will give me all that you have, then I (God) will give you all that I have." (This, of course, is the best bargain in all eternity.) Understood on this level, the oath in "oath and covenant" is the oath that God swore to Abraham (see Genesis 22:16–18; see also 1 Chronicles 16:15–18; Luke 1:70–75; Acts 2:30; Hebrews 6:12–20), which, because it includes the promise of posterity, must include both husband and wife, and of which we may be assured we are jointly heirs, if we keep the terms of the new and everlasting covenant as did Abraham and Sarah.

In yet another context, although the covenant in "oath and covenant" is still the new and everlasting covenant, the oath is neither God's conditional promise that he will keep his word nor is it any guarantee that we are also entitled to the promises he swore to Abraham, Isaac, and Jacob that they would be exalted. Rather, it is the oath of God sworn to us by his own voice (keeping in mind D&C 84:42; 1:38) that we are "sealed up unto eternal life," receiving this "more sure word of prophecy . . . by revelation and the spirit of prophecy, through the power of the Holy Priesthood" (D&C 131:5). This application of the phrase "oath and covenant" concerns those who have been sealed up to eternal life, or whose calling and election has been made sure. One example of this is the oath of God to the greatest priest of all: "Inasmuch as not without an oath he [Christ] was made priest: (For those [Aaronic] priests were made without an oath; but this [the Melchizedek high priest] with an oath by him that said unto him, The Lord sware and will not repent, Thou art a priest for ever after the order of Melchisedec)" (Hebrews 7:20–21; see also Psalm 110:4). To exercise the fulness of the Melchizedek Priesthood forever is equivalent to being exalted. In such cases, God's oath effectively seals up those who receive it to eternal life, and the effective terms of the covenant in this instance would become something like this: "You *will* be exalted; I swear it. Only you can now break this seal by using your inviolable agency to choose perdition. But if you do not commit murder or sin against the Holy Ghost, you shall be exalted" (see D&C 68:12; 132:26).[49]

Joseph Smith expounded on this deeper application of "oath and covenant of the priesthood" in a letter to his uncle Silas Smith, dated 26 September 1833, a year after Doctrine and Covenants 84 was received: "Why was it that the Lord spake to [Jacob] concerning the same promise, after he had made it once to Abraham, and renewed it to Isaac? Why could not Jacob rest contented upon the word spoken to his fathers? . . . [Paul] was careful to press upon [the Hebrew Saints] the necessity of continuing on until they, as well as those who then inherited the promises, *might have the assurance of their salvation confirmed to them by an oath from the mouth of him who could not lie;* for that seemed to be the example anciently, and Paul holds it out to his Hebrew brethren as an object attainable in his day. . . . Abraham, Isaac, and Jacob had the promise of eternal life confirmed to them by an oath of the Lord, but that promise or oath was no assurance to [the Hebrew Saints] of their [own] salvation; but they could, by walking in the footsteps, continuing in the faith of their fathers, *obtain, for themselves, an oath* for confirmation that they were meet to be partakers of the inheritance with the saints in light."[50]

A decade later, in a sabbath address at Nauvoo on 21 May 1843, Joseph further taught that "to obtain a promise from God for myself that I shall have eternal life . . . is the more sure word of prophecy."[51]

And finally, another context for the phrase "oath and covenant of the priesthood" can be found even within the parameters of the lesser, preparatory law. This was the case when Israel, with their lesser priesthood and law, entered the land of Canaan after the fulness of the gospel and the Melchizedek Priesthood had been taken from them: "That thou shouldest enter into covenant with the Lord thy God, and into his oath, which the Lord thy God maketh with thee this day. . . . Neither with you only do I make this covenant and this oath; but with him that standeth here with us this day before the Lord our God, and also with him that is not here with us this day" (Deuteronomy 29:12, 14–15).

Thus, the "oath and covenant of the priesthood" may be

correctly understood in more than one context and with more than one application, depending on the spiritual situation of those who receive it and with some degree of applicability to every member. Nevertheless, all of these different applications understood in all their different contexts actually amount to about the same arrangement. If we will make and faithfully keep the covenants presented to us, God guarantees by his own oath that we shall receive all things and be exalted in his celestial kingdom. This is the common promise to all who receive the oath and covenant of the priesthood, in whatever spiritual context they may do so. And this glorious arrangement with God, confirmed by his own oath, will be kept—worlds without end.

41. Shall not have forgiveness of sins in this world nor in the world to come. Just as the phrase "oath and covenant of the priesthood" has more than one context and application, so does the penalty for violating this covenant. Applied to those who have been sealed up to exaltation and who then "altogether turneth therefrom" (v. 41), it could refer to their becoming sons of perdition, to suffering the second death, and to going with Satan and his angels into outer darkness at the Last Judgment.

The key wording here is "altogether turn[ing] therefrom." This phrase means "without subsequent repentance" (the Hebrew word for repent is *shuv*, "to turn"). Those who turn away from their covenants and who will not subsequently turn back again, or repent, will not have forgiveness—ever. Should they subsequently repent, however, then they did not turn away *altogether* but only for a time. In such cases, everlasting punishment could be avoided.

For the average Church member who has not been "sealed up to eternal life," however, verse 41 does not imply perdition. If such an individual violates his covenants, *and never subsequently repents,* "he will never again have the opportunity of exercising the priesthood and reaching exaltation. That is where his forgiveness ends. He will not again have the priesthood conferred upon him, because he has trampled it under his feet; but as far as other things are concerned, he may be forgiven."[52] Nevertheless, as always, should such a person repent or "turn" again, he may still be forgiven and receive celestial blessings in eternity.

42. Wo unto all those who come not unto this priesthood. Does "this priesthood" refer to the priesthood defined as God's authority or to the priesthood defined as God's servants? It probably means both.[53] Those who will not heed the servants of God cannot receive the blessings of the gospel (see D&C 1:14), and those who will not receive the oath and covenant of the priesthood cannot be exalted in the celestial kingdom.

42. Which I now confirm upon you . . . by mine own voice. This important statement may reflect what was said about receiving the oath and covenant of the priesthood in verses 39–40. The elders present on 23 September 1832, when Doctrine and Covenants 84 was given, received confirmation of their priesthood covenant by the voice of God himself. Having been taught the principle in verses 33–40, they then received its blessings to some degree, as recorded in verse 42 (see also v. 48).

The voice of God in this case came through the mouth of his servant Joseph Smith. When the living prophet speaks under inspiration of God, it is the voice of the Lord (see D&C 1:38).[54] It is true that some have heard the voice of God himself from his own lips (see, for example, 2 Nephi 31:15–20; 3 Nephi 15:24; Moses 1:31; 6:66–69), but this is not necessary for exaltation in the celestial kingdom. Many have heard the voice of God bearing witness or confirming the surety of their covenants upon them through the mouths of his servants the apostles and prophets, as did these elders in Kirtland in 1832.

42. Charge. That is, instructions. It would seem from this and other passages that at times God does direct his angels to watch over his servants (see v. 88; D&C 109:22; Matthew 18:10).

44. Every word that proceedeth forth from the mouth of God. This phrase means not only those words voiced by God himself in personal revelation but also his words as voiced by his authorized servants (see D&C 1:35–38; 21:4–5).

45. The word of the Lord is truth . . . light . . . spirit. The source of all spiritual and physical energy on all levels of existence in this creation, from the subatomic to the intergalactic, is Jesus Christ, the creator of heaven and earth. Heat, light, energy, truth, glory, and spirit (all symbolized by the power of the sun) characterize the works and the forces of God in the universe. All of these come from the creative force of the light or Spirit of Christ (see D&C 88:6–13; 93:23–40).[55] On the other hand, entropy (loss of energy), falsehood, cold, and darkness beyond the sphere of God's influence all characterize the nature, works, and destiny of Satan and perdition.

46–48. The Spirit giveth light to every man. Every human being born into the world has a certain measure of light, life, energy, and intelligence. Because all these forms of energy derive from the light of Christ, which permeates the physical creation, it follows that every human being has some measure of the light or Spirit of Christ. If humans will heed this inborn light-energy, they will be led upward to more intense forms of the divine power until they eventually are led to the Father, the ultimate source of all light. He will confirm them in the new and everlasting covenant, which in turn brings to them a fulness of celestial light, life, truth, and glory.

48. Not for your sakes only. God reveals himself to some and gives them the blessings of eternity, not just for their sakes but so they can, in turn, take those same blessings to all the inhabitants of the world. This obligation comes with the blessings of the gospel and is, indeed, inseparable from them. We cannot receive the blessings of eternity without fulfilling in some way our obligation of taking those blessings to others.

49–53. The whole world lieth in sin. As a result of the Fall, every human being has committed sin. The only way sin may be removed is through the atonement of Christ. Hence, "whoso cometh not unto me is under the bondage of sin" (v. 51). Everyone in the whole world who has not received the gospel is in bondage to sin. This sin brings misery to their lives, and they groan under its influence. But some people see this bondage for what it is and seek to be freed from sin; others have no desire to be set free. Those who seek deliverance from bondage follow the influence of the light of Christ in their lives and seek ever greater light until they hear the gospel and recognize in it the voice they have heard faintly and followed before. Those who love their sins and have not sought deliverance have not heeded the promptings of the light of Christ and do not recognize his voice when they hear it. The distinction between "righteous" and "wicked" in these verses is not based on whether they sin or not. They *all* lie under the bondage of sin (see v. 49). But the righteous are those who hate their sins and who seek deliverance from their bondage. They recognize the voice that proclaims deliverance and enter into the covenant that bestows it. The wicked just turn away.[56]

54. Your minds . . . have been darkened because of unbelief. The focus shifts here from the world (see vv. 46–53) to the Church. Even faithful members of the Church can be faulted for sometimes resisting the word of the Lord. The error mentioned here is not one of ignorance but of wilful resistance to or rejection of some portion of the Lord's revealed word. In the context of the Church in 1832, it is likely that a part of this unbelief involved the principles of consecration and the establishment of Zion (see D&C 58:15; 85:8).

Members of the Church in many dispensations, including our own, have come under condemnation for refusing to accept the whole doctrine of Christ. Though they may claim testimonies that the Church is true, some members bristle at the authority of the apostles and prophets, or even of their own bishops. Some resist the very idea of consecration or reject their responsibility to establish Zion upon the earth. Some reject the doctrine of only one true Church; others dislike celestial marriage, or of having heavenly parents, or the doctrine of becoming like God.

Although the specific doctrines being resisted in 1832 are not enumerated, the Book of Mormon gives an example of wilful unbelief in the days of Zenock: "For behold, [Zenock] said: Thou

art angry, O Lord, with this people, because they will not understand thy mercies which thou hast bestowed upon them because
of thy son" (Alma 33:16). If the gospel is true, then it is *all* true,
the difficult doctrines as well as the easy ones, the tender ones as
well as the hard.

54. You have treated lightly the things you have received.
Not only do the members of the Church today sometimes resist
portions of the doctrine of Christ, but they also sometimes treat
lightly what they have received from God. It isn't enough to
"know" that the Book of Mormon is true if we have never read it,
neither knowing nor caring what it says. Treating lightly the things
we have been given include such behaviors as having the scriptures on our shelves but never studying them, or knowing that
there are apostles and prophets in Salt Lake City but never listening to them at conference or reading their messages in Church
publications. Actions such as these do bring us under condemnation, in the same way as the early members of the Church were
brought under condemnation (see vv. 55–56).

55. Vanity and unbelief. *Vanity* means "emptiness." *Vanity*
also describes behavior that is empty and ultimately accomplishes
nothing, just as the related phrase "in vain" means "all for nothing." *Vanity* and *vain* are often applied to preoccupation with
appearance rather than reality, because all such concern is ultimately pointless. Everybody ages, and God doesn't care how
pretty we were. In the religious sense, in this passage "vanity"
means to make nothing out of something, to prize appearance
over reality, or to prize that which is of little or no value more
highly than the riches of eternity.

Unbelief is refusing to believe the doctrines that have been
revealed (see v. 54).[57] Many Saints treat the doctrines of the kingdom as if they were a buffet lunch, selecting what they like and
rejecting what they don't. The twin evils of vanity and unbelief
have brought the whole Church under the condemnation of God.
Those who are guilty of vanity and unbelief are "walking in darkness at noon-day" (D&C 95:6), having knowledge given to them

but preferring ignorance, having light shined upon them but preferring the dark.

56. The children of Zion, even all. The immediate historical setting of these verses is the vanity and unbelief of the members of the Church in Zion (Missouri) who were then resisting the instructions of the Prophet Joseph Smith about the establishment of Zion (see v. 76; D&C 58:15 and Commentary). But in a secondary sense, "the children of Zion" included the whole Church at that time and still refers to the collective Church today. To some extent the members of the Church, both then and now, are still guilty of the sins of vanity and unbelief and suffer the condemnation of God for it.

57. They shall remain under this condemnation. President Ezra Taft Benson applied these verses to the Church today: "The Lord declares that the whole Church and all the children of Zion are under condemnation because of the way we have treated the Book of Mormon. This condemnation has not been lifted, nor will it be until we repent. (See D&C 84:51–81.)

"The Lord states that we must not only say but we must do! We have neither said enough nor have we done enough with this divine instrument—the key to conversion. As a result, as individuals, as families, and as the Church, we sometimes have felt the scourge and judgment God said would be 'poured out upon the children of Zion' [D&C 84:58] because of our neglect of this book."[58]

Elder Dallin H. Oaks further declared: "The subject I believe we have neglected is the Book of Mormon's witness of the divinity and mission of Jesus Christ and our covenant relationship to him. . . . In too many of our classes, in too many of our worship services, we are not teaching of Christ and testifying of Christ in the way we should. This is one way we are failing to 'remember the new covenant.'"[59]

57. The new covenant, even the Book of Mormon. The fulness of the gospel is found in the Book of Mormon (see Commentary on D&C 1:23). If the Saints will just read the Book of Mormon, they will learn the doctrine of Christ. The fulness of the gospel can also be found in the Bible (see Introduction to the Book of Mormon) and the other scriptures of the Church, but the Book of Mormon has been revealed in the last days specifically as a witness for our dispensation.

57. And the former commandments. *Commandment* sometimes equals *revelation* in the language of the Doctrine and Covenants.[60] "The former commandments" may mean the revelations of Joseph Smith, soon to be printed in the 1833 Book of Commandments, or "former" may mean prior to the Book of Mormon and would thus indicate the revelations given by God in the Bible, which also contains "the fulness of the everlasting gospel" (Introduction to the Book of Mormon).

57. Not only to say, but to do. Through studying the Book of Mormon and the other scriptures, and by heeding the words of the apostles and prophets, we will first avoid unbelief, for we will learn what the Lord has said. Then, as we conform our lives to what we have learned, we will also avoid vanity, for the false priorities of our lives will be corrected, and we will live the gospel, keep the commandments, and shun the vanities of life. We will stand for something, rather than nothing.

58. Meet. Appropriate.

58. Otherwise there remaineth a scourge and judgment. The members of the Church in 1832 were warned that if they did not repent of their vanity and unbelief, they would be judged and scourged. By 1838 almost all of the members were living in Missouri, but they had still been unable to establish Zion. On 27 October 1838, the infamous Extermination Order was issued by Governor Lilburn W. Boggs. In January 1839, Brigham Young and the Quorum of the Twelve (as Joseph Smith was in Liberty Jail) organized a committee for the removal of Church members from Missouri. By the end of April, the last members had left Far West, Missouri. This was the scourge visited upon them partly for their vanity and unbelief and partly for failing collectively to accept and implement the doctrines of Zion.[61] But since President Ezra Taft

Benson pointed out the continuing condemnation of the contemporary Church in the areas of vanity and unbelief, it follows that if the Church does not repent collectively in our day, we also await a scourge and judgment preceding the second coming of the Savior (see 1 Peter 4:17).

59. Shall the children of the kingdom pollute my holy land. In both the Old and the New Worlds, the land of promise was given to a chosen people with both a promise and a warning. If the inhabitants would dwell upon the land in righteousness, they would be blessed as promised, but if they turned to wickedness, they would be scoured off the land (see Leviticus 18:24–28; Deuteronomy 29:24–28; 2 Nephi 1:7; Ether 2:9). Wickedness will ultimately not be tolerated in the land of promise.

61. I will forgive you of your sins. Once again the great mercy of God is manifested as he forgives the elders present their sins on condition that they will remain faithful and do their duty under the covenant.

63. As I said unto mine apostles. In 3 Nephi 15:24 and John 15:14–15, these references apply to both the Twelve in the Old World and to the Twelve in the New World. It should be remembered that the passage that follows was given to the leaders of the Church and not necessarily to the general membership. The Quorum of the Twelve had not yet been established in the early Church when Doctrine and Covenants 84 was received, so the high priesthood of the Church largely functioned as its general authorities. In any case, what follows are instructions for the leaders of the Church in modern times as well as in ancient times.

There are many unmistakable parallels in Doctrine and Covenants 84 to passages of the New Testament. The Lord explains in this verse why this is so. He is giving to the leaders of the latter-day Church the same instructions he gave to the leaders of the primitive Church at a similar point in their development.

63. Ye are my friends. Those who enter into and keep the covenants of Abraham may in time become, like Abraham, not just God's servants, or even his children, but his friends (see v. 77; James 2:23; Exodus 33:11).

65. These signs shall follow them that believe. The signs listed here are apostolic privileges. Perhaps "them that believe" refers to those who have been converted, called, commissioned, and in turn sent out as the Lord's special witnesses. In any case, the apostolic blessings and keys listed here *may* be passed to or enjoyed by others, but we should not assume that they are *always* available to every missionary or to every member.

66. In my name. The powers of heaven cannot be controlled by human beings, except as they are able to invoke the authority of Jesus Christ. Human beings do not perform these works; Jesus Christ performs them through his servants.

71. Poison . . . shall not hurt them. This promise must have been particularly meaningful to the Prophet Joseph Smith, who had been poisoned at an inn three months earlier and had been healed by the power of the priesthood.[62]

73. They shall not boast themselves of these things. The signs of priesthood power are not to be used to get glory or to boost our own egos. Neither should those who perform such signs boast that *they* have done them, for they have not. God has performed them through his servants. All credit should be reverently given to God and nothing taken for ourselves.

73. Neither speak them before the world. If the priesthood leaders of the Church have such powers, and if the keys of such powers can be extended to others in the ministry, then why don't we hear more about it? Why don't we see such miracles documented on TV? Because those who enjoy the authority of God to perform signs and miracles are expressly commanded *not* to parade them before the public. The working of signs and miracles have very little to do with conversion (see D&C 63:7–12). These powers of God are for the benefit of those who possess them and those for whose blessing they are invoked. They are not media events. Like most sacred things, they are to remain private and personal.

74. Shall be damned. This phrase does not refer to permanent consignment to hell. Faith in Christ, repentance, baptism, and receiving the Holy Ghost are prerequisites for dwelling with the Father and the Son. Because everyone will have an opportunity to be baptized, those who prefer to remain in the dark and reject their opportunities will inherit kingdoms less glorious than the celestial, but they inherit kingdoms of glory, nonetheless.[63]

76. From you it must be preached unto them. Once again the Lord lays upon the Saints the obligation of taking the gospel to the world.

76. And your brethren in Zion for their rebellion. Reference is made here to the tension that had developed between Sidney Rigdon, Edward Partridge, and others in Missouri. These tensions had for the most part been resolved by the parties involved during the conference in Independence the preceding 24 April (1832).[64] Although the historical record shows that all parties were conciliatory at that time, it seems that the Saints in Zion soon rekindled some hard feelings.

The commandment contained here to upbraid or reprimand the Saints in Missouri for their unbelief was followed by two letters to them, both dated 14 January 1833. One of these was from Joseph Smith, and it contained the text of Doctrine and Covenants 88. The other was from Orson Hyde and Hyrum Smith, writing for the Church in Kirtland. The text of these letters calling the Missouri Saints to repentance can be found in *History of the Church,* 1:316–21.[65]

77. That ye become even as my friends. The Church leaders of 1832, many of whom were eventually ordained apostles, are commanded here to go out as did the apostles of old.

78. Purse or scrip. Means of carrying money and belongings. We might say "without wallet or suitcase" today. The missionaries of that day were not to take provisions with them beyond the clothes on their back, not even enough for one day.

79. To prove the world. An older meaning of *prove* is "to test or try." The sense here is to preach the gospel to the world and by doing so to divide the listeners into sheep and goats: those who belong to the Savior's flock and those who do not. The test applied by the preacher "proves" the character of the listener sufficiently to establish the facts (or provide "proof") at the Judgment Day.

79. The laborer is worthy of his hire. The missionary preaching was to be supported by those who received the message. The full-time labor of the missionaries in taking the gospel to the world was worth the support of those who heard their message. That hardly amounts to a "paid ministry" because the brethren received only their bare sustenance and accumulated nothing—having no purse to put it in (see v. 78).

81–84. Take ye no thought for the morrow. Remember that these instructions and promises are for the leaders of the Church and other missionaries sent out by them, as they travel without purse or scrip (see JST Matthew 6:25; 3 Nephi 13:25). These instructions and promises are *not* intended as commandments or advice for the Saints generally in living their everyday lives. Otherwise, we would not worry about such things as a year's supply. We would set no goals, make no plans, prepare for no future possibilities. If such advice were to be generally applicable to the Church, there would be no bishops' storehouses, no scheduled meetings or conferences, or even plans for the eventual establishment of Zion. On the contrary, the Lord expects his Saints to be wise stewards and to take appropriate "thought for the morrow" and beyond. These instructions are for full-time missionaries who travel without purse or scrip.

85. Neither take ye thought beforehand what ye shall say. Once again, these instructions apply to missionaries who cannot anticipate in advance what topics or questions may arise in the course of their work. This instruction should not normally be applied to speaking, preaching, or teaching assignments within the Church, where a great deal of thought and preparation is expected of those who magnify their callings.

86. Unto all the faithful who are called. The commandment concerning purse or scrip (see vv. 78–86) is applied to all subsequent missionaries. However, on 16 September 1860, President Brigham Young said that missionaries should no longer follow the practice of asking members in the mission field for support. Instead, that support should come from members at home. The laws of the United States and other nations (for example, vagrancy laws and visa requirements) also made traveling without purse or scrip socially unfeasible and a hindrance to the work.

87. I send you out to reprove the world. "'Reprove' . . . is to 'convict.' God's messengers, as it were, are lawyers before the bar of God. It is their duty to 'convict' the world of sin, and to warn all men of the 'judgment which is to come.' They are not sent out to entertain the world with philosophical lectures, or ethical discourses, or flowery oratory, or amusing anecdotes. Their one duty is to secure conviction and, if possible, repentance and salvation."[66]

88. Mine angels round about you. The ministry of angels is real, even though we may be unaware of their presence and their aid.

89–91. Note the similarity between these verses and Matthew 25:34–46 ("Come ye blessed . . ."), which passage is not usually perceived in terms of missionary work. Yet it is clear by the parallels here that missionary work is an important setting and application for the passage in Matthew.

92. Cleanse your feet even with water. This is an apostolic responsibility not extended to other missionaries. The action described here is a variation on shaking the dust off the feet.[67]

94–97. See Doctrine and Covenants 1:1–23, 33–38; 5:19; 45:31 and Commentary.

97. Cut short in righteousness. A reference to the second coming of Christ.[68]

98. All shall know me, who remain. When the Lord returns and cleanses the earth by fire, all who remain to inhabit his millennial kingdom will be his. Although not all will be Church members, for many good people of other faiths will be worthy of his millennial kingdom, it will not take long for the truth to spread among the good people of all the earth.

98. Sing this new song. When the kingdom is established upon the earth, it will be possible for the first time to sing of the Lord's mighty works as already accomplished instead of as future. The new song that will be sung will celebrate the works of the victorious Christ. From that perspective, the Saints will sing specifically of the following: He has established Zion. He has redeemed his people by his grace through their faithfulness to his covenant (see D&C 20:30). He has redeemed his people by casting out Satan and bringing them from mortal time into eternity. He has reunited what was separated or lost—the house of Israel, the family of Abraham, the Zion above and the Zion below, God and his people. He has glorified the earth upon which he now stands, and he has done it all with perfect mercy, justice, grace, truth, and peace. Said President Rudger Clawson of the Quorum of the Twelve: "I declare to you, my brethren and sisters, that this new song . . . is one of the greatest songs that was ever written, and I have no doubt that it is a greater song than anything that ever can be written, because it sets forth the works of Almighty God and the consummation of all things."[69]

99. The Lord hath brought again Zion. The establishment of the millennial kingdom is the establishment of Zion permanently and perfectly upon the earth. Zion will be established in more than one way, however. It will be "brought down . . . from above," referring to the return of the City of Enoch, the heavenly Jerusalem, which the Lord shall bring with him at the time of his return.[70] Zion will also be "brought up . . . from beneath," referring to the Zion established upon the earth by faithful Saints, living and dead, who will be lifted up from the earth at the last day (see 1 Thessalonians 4:16–17). These are the Saints who have kept their covenant with the Lord to build Zion, even if it is only in their own homes or neighborhoods. Undoubtedly, it will include the righteous of other faiths who would have accepted the gospel on earth and worked to build Zion if only they had had the opportunity (and who subsequently did so in the world of spirits) (see D&C 137:6–7).

99. The Lord hath redeemed his people, Israel. The Lord, of course, is Jesus Christ. To redeem is to buy back. Thus, Israel will sing the song of Jesus' redeeming them from death, sin, and hell. They are redeemed from death by the resurrection, which will begin when the physical kingdom is established. They are redeemed from sin by the cleansing of baptism in his name. They are redeemed from hell by their second birth, for they belong to Christ and not to Satan. The wicked, those who are filthy still when Christ comes, will remain in Satan's power, in hell, for the thousand years of the Millennium (see D&C 76:84–85, 106; 88:101; Revelation 20:5).

99. The election of grace. In speaking of Christ's redemption of Israel, the new song uses the same language as does Paul in Romans 11:5. That election, or selection, or being chosen to inhabit Zion and the millennial kingdom, is here attributed directly to the grace of the Lord Jesus Christ "brought to pass by the faith and covenant of their fathers."[71]

We do not save ourselves. Jesus Christ saves us, redeems us, and glorifies us. It follows that because he performs these mighty works of salvation and redemption, we should rely upon his merits and celebrate and praise him in the new song rather than ourselves and our own accomplishments (see 2 Nephi 2:8; Alma 22:14; Moroni 6:4).

99. Brought to pass by the faith and covenant of their fathers. God's grace is not random but is associated with the mercy and justice of God (see v. 102). It is true that we cannot save ourselves, but we can choose to have faith in Christ and to enter and keep his covenant. If we are faithful to our covenants, which are the same covenants God made with our fathers Abraham, Isaac, and Jacob, Christ will redeem us by his grace. And by doing so he graciously keeps his promises both to us and to the fathers.

100. Time is no longer. It is common for Latter-day Saints to divide the future into "time" and "eternity." From this point of view, time is the present, fallen, and mortal world, whereas eternity is the world to come. (Though in the larger scope of things, our mortal time is also a part of eternity.) To say "time is no longer" does not mean that time is no longer reckoned after the beginning of the Millennium, for the Millennium itself is to last for a thousand years, and so someone has to be counting something (see Abraham, Facsimile 2, fig. 1). Rather, "time is no longer" means that the world and the time of our probation have come to an end, because Satan is bound, and there is no more delay to the establishment of Zion on earth (see D&C 19:2–3).

100. The Lord hath gathered all things in one. From the beginning, the establishment of Zion has been an attempt to gather together in one community those who have come to God and Christ and thus share one heart and one mind (see Moses 7:18). This unity of all into one is an eternal goal and will be largely accomplished in the great millennial kingdom (see D&C 27:13; 38:27; 41:6).[72]

101. The earth hath travailed. The earth is itself a living entity, which is said to suffer under the curse of the Fall and the sins committed upon its face by its inhabitants (see Moses 7:48–49). From the Fall until the second coming of Jesus Christ, the earth has been unable to exercise its real strength, which would make this world a paradise, as it was once in Eden and will be again in the Millennium. As we draw closer to the coming of the Savior and as the world ripens in sin, the earth's pains are compared to the increasing pangs of childbirth. Natural disasters will reflect the travail of the earth, becoming increasingly more severe as the end approaches. Then, with the coming of the Savior, it will be over, and the earth, like the mother she is, will be delivered and bring forth "her strength" for the new millennial age.

101. Clothed with the glory of her God. When the risen Christ returns, he will bestow the glory of a terrestrial world on the earth, making earth once again a paradise, as it was in Eden before the Fall.

102. To our God. To Jesus Christ as he appears here both in his own right and also as the image and representative of his Father in all things.

102. For he is full of mercy, justice, grace. When Christ stands victorious over all things at the last day, he will have obeyed perfectly, as he has already, all the laws and principles of the celestial kingdom. His mercy, justice, grace, truth, and peace will be perfect and infinite. Justice will not have been compromised in any degree by his exercising perfect mercy and grace. Truth will not have been compromised in any degree to bring about perfect peace.

103–5. Those who served missions were not to benefit personally thereby. If large sums of money were given to them, they were to be sent home for the support of their families or be sent to the bishops' storehouse for the building of Zion. If someone donated other goods, such as a coat, the missionary could keep the better of two, but he could not accumulate possessions. What he did not need, he was to give away.

Specifically, at the time this revelation was received, W. W. Phelps and Oliver Cowdery were in Independence, Missouri, preparing to print the Book of Commandments, which would contain the revelations received through the Prophet Joseph Smith. They were also publishing the newspaper *The Evening and the Morning Star,* in which some of the revelations appeared. This verse commands missionaries in 1832 to send any donated funds to these two brethren to assist them in paying the cost of printing the scriptures.

106. Take . . . him that is weak. People grow in spirituality through the example and training of others who are strong. Most faithful and obedient Saints are future leaders in the Church, if they are properly trained and nourished spiritually. A willing heart, a good example, and the power of the Holy Ghost can make the weak in spirit become strong. This principle can be applied today in the organizations and programs of the Church to effectively prepare members to serve in whatever capacity they are called to, be it a nursery leader or a general authority, as every calling in the Church is important in the eyes of the Lord.

108. This is the way that mine apostles. Examples would be Paul and Barnabas taking young John Mark with them (see Acts 13:5) or Paul later training Timothy and Titus (see Acts 16:1; Titus 1:4).

109–10. Let every man stand in his own office. These verses allude to and summarize the teaching of Paul to the Corinthians (see 1 Corinthians 12:12–27) in his famous analogy of the Church as the body of Christ and the Saints as its "members" (a word originally meaning "body part"). Every person in the Church has an office, a calling, or a function. Each part is needed, and if each "member" stands in his or her own calling and magnifies it, then all the parts work together and the body of Christ (the Church) functions effectively. But if anyone neglects his or her own duty or covets the calling of another, then the body of Christ (the Church) is handicapped. Let the head of the Church (who was Joseph Smith in 1832) be the head, and don't let the neck and shoulders or any other "member" try to be the head, or we deform and handicap the body of Christ, which is the Church. Let each "member" learn his or her own duty and perform it without jealousy or covetousness and without trying to perform or influence the duty of another.

112–16. These verses are directed specifically to Bishop Newel K. Whitney in Kirtland. His primary duty will be to care for temporal needs within the Church (see v. 112). He may hire someone to take care of the retail store, Newel K. Whitney & Co., while he does the business of the Church (see v. 113). Despite his primary duties, Bishop Whitney is also called on a preaching mission to New York City, Albany, and Boston. President Wilford Woodruff once stated that these three cities would be destroyed by earthquake, fire, and tidal wave, respectively.[73] These calamities are likely to be associated with the natural disasters immediately

preceding the end of this world (see v. 101). The mission commanded in verse 114 was undertaken by Bishop Whitney almost
immediately and lasted less than two weeks. He was accompanied
on this mission by Joseph Smith, who recalled "a hurried journey
to Albany, New York and Boston, in company with Bishop
Whitney, from which I returned on the 6th of November, immediately after the birth of my son Joseph Smith, the third."[74]

117. The desolation of abomination. This term is also found
as "the abomination that maketh desolate" (Daniel 11:31; 12:11)
and "the abomination of desolation" (Matthew 24:15; Mark 13:14;
Joseph Smith–Matthew 1:12, 32). Idolatry, murder, sexual sin,
and perversion of rituals are among those sins described in the
Old Testament as abominations. An abomination of desolation is
sin so repugnant to God that his Spirit is completely withdrawn,
destruction follows, and the land is left desolate, or empty, of its
inhabitants.

The prophet Daniel described an event that would precede
the coming of the Messiah as "the abomination that maketh desolate" (Daniel 11:31; 12:11). This specific event would consist of
desecration of the temple and the perversion of its worship, which
would leave the temple desolated of God's Spirit. This, in turn,
would lead to the eventual political destruction of the people of
the Holy Land. Jews anciently understood the abomination of
desolation as idolatry, bloodshed, and other heinous sins committed in the Temple, particularly the attempts by pagan rulers to
institute idolatry in the Jerusalem Temple, as in the cases of the
Seleucid Greek king Antiochus IV (ca. 167 B.C.) and the Roman
emperor Caligula (ca. A.D. 42).

When Jesus referred to the abomination of desolation, however, he added a warning: "Whoso readeth, let him understand"
(Matthew 24:15), thus indicating the possibility of another meaning for the term beyond the physical desecration of the Jerusalem
Temple (which took place in A.D. 70). The apostle Paul alludes to
this additional dimension of the abomination of desolation in
2 Thessalonians 2:3–11. In Paul's reference, the temple which will

be desolated is equated with the Church of Jesus Christ (see 2 Thessalonians 2:4; see also Ephesians 2:19–22; 1 Corinthians 3:16–17; 2 Corinthians 6:16; 1 Peter 2:5). The abomination is the "falling away," or apostasy, of the members (2 Thessalonians 2:3), which sets up a false idol in the temple (the Church). This false idol is the "man of sin," or "son of perdition" (2 Thessalonians 2:3), who usurps the rightful place of God, the "Man of Holiness" (Moses 6:57). This idol, of course, is the wicked one, or Satan (see 2 Thessalonians 2:8–9), who deceives the members of the Church into believing a false gospel. According to Paul, this "mystery of iniquity" was already at work in the Church as he wrote to the Thessalonian Saints (2 Thessalonians 2:7) and was in fact almost complete.

Thus, while the "abomination of desolation" refers on one level to the desecration of the physical temple of God (which took place as prophesied in A.D. 70), on another level it refers to the desecration of the spiritual temple, the Church of Jesus Christ, and to the perversion of its doctrines and ordinances in a Great Apostasy (which also took place as prophesied; see D&C 1:15–16). The servants of God, newly called in this dispensation, are to reveal to the world that there has been an apostasy, call the world to repentance, and show them how to avoid the additional desolations that will inevitably precede the coming of the Messiah (see Joseph Smith–Matthew 1:32).

On a more general level, the principle could be stated that whenever people commit abominations, they bring upon themselves desolation. The Spirit of God withdraws, their priesthood is no more, and they are left to themselves and to the consequences they have freely chosen.

120. Alpha and Omega. See Commentary on Doctrine and Covenants 19:1.

---

1. Cannon and Cook, *Far West Record,* 47–48.
2. See Smith, *History of the Church,* 1:271–72.
3. See Anderson, *Joseph Smith's Kirtland,* 34–36.

4. *Times and Seasons* 5 (1 Oct. 1844): 660; see also Whitney, *Times and Seasons* 5 (15 Oct. 1844): 686.

5. Charles C. Rich Papers, as cited in Cook, *Revelations of the Prophet Joseph Smith,* 174.

6. Jessee, *Personal Writings,* 272–73; spelling, punctuation, and grammar standardized. It should perhaps be noted that Sidney did not need to repent of his depression, only of the false statements he made under its influence.

7. See Van Wagoner, *Sidney Rigdon,* 116–18.

8. See Background to D&C 99.

9. Smith, *History of the Church,* 1:286–87.

10. See MS 1, as cited in Woodford, "Historical Development," 2:1061, and Kirtland Revelation Book, 24; see also the discussion in Cook, *Revelations of the Prophet Joseph Smith,* 176–77.

11. See Commentary on D&C 77:66.

12. Smith, *History of the Church,* 2:262; Ether 13:1–12.

13. See also D&C 36:2 and Commentary.

14. McConkie, *Ensign,* Apr. 1979, 65.

15. See Commentary on D&C 45:21.

16. Smith and Sjodahl, *Doctrine and Covenants Commentary,* 497.

17. See Commentary on D&C 36:2; see also Dahl and Cannon, *Encyclopedia of Joseph Smith's Teachings,* 506.

18. Smith, *Teachings of the Prophet Joseph Smith,* 181.

19. See Dahl and Cannon, *Encyclopedia of Joseph Smith's Teachings,* 507.

20. See Commentary on D&C 76:57.

21. See, for example, *Times and Seasons* 5 (15 Dec. 1844): 746.

22. See Ginzberg, *Legends of the Jews,* 1:232; 5:225–26.

23. See *Quaestiones,* 14.18.

24. Robinson, "Apocryphal Story of Melchizedek," 26–39.

25. The First Presidency [Joseph F. Smith, John R. Winder, and Anthon H. Lund], *Improvement Era,* Nov. 1909, 80.

26. Smith, *History of the Church,* 3:386.

27. Smith, *Teachings of the Prophet Joseph Smith,* 180.

28. See Robinson, *Are Mormons Christians?* 60–70.

29. Dahl and Cannon, *Encyclopedia of Joseph Smith's Teachings,* 506–7.

30. See Commentary on D&C 15:6.

31. Smith, *Teachings of the Prophet Joseph Smith,* 180–81; see also D&C 84:26.

32. See Commentary on D&C 42:18; 76:69.

33. See Oaks, in Conference Report, Oct. 1998, 48–52.

34. See Commentary on D&C 20:30.

35. See Commentary on D&C 76:69.
36. See Dahl and Cannon, *Encyclopedia of Joseph Smith's Teachings,* 507.
37. See Dahl and Cannon, *Encyclopedia of Joseph Smith's Teachings,* 351–56.
38. See Dahl and Cannon, *Encyclopedia of Joseph Smith's Teachings,* 286.
39. McConkie, *Doctrinal New Testament Commentary,* 1:89.
40. Smith, cited in Dahl and Cannon, *Encyclopedia of Joseph Smith's Teachings,* 352.
41. Smith, cited in Dahl and Cannon, *Encyclopedia of Joseph Smith's Teachings,* 354.
42. See Commentary on D&C 68:15.
43. See Commentary on D&C 84:6.
44. Brown, in Conference Report, Apr. 1963, 90.
45. Asay, in Conference Report, Oct. 1985, 58.
46. See Commentary on D&C 76:74, 82.
47. Romney, in Conference Report, Oct. 1960, 73.
48. See Commentary on D&C 84:20; 76:58–59.
49. See Commentary on D&C 58:12; 132:26.
50. Smith, cited in Dahl and Cannon, *Encyclopedia of Joseph Smith's Teachings,* 566.
51. Smith, cited in Dahl and Cannon, *Encyclopedia of Joseph Smith's Teachings,* 368; see also D&C 132:49; Mosiah 26:20.
52. Smith, *Doctrines of Salvation,* 3:141–42.
53. See Commentary on D&C 84:35.
54. See Commentary on D&C 1:38.
55. See Commentary on D&C 88:6–13; 93:23–40.
56. See Commentary on D&C 21:8; 49:8, 20; 82:2–7; see also Romans 3:23.
57. See Commentary on D&C 84:54.
58. Benson, *Teachings of Ezra Taft Benson,* 64.
59. Oaks, *Ensign,* Mar. 1994, 60–67.
60. See Commentary on D&C 58:29.
61. See Smith and Sjodahl, *Doctrine and Covenants Commentary,* 509.
62. See Smith, *History of the Church,* 1:271–72.
63. See Commentary on D&C 19:7.
64. See Commentary on D&C 82:1.
65. See also Background to D&C 85.
66. Smith and Sjodahl, *Doctrine and Covenants Commentary,* 518; see also D&C 84:79; 1.
67. See Commentary on D&C 24:15.
68. See Commentary on D&C 52:11.

69. Clawson, in Conference Report, Apr. 1932, 89.
70. See Commentary on D&C 42:9; 45:66.
71. See Commentary on D&C 3:20; 17:8; 20:30, 32; 76:69.
72. See Commentary on D&C 27:13; 38:27; 41:6.
73. See *Deseret News*, 12 Nov. 1884, 679; see also Cook, *Revelations of the Prophet Joseph Smith*, 177.
74. Smith, *History of the Church*, 1:295.

DOCTRINE AND COVENANTS

85

BACKGROUND

Since September 1832, Joseph and Emma had been living in Kirtland, Ohio, in quarters above Newel K. Whitney's store. On 6 November 1832, Joseph Smith returned to Kirtland from a brief mission to New York, Albany, and Boston to which the Lord had called Bishop Whitney and on which the Prophet accompanied him.[1] Sometime during the next three weeks, Joseph received letters from Church leaders in Missouri (Zion), which caused him to reflect upon the situation of the Saints there. On 27 November 1832, Joseph wrote to William W. Phelps concerning several things which were "lying with great weight upon [his] mind."[2] Although the original of Joseph's letter to Phelps has not been preserved, the file copy made by Joseph's scribe, Frederick G. Williams, is in the possession of the Church, and the full text has been published several times.

Brother Phelps received Joseph's letter in December 1832 and promptly published portions of it in the January 1833 issue of *The Evening and the Morning Star.* The full text of the letter, except a postscript, was also published at Nauvoo in the *Times and Seasons* for 15 October 1844.[3] In 1876 Orson Pratt was directed by President Brigham Young to include portions of the Phelps letter, roughly equivalent to what had appeared in *The Evening and the Morning Star* in 1833, as section 85 in the Doctrine and

Covenants. Section 85 did not appear in editions of the Doctrine and Covenants before 1876, but its inclusion as a divine revelation is clearly justified by the Prophet's language in verses 5–6 ("saith the Lord of Hosts," "thus saith the still small voice") and by his declaration in verse 10 that "these things I say not of myself."

Although the Prophet's letter was addressed to W. W. Phelps, the portions of it that make up Doctrine and Covenants 85 consist of instructions originally directed to John Whitmer, the Church historian, or "the Lord's clerk" (v. 1), who was then living in Missouri. These instructions emphasize the importance of obeying the law of the Lord governing inheritances in Zion and of documenting compliance with that law through scrupulous record keeping. It should be noted, perhaps, that just before Doctrine and Covenants 85 was received, Brigham Young, Joseph Young, and Heber C. Kimball traveled from Mendon, New York, to Kirtland to meet the Prophet Joseph Smith. They found the Prophet in a field behind the Whitney store where he was chopping wood with his brothers. Though all three had previously joined the Church (in April 1832), this was the beginning of their close association with the Prophet in Kirtland.

COMMENTARY

1. The Lord's clerk. At the time Doctrine and Covenants 85 was written, this title referred to John Whitmer, who had been called as the Church historian in Doctrine and Covenants 47.

1. To keep a history. On the very same day the Church was organized, the Lord directed that a record should be kept of its affairs (see D&C 21:1). As Church historian, John Whitmer already knew that he was to keep a general history of the Church in Missouri, for this had been specified when he was called (see D&C 47:1). In this revelation, however, Whitmer is instructed to keep other kinds of records as well, including financial and membership records for the Saints in Missouri (see vv. 1–5).

1. Those who consecrate properties, and receive inheritances. Financial transfers or conveyance of other resources between the Church and its members are to be matters of permanent Church records. This principle would include financial transfers made under the law of consecration in 1831, or under the laws of tithing, fast offering, and so forth, in the contemporary Church.

2. Their manner of life. The Church was also to keep what would today be called membership records, which would include an indication of an individual's standing in the Church. Church records were also to indicate those who left the Church after making sacred covenants.

3. Contrary to the will and commandment of God. The Lord had told his people very clearly how they were to establish Zion (see D&C 42; 48; 51; 56–59; 63; 70; 72). The law of consecration and the stewardship of property were sufficiently explained in these revelations and in instructions from the Prophet Joseph Smith. It was intended originally that "go[ing] up unto Zion" (D&C 72:24) from the East would be a privilege for those Saints who had prepared themselves both materially and spiritually and who would consecrate all their possessions to the bishop in Zion upon arriving there (see D&C 72:15). Those who went up to Zion were supposed to be debt-free and also were to have the means to purchase land in Missouri upon their arrival. Ideally, they were to bring with them enough food and clothing to last for a year.[4] Most important, they were supposed to be *called* to go up and were to arrive in Missouri with recommends from the Church in Kirtland attesting to their worthiness and good standing (see D&C 72:3–6, 16–18, 24–26).

Unfortunately, enthusiastic but disobedient members were emigrating to Missouri on their own without observing the Lord's law, without being called, and without sufficient financial resources or preparation. Their disobedience and the consequent financial drain they placed on the Missouri Church threatened the very establishment of Zion.[5] Whatever their motives may have been, the Lord commands here that such individuals were not to be accepted as members in good standing when they arrived in Missouri. No one should have claim upon the blessings of Zion who will not observe the principles of Zion or make and keep the covenants of Zion. Had this commandment been observed by the Saints in Jackson County, the financial pressures which frustrated the establishment of Zion there would have been greatly reduced.

4. Neither is their genealogy to be kept. This reference is not to genealogical records in the modern sense but rather to family membership records.

5. The book of the law of God. In Joshua 24:26, we are told that Joshua wrote in "the book of the law of God" an account of the covenant by which Israel entered the promised land. That same term is used here in a similar fashion to indicate a physical record of those who received inheritances in Missouri by covenant according to the law of God, that is, Doctrine and Covenants 42.[6] Apparently, the terms "book of the law of God" (vv. 5, 7), "book of remembrance" (v. 9), and "book of the law" (v. 11) all refer to the same record of those who have entered the covenant of consecration and are to receive inheritances in Zion.

7. One mighty and strong. See Commentary on Doctrine and Covenants 36:1. It should be noted that in the Old Testament "the mighty One of Israel" is distinctly and exclusively Jehovah, or the premortal Jesus Christ (Isaiah 1:24; see also 1 Nephi 22:12; D&C 36:1). Psalm 24:8 uses the title "strong and mighty" for Jehovah (see also Psalm 89:6, 8), while Doctrine and Covenants 65:1 refers to Christ as "mighty and powerful." Jehovah, or Christ, is called "the mighty God of Jacob" (Genesis 49:24), "the mighty God" (Isaiah 9:6; 10:21; 28:2–17), "a mighty and strong one" (Isaiah 28:2), "mighty in strength" (Job 9:4), and one who "goes forth in mighty power" (Mosiah 13:34). Dozens of additional examples might be cited to support the identification of the archetypical "one mighty and strong" as the Lord Jesus Christ, for there is none mightier or stronger than he. Moreover, it is Jesus, the millennial king, who will "hold the scepter" (v. 7; see also D&C

106:6; Numbers 24:17; Hebrews 1:8), whose "mouth utters eternal words" (D&C 85:7; see also Psalm 78:2; Matthew 13:35), and who is described as "a fountain" in scripture (v. 7; see also Jeremiah 2:13; 17:13; Zechariah 13:1; Ether 8:26).

More telling, however, is the identification of "the one mighty and strong" here in Doctrine and Covenants 85 as Jesus Christ. A comparison of verses 7–9 and their parallels elsewhere shows that the coming of "one mighty and strong" is described in section 85 in precisely the same language used elsewhere to describe the coming of Christ (see also Joseph Smith–Matthew 1:53–54).

The idea proposed by some that the "one mighty and strong" is some intermediary character who will arrive prior to the second coming of the Savior in order to straighten out the Church is incorrect. This is a distortion that persists only because it allows dissidents to envision the Church as presently in need of correction—and to declare themselves or someone else as the "one mighty and strong" called to steady the ark. But verse 8 makes it clear that the ark needs no one to steady it, just as it reveals the fate of any who may try. No one may steady this ark until the coming of Jesus Christ, the One Mighty and Strong, who will settle all accounts, right every wrong, and reward all his faithful Saints at his glorious coming. As a First Presidency message on this topic issued in 1905 and reprinted in 1907 stated very firmly: "Certainly this prophecy does not allude in any way to any President of the Church, past, present, or to come."[7] Thus, it would be impossible to interpret the coming of "one mighty and strong" as a change in LDS Church leadership prior to the second coming of Christ.

Still, though the Savior himself is the archetypical "one mighty and strong," when the Savior does come, he will establish an administration over his kingdom, and in that day whoever he appoints to act with his authority will also, by extension, be "mighty and strong." In this sense—as an extension of Christ himself—a millennial presiding bishop might also be referred to as "one mighty and strong."

7. To arrange by lot the inheritance of the saints. See Numbers 26:55–56; 33:54. "By lot" means by chance, as in drawing straws or drawing names from a hat. Arranging things by lot eliminates the possibility of any human influence or favoritism on the outcome. At the same time, since there is no random chance with God and he controls all things, the outcome will reflect his divine judgment.

Since the inheritances of all consecrated Saints are to be equal (adjusting for individual "circumstances, wants, and needs"; see D&C 51:3), there is no need to worry that a selection "by lot" will unfairly favor some or disadvantage others. In a sense, selecting equal inheritances "by lot" allows God to arrange his people however he wishes without the influence of preexisting bias on the part of the Saints.

8. That man. Latter-day Saint tradition has tended to identify "that man" in verse 8 as specifically and exclusively referring to Edward Partridge; however, a contemporary document indicates that this is too narrow an understanding. Over a year after Joseph wrote his letter containing Doctrine and Covenants 85 to W. W. Phelps, Oliver Cowdery wrote to John Whitmer to clarify the duties of the clerk as they had been given in that revelation. Concerning verse 8 specifically, Oliver wrote: "Brother Joseph says, that the item in his letter that says, that the man that is called &c. and puts forth his hand to steady the ark of God, does not mean that any one had at the time, but it was given for a caution to those in high standing to be ware, lest they should fall by the shaft of death."[8] Although the warning contained in verse 8 undoubtedly was intended for Bishop Partridge and his associates in Missouri, it was a warning only, and the phrase "that man" was not intended to single out an individual or to indicate that such a sin had already been committed.

There is no doubt that Edward Partridge experienced some difficulty in following all the instructions of the Prophet Joseph Smith, and it is likely that the warning in verse 8 was intended primarily for him. But Bishop Partridge was faithful, repented of his unbelief, and died in good standing in the Church.[9]

8. To steady the ark of God. The reference is to an incident recorded in 2 Samuel 6:6–7. When David brought the ark of the covenant to Jerusalem, Uzzah, one of the teamsters driving the wagon (see 2 Samuel 6:3), took it upon himself to steady the load by touching the ark himself rather than waiting for a priest to do it. For this presumption, Uzzah was struck dead "like as a tree that is smitten by the vivid shaft of lightning" (v. 8; see 2 Samuel 6:8). It doesn't matter how sincere our belief may be that those who hold the keys are wrong; when we presume to invade their stewardship and correct what we think to be "errors," we, like Uzzah, are steadying the ark. Even where there may be genuine problems, these must be resolved in the Lord's appointed way, through priesthood channels, and not by self-appointed judges or spiritual vigilantes.

9. Shall find none inheritance in that day. If a person's Church records show faithful obedience to the financial laws of God, then that individual will have a claim upon the Lord for an inheritance in his kingdom. Those Saints who have not kept their financial covenants will have no valid claim and will receive no inheritance in Zion or in the celestial kingdom. President Joseph F. Smith indicated that for contemporary Saints this referred particularly to the law of tithing.[10]

12. The children of the priest. When the Jews returned from their captivity in Babylon to Jerusalem beginning around 539 B.C., it was necessary to reconstitute the priesthood for service in the temple according to the genealogies and other records which had been kept during the captivity. At that time it was discovered that many who claimed the priesthood by right of descent could not prove their claim by the official records (see v. 11; D&C 128:6–7; Revelation 20:12; Daniel 7:10; 2 Nephi 29:11; 3 Nephi 27:25–26). These individuals were therefore dismissed from the priesthood as "polluted" or of irregular (non-Levitical) descent (Ezra 2:62; Nehemiah 7:64).

1. See Commentary on D&C 84:114.

2. Jessee, *Personal Writings*, 285–87; see also Smith, *History of the Church*, 1:297–99; *The Evening and the Morning Star,* Jan. 1833; *Improvement Era,* Oct. 1907, 928–42; Woodford, "Historical Development," 2:1079–83.

3. See *Times and Seasons* 5 (15 Oct. 1844): 673–74.

4. See *The Evening and the Morning Star,* Jan. 1833 and July 1833.

5. See Jessee, *Personal Writings,* 284; Cook, *Joseph Smith and the Law of Consecration,* 14–22.

6. See Cook, *Revelations of the Prophet Joseph Smith,* 178.

7. Clark, *Messages,* 4:107–20; see also *Improvement Era,* Oct. 1907, 928–29, 933, 939–42.

8. Cited in Cook, *Revelations of the Prophet Joseph Smith,* 179.

9. See Commentary on D&C 58:15; 82:1; 84:55–57, 76; compare D&C 124:19; Smith, *History of the Church,* 2:302–3.

10. See Smith, in Conference Report, Oct. 1899, 42.

86

BACKGROUND

During December 1832, the Prophet continued to work in Kirtland on his translation of the Bible, with Frederick G. Williams as scribe. In that same month, Joseph received three revelations focused directly upon events associated with the end of the world. Doctrine and Covenants 86 explains the parable of the wheat and the tares; section 87 describes the wars and destruction that were soon to rage over the earth; and section 88 discusses the redemption of Christ and other events relating to his second coming.

The parable of the wheat and the tares is found in Matthew 13:24–30, 36–43. Doctrine and Covenants 86 clarifies the timing and the sequence of the elements symbolized in that parable. In particular, verse 7 explains that it is the wheat, the children of the kingdom, who are to be gathered first, whereas the tares left over will then be bundled for burning. This reverses both the order and focus of the parable as it is given in the King James Version but also brings the parable into agreement with other scriptures.[1] Concerning this revelation, Joseph wrote simply, "On the 6th of December, 1832, I received the following revelation explaining the parable of the wheat and tares."[2]

COMMENTARY

1. The parable of the wheat and of the tares. See Matthew 13:24–43. Tares are a type of weed which closely resemble wheat in its developing stages, but which are clearly recognizable from wheat in their mature forms. Tares have a bitter taste, and, when eaten in appreciable amounts, are noxious to humans, causing dizziness and vomiting. The separation of wheat and tares in a crop must wait until the plants are mature at harvest, so that immature wheat will not be mistaken for tares and so that aggressive weeding will not uproot some of the wheat as well.

2. The field was the world. Doctrine and Covenants 86 changes the present tense of the King James interpretation to the past tense. This change indicates that the parable has a dual application, one for the meridian of time which has passed, and one for "the last days" (v. 4) in which we now live. When the good seed was sown in the former dispensation, the tares succeeded in choking the wheat and in driving the Church into the wilderness; in the second instance, "in the last days," quite a different outcome is predicted.

2. The apostles were the sowers of the seed. In the King James interpretation of the parable, the Lord identified himself as the sower of the good seed (see Matthew 13:37). However, after he had personally taught his apostles, he sent them out after his resurrection to "teach all nations" (Matthew 28:19), so the reference here is probably to the spread of the Church in the apostolic period. Moreover, according to Doctrine and Covenants 1:38, the one who is commissioned and sent is the same as the one who sends him ("whether by mine own voice or by the voice of my servants, it is the same"), so the point is moot.

3. After they have fallen asleep. As long as the apostles lived, the good seed or the children of the kingdom (see Matthew 13:38) remained. Only after those who held the keys of the Lord's work had been removed and the ordinances could no longer be performed with authority could Satan complete his work of choking out the good seed and driving the Church into the wilderness.

The elimination of the apostles and prophets was a final step in the completion of the Great Apostasy.

3. The apostate, the whore, even Babylon. Another scriptural designation for this entity is the "great and abominable church" (1 Nephi 14:3; 22:14), or the "church of the devil" (1 Nephi 14:10; see also Commentary on D&C 1:16; 18:20). A generation in the early history of Christianity knew the truth of the gospel and then wilfully perverted it, thus bringing about the Great Apostasy (see 2 Thessalonians 2:3–12).

3. To drink of her cup. See Commentary on Doctrine and Covenants 29:17; 35:11.

3. In whose hearts, the enemy, Satan, sitteth to reign. This is likely an allusion to 2 Thessalonians 2:4. In that passage, the "temple" in which Satan "sitteth" is the Church which is made up of the members collectively (see, for example, 2 Corinthians 6:16, where "ye," as always, is plural). When Satan instead of Jesus sits and reigns in the hearts of the members collectively, the Church of the Lamb has become "the church of the devil" (1 Nephi 14:10).

3. Soweth. When applied to human beings, as it is here, *sowing* must be understood as an act of begetting. Thus, the good seed are the wheat who have been "spiritually begotten" or "born of him" to "become his sons and his daughters" (Mosiah 5:7; see also Ether 3:14). On the other hand, those who are sown by Satan are the tares who are begotten as his own children through their apostasy (see John 8:44; Moses 7:37).

3. Drive the church into the wilderness. See Commentary on Doctrine and Covenants 33:5.

4. In the last days, even now. In the latter days, the good seed has been planted a second time upon the earth through the restoration of the gospel.

5. The angels are crying unto the Lord. See Commentary on Doctrine and Covenants 38:12.

6. Pluck not up. Compare Doctrine and Covenants 77:9 and Commentary.

7. First gather out the wheat. This verse changes the order of events in the parable as given in the King James Version. By doing so, the parable is brought into conformity with other scriptures, and the focus is moved from the burning of the wicked to the gathering of Israel.

7. The field remaineth to be burned. After the grain had been harvested, the fields of stubble and trash were burned, together with any weeds (tares) that remained. This practice eliminated the trash, destroyed the seeds of unwanted plants, sterilized the fields of some kinds of diseases and insect pests, and added valuable nutrients to the soil for the following year's crop.

8–11. These verses are closely related to the prophecy of Isaiah concerning the "messianic servant" (Isaiah 49) of the Lord and the ultimate redemption of Israel. The messianic servant is Jesus Christ. However, in his role as the prophet of the last dispensation, Joseph Smith is himself a type or shadow of the suffering servant who is Christ, a "light unto the Gentiles" and "a savior" (v. 11).[3]

8. You, with whom the priesthood hath continued. It was not the priesthood itself that had continued down through the lineage of Joseph and his associates (in which case there would have been no need for a restoration). Rather, it was the right by lineage to receive and hold the priesthood—when it was revealed—which these individuals had inherited from their ancestors. Doctrine and Covenants 86 is directed to the Lord's servants (see v. 1) in the latter days. Just as Joseph Smith is a direct descendant of the biblical Joseph (see 2 Nephi 3:6–7), and through Joseph a descendant also of Abraham, Isaac, and Jacob, so also are many other priesthood leaders and members in these latter days descendants of the ancient patriarchs. For these literal descendants of the patriarchs or fathers, the right to receive the priesthood comes with their lineage because of the promises made to the fathers concerning their posterity. When the literal descendants of the fathers turn to God in righteousness and seek their rights as heirs, God is obligated to reveal the gospel and the priest-hood to them (see Abraham 1:2–4).

God promised Abraham, Isaac, Jacob, and Joseph that the gospel and the priesthood would be restored in the latter days to their direct, biological descendants and that through their family the gospel and the priesthood would then be taken to the rest of the world (see Abraham 2:9–11). In this dispensation, God's promise to the patriarchs has been fulfilled by the restoration of the priesthood to direct descendants of Abraham and Joseph.

However, the fulfillment of this promise to the patriarchs that the gospel and the priesthood would be restored to their descen-dants first, in no way excludes other lineages from learning the gospel, coming to Christ, and receiving the priesthood and its blessings. In fact, it is the intent of God, and the mission of Israel that this very thing happen, through the leadership of these right-ful heirs in the latter days (see Abraham 2:10; Isaiah 49:12, 21–22; see also Commentary on D&C 19:27; 64:36).

9. Ye are lawful heirs. Joseph Smith and other Church lead-ers are literal descendants and therefore rightful heirs of the promises made by God to the fathers.

9. Hid from the world with Christ in God. The true sig-nificance of many things is known to God but hidden from the world. Among these hidden things are the true nature, lineage, identity, and importance of the Prophet Joseph Smith and of his associates in the leadership of the Lord's Church and kingdom upon the earth. Some hidden things might require knowledge of the premortal life, of foreordination, or of the postmortal spirit world in order to be understood at all, and these are things that the world does not know. The world perceives only the temporal, and therefore a true understanding of the Lord's servants and the importance of their work is hidden from the world's view (com-pare Isaiah 49:2; Colossians 3:1–3).

10. Your life and the priesthood have remained. "Your" here is plural, as is also indicated by the use of "ye" (which is plural) in verses 9 and 11. Because the Lord's servants (see v. 1) are rightful heirs of the promises made to the fathers, their lineage, speaking collectively, will continue to hold the keys and administer the kingdom until the Savior comes.

10. The restoration of all things. This glorious time began with the restoration of the gospel and of the priesthood in the latter days but will not be complete until all things have been restored. This would include the restoration of spirits to their bodies at the resurrection (see Alma 40:23–24), the restoration of the kingdom of David to its rightful ruler (see Acts 2:6–7), and the restoration of the earth to its paradisiacal glory (see Articles of Faith 1:10). In its fullest sense, therefore, the restoration of *all* things can only take place after the second coming of Christ and the establishment of his millennial kingdom upon the earth.[4]

1. See Matthews, *Plainer Translation,* 82.
2. Smith, *History of the Church,* 1:300.
3. See Jackson, "Revelations Concerning Isaiah," in Millet and Jackson, eds., *Studies in Scripture,* 1:326–30.
4. See Commentary on D&C 13:1.

BACKGROUND

During December 1832, while Joseph remained in Kirtland working on his translation of the Bible, national and world events caused the attention of many of the Saints, including the Prophet, to turn toward thoughts of the last days. According to Joseph, "Appearances of troubles among the nations became more visible this season than they had previously been since the Church began her journey out of the wilderness. The ravages of the cholera were frightful in almost all the large cities on the globe. The plague broke out in India, while the United States, amid all her pomp and greatness, was threatened with immediate dissolution. The people of South Carolina, in convention assembled (in November), passed ordinances, declaring their state a free and independent nation; and appointed Thursday, the 31st day of January, 1833, as a day of humiliation and prayer, to implore Almighty God to vouchsafe His blessings, and restore liberty and happiness within their borders. President Jackson issued his proclamation against this rebellion, called out a force sufficient to quell it, and implored the blessings of God to assist the nation to extricate itself from the horrors of the approaching and solemn crisis."[1]

Historically, the "solemn crisis" Joseph referred to was the so-called Nullification Controversy of 1832, in which the state of

South Carolina had declared for itself the right to nullify any federal law with which it disagreed, holding the rights of individual states to be superior to those of the nation collectively.[2] In November 1832, South Carolina declared that it had nullified certain federal tariffs and trade policies, almost precipitating a civil war.

Joseph Smith never connected his predicted rebellion of South Carolina (see v. 1) with trade and tariff issues, however. Rather, he identified slavery as the likely cause of the coming troubles. In 1860 Brigham Young informed the Saints that at the time Doctrine and Covenants 87 was received, the Prophet and his brethren had been pondering the question of slavery: "Brother Joseph had that revelation concerning this nation [D&C 87] at a time when the brethren were reflecting and reasoning with regard to African slavery on this continent, and the slavery of the children of men throughout the world."[3] On 2 April 1843, eighteen years prior to the Civil War, Joseph further clarified that on Christmas Day 1832, as he had been praying to know about the wars that were to come upon the nations, a voice had revealed section 87 to him (see D&C 130:12–13).[4] He further clarified at that time also that the rebellion of South Carolina would probably begin over the issue of slavery. Thus, in Joseph's own mind, the coming war was going to be fought, not over the tariff issues raised by the Nullification Crisis, but over slavery. Joseph's own brief account of receiving Doctrine and Covenants 87 merely states that "on Christmas day [1832], I received the following revelation and prophecy on war."[5]

However, Joseph's revelation on war was not published in 1835, nor in subsequent editions of the Doctrine and Covenants until 1876, although it was published in 1851 by Franklin D. Richards in England. In an address in 1860, Brigham Young referred to the still-uncanonized revelation: "Brother [Orson] Hyde spoke of a revelation which he tried to find in the Book of Doctrine and Covenants. That revelation was reserved at the time the compilation for that book was made by Oliver Cowdery and others in Kirtland. It was not wisdom to publish it to the world, and it remained in the private *escritoire*."[6] Perhaps it was feared in the early days that a revelation about the wars that were to fall upon the Gentiles would be interpreted as threats against non-members and have an incendiary effect upon the enemies of the Church. Other verses had also been held back from Joseph's revelations for similar reasons.[7]

Even though section 87 was not included in the Doctrine and Covenants until 1876, it is very well attested before that time and is, in fact, one of the most reprinted sections in that volume of scripture. The earliest extant copy of the revelation, in the handwriting of Sidney Gilbert, was made some time before 12 June 1833.[8] When the Civil War did begin, the exact and detailed correctness of Joseph's prophecy caused it to be considered an "oddity" by the national media, and Doctrine and Covenants 87 was printed and reprinted in non-LDS newspapers along with the question, "Have we not had a prophet among us?"[9]

In Joseph's own day, however, in consequence of the information received in Doctrine and Covenants 87, he was commanded by the Lord to write a warning letter to the nation. This he did ten days after receiving section 87.[10] His letter, to a Mr. N. E. Seaton (or, possibly, Sexton) was sent to Rochester, New York, and published in Seaton's newspaper there. Moreover, Joseph exhorted other persons in his own lifetime to warn their friends and relatives in South Carolina to repent and to flee the carnage that was coming to that area. For example, Wilford Woodruff's journal for 30 December 1860 records the following: "Brother Emmett Murphy [p]reached in the morning [and] gave an account of his receiving the gospel, his gathering to Missouri, his visit to Joseph in Prison, [and] the advice of Joseph the Prophet to him to go to South Carolina and Georgia and warn his friends of the wrath and desolation that the people in that land [would suffer] and to gather out his Friends to Zion, for the wars and rebel[l]ion would begin in South Carolina."[11]

Joseph Smith later prophesied that the coming war would

devastate Jackson County, Missouri, for its persecution of the Saints so that "[t]he fields and farms and houses will be destroyed, and only the chimneys will be left to mark the desolation."[12] This prophecy was fulfilled in every horrible detail.

Doctrine and Covenants 87 was first published in the first edition of the Pearl of Great Price, which was printed in England in 1851. It became part of the Doctrine and Covenants in 1876 when it was included by Orson Pratt at the direction of President Brigham Young.

COMMENTARY

1. The wars that will shortly come to pass. As the introduction to section 87 in the Doctrine and Covenants indicates, this is not just a revelation on the Civil War, but on war generally as it will apply to the Saints in the latter days. The Civil War will mark the *beginning* of a series of conflicts that will in time make "a full end of all nations" (v. 6). Thus, at the present time, the world is in the middle of a series of wars that began with the Civil War and that will continue until the whole earth is engulfed in armed conflict. The term "shortly" is used in reference to the Civil War specifically as the beginning of the series of wars to come. The actual time elapsed between this prophecy and the beginning of its fulfillment at the start of the American Civil War was 28 years.

1. The rebellion of South Carolina. On 17 November 1860, South Carolina passed an ordinance of secession and in the following month became the first state to secede from the Union. On 12 April 1861, Southern troops fired on the Union garrison at Fort Sumter in the harbor at Charleston, South Carolina, thus beginning the great War between the States.

1. The death and misery of many souls. There were more casualties of American citizens in the American Civil War than the combined totals for all other armed conflicts involving the United States from the Revolutionary War to the present day.[13] Of the approximately 2.4 million men who fought in the Civil War, almost half were killed or injured. At the time, this number represented a large percentage of the adult male population of the United States. In Missouri alone there were at least 487 separate battles, and Illinois lost no fewer than 35,000 men.[14] In addition, the economic hardships and negative social consequences of the Civil War continued to be felt well into the twentieth century in some parts of the country.

2. Beginning at this place. That is, beginning with the start of the Civil War in South Carolina. It is not surprising that the American Civil War marks the beginning of the wars of the last days, for the Civil War is generally accepted as the first "modern" war. For the first time, technology, tactics, politics, and other factors combined to make it possible to destroy hundreds of thousands and, later, even millions of persons in a relatively short time.[15] The world wars, holocausts, and "killing fields" endured since the Civil War would not have been possible on such a scale at an earlier time in the earth's history before the advent of "modern" technology, politics, and warfare.

3. The Southern States will call on other nations. Two separate historical periods are described in this verse. The first of these is the Civil War, during which the Southern States would enlist the aid of other nations, including Great Britain, against the Northern States. History shows that the South did seek aid and alliances from Great Britain and also from France, Holland, and Belgium. These nations offered passive support to the South but would not enter into official political and military alliances unless the Confederacy could demonstrate some likelihood of ultimate victory.

A second historical period is described in the last half of this verse, when "they shall also call upon other nations" to defend themselves from still "*other* nations." When the events described in this verse take place, war will become worldwide. Brother Sidney B. Sperry noted that the pronoun "they" in this passage refers not to the South but to the nations to which the South had previously appealed, that is, to Great Britain and France, Holland, and Belgium.[16] This seems likely, since the South never sought military aid against "other nations" (foreign powers) but only against the Northern States. Thus, the prophecy in verse 3 indicates that during the Civil War the South would call upon Britain as well as on other nations. Then, at a later time, Britain, France, Holland, and Belgium would in turn also call upon other nations for help against their enemies, and war would at that time be poured out upon the whole world. In fact, Great Britain and these other nations did seek the aid of other nations at least twice in the twentieth century, and on each occasion the result was a world war.

4. After many days. In contrast to the beginning of the Civil War which would happen "shortly" (v. 1), it is clear that the events described in verse 4 are separated from the Civil War and its following world wars by "many days."

4. Slaves shall rise up against their masters. The time frame here is the key to understanding this statement. "Many days" after the Civil War and "many days" after the world wars in which Britain and her allies call upon other nations for help, *then* will slaves rise up against their masters. In chronological context, it will be seen that the reference cannot be to the black slaves of the nineteenth century South, who for the most part did *not* rise up against their masters, but to all inhabitants of the earth who are in political or economic bondage in a period after the world wars. Brigham Young stated that Joseph Smith and the brethren had been pondering the slavery both of black Africans in the Americas and of all the peoples of the world when this revelation came to him.[17] In other terms, a worldwide outbreak of demands for independence and self-determination on the part of every conceivable ethnic, political, racial, economic, linguistic, or religious group will tear the nations of the world apart and engulf the earth in blood and war. We have seen this process at work specifically in such former Communist Bloc countries as Chechnya, Azerbaijan, Bosnia, and so forth. No doubt we will see more in the future.

4. Who shall be marshaled and disciplined for war. Satan loves war, and wherever Satan has gained influence on the earth there will be elaborate and expensive preparations for war. As the nations of the earth prepare to wage war with each other, it appears that their own minorities, splinter groups, and "breakaway republics" will cause internal dissension and collapse.

5. The remnants who are left of the land. These are the remnants of the twelve tribes of Israel, who are scattered throughout the nations of the earth, and particularly the remnants of the Nephites in the New World. When the times of the Gentiles have been fulfilled in the latter days, and the gentile nations have had their opportunity to accept or reject the gospel, then the power of the Lord will rest once again upon the remnants of Israel, the Jews, the Lamanites (who are the descendants of Nephi as much as of Laman; see Commentary on D&C 3:17–20), and others. These remnants of the house of Israel will rise up among the Gentiles like a lion among the sheep. The justice of the Lord will then fall upon the Gentiles who have rejected his gospel, just as it fell anciently upon the ten tribes, the Jews, and the Nephites when they rejected it. Read 3 Nephi 20:10–20 for a full description of these events as prophesied by Christ to the Nephites (see also 3 Nephi 5:23–24; Mormon 5:24).

A copy of Doctrine and Covenants 87 reprinted in the *Millennial Star* for 28 January 1860 further indicated that "the remnants" mentioned could be understood as the house of Joseph, Lamanites or Native Americans, while "the Gentiles" are the populace of the United States.[18]

6. The inhabitants of the earth shall mourn. In the end time, both man-made disasters, such as wars, and natural disasters, such as earthquakes and plagues, will increase until the whole world mourns. Joseph Smith described these future events thus: "The time is soon coming, when no man will have any peace but in Zion and her stakes.

"I saw men hunting the lives of their own sons, and brother murdering brother, women killing their own daughters, and daughters seeking the lives of their mothers. I saw armies arrayed against armies. I saw blood, desolation, fires. The Son of Man has said that the mother shall be against the daughter, and the daughter against the mother. These things are at our doors. They will follow the Saints of God from city to city. Satan will rage, and the spirit of the devil is now enraged. I know not how soon these things will take place; but with a view of them, shall I cry peace? No; I will lift up my voice and testify of them. How long you will have good crops, and the famine be kept off, I do not know; when the fig tree leaves, know then that the summer is nigh at hand."[19]

A first taste of these conditions would be experienced with the Civil War and the world wars, but the full realization of the "consumption decreed" (v. 6) will only be experienced as we approach the world's last day. Thus, it will be necessary for the Saints to recognize the signs of the times through their study of the scriptures and by listening to the words of the prophets and gather to the stakes of Zion for safety.

6. Chastening hand of an Almighty God. The destruction of the nations will not be an arbitrary act. It will be the just punishment meted out to them by God for rejecting the gospel, killing the prophets, and persecuting the Saints (see v. 7). According to Doctrine and Covenants 63:33, in these wars "the wicked shall slay the wicked." In the beginning of this dispensation, the American Civil War marked a judgment upon the United States for their treatment of the Saints, just as worldwide consumption of the nations will mark God's judgment upon all nations for the same sins as we draw closer to the end.

6. A full end of all nations. The only political entity that will pass from this fallen, telestial world into the glorious, terrestrial Millennium intact will be the kingdom of God. All nations, including the United States, will be consumed in the chaos and destructions that precede the coming of Jesus Christ. In the Millennium, there will be only one kingdom and one King.

It is possible that events preceding the Savior's glorious appearance to the Nephites will prove to parallel events preceding his glorious coming in our own dispensation. These parallels might include the rise of gangs and conspiracies (see 3 Nephi 1:27–30; 6:27–28), the increasing wickedness of the people (see 3 Nephi 2:1–3), wars, famines, and sieges (see 3 Nephi 4:2–5), the worst battles in Nephite history (see 3 Nephi 4:11), corruption of the legal system (see 3 Nephi 6:11–12, 21–30), the collapse of government and division into smaller groups (see 3 Nephi 7:2–6), the growth of the Church (see 3 Nephi 7:24–26), and, finally, unexpected natural disasters and the destruction of the wicked (see 3 Nephi 8–10).

7. The cry of the saints, and of the blood of the saints. God is a God of justice, and those who reject his mercy offered in the gospel covenant must suffer his justice when they have ripened in iniquity. Elder George Q. Cannon wrote: "There is no sin that a nation can commit, which the Lord avenges so speedily and fearfully, as he does the shedding of innocent blood, or, in other words, the killing of his anointed and authorized servants. No nation which has been guilty of this dreadful crime has ever escaped his vengeance."[20]

7. The Lord of Sabaoth. In the Old Testament, "Sabaoth" is a Hebrew word usually meaning "hosts" or "armies," and "the Lord of Sabaoth" is usually translated as "the Lord of Hosts." However, there are no vowels in ancient Hebrew, and the root consonants s-b-t are also found in the words for "sabbath," "seven," "oath," and others. This similarity of spelling and pronunciation makes wordplay between these ancient terms possible. It is likely that here, in the revelation on war, the term Sabaoth should be understood primarily as "hosts" or "armies."

8. Stand ye in holy places, and be not moved. According to President Ezra Taft Benson, "Holy men and holy women stand in holy places, and these holy places include our temples, our chapels, our homes, and the stakes of Zion."[21] To stand in holy places is to stand in the spiritual Zion we have sacrificed to create, build up, and serve in our own homes, wards, and stakes of the Church.

8. It cometh quickly. See Commentary on Doctrine and Covenants 33:18.

1. Smith, *History of the Church,* 1:301.
2. See the detailed treatment of the political issues in Smith and Sjodahl, *Doctrine and Covenants Commentary,* 533–37; Cannon, "Prophecy of War," in Millet and Jackson, *Studies in Scripture,* 1:335–39.
3. Young, *Journal of Discourses,* 8:58; see also Journal History, 20 May 1860, as cited in Woodford, "Historical Development," 2:1105.
4. See Smith, *History of the Church,* 5:324, 6:116; Grant, *Journal of Discourses,* 2:147.
5. Smith, *History of the Church,* 1:301.
6. Young, *Journal of Discourses,* 8:58.
7. See Background to D&C 5.
8. See Woodford, "Historical Development," 2:1114.
9. "A Mormon Prophecy," *Philadelphia Sunday Mercury,* 5 May 1861.
10. See Smith, *History of the Church,* 1:312–16.
11. Cited in Woodford, "Historical Development," 2:1108.
12. See the excellent article by Grey, "Joseph Smith and the Civil War," 1–22, esp. 12–13; see also Roberts, *New Witnesses for God,* 1:298–99.
13. See Cannon, "Prophecy on War," in Millet and Jackson, eds., *Studies in Scripture,* 1:337.
14. See the sources in Grey, "Joseph Smith and the Civil War," 20; compare Webb, *Battles and Biographies of Missourians,* 5; Howard, *Illinois,* 298.
15. See Rubenstein, *Cunning of History,* 7.
16. See Sperry, *Compendium,* 419–20.
17. Young, *Journal of Discourses,* 8:58.
18. See "Dark Day of the United States," *Millennial Star,* 28 Jan. 1860, 51.
19. Smith, *History of the Church,* 3:391.
20. *Millennial Star,* 4 June 1864, 361.
21. Benson, "Prepare Yourselves for the Great Day of the Lord," 68.

DOCTRINE AND COVENANTS

88

BACKGROUND

During December 1832, Joseph Smith continued his work on the Joseph Smith Translation at Kirtland, Ohio, and continued to receive in connection with that work some remarkable visions concerning the future of the world.[1] Doctrine and Covenants 86 dealt with the second coming of the Savior, the gathering of the wheat and the tares, and the Final Judgment. Section 87 dealt with the wars and horrors that would precede the Lord's coming and which were soon to be poured out upon the nation and upon the world. According to Jedediah M. Grant, "The prophet stood in his own house when he told several of us of the night the visions of heaven were opened to him, in which he saw the American continent drenched in blood, and he saw nation rising up against nation. . . . The Prophet gazed upon the scene his vision presented, until his heart sickened, and he besought the Lord to close it up again."[2]

Naturally, after Joseph had seen such terrible things lurking in the future of the world, both he and those with whom he shared these visions (see D&C 86–87) were concerned for the future of the Church and the Saints. Consequently, on 27 December, two days after Doctrine and Covenants 87 had been received, a council of ten leading high priests met to plead with the Lord for additional understanding, and God blessed them—

and all his Saints—with a great revelation for the coming New Year. However, this was not a revelation of future doom and woes, but a revelation of peace and comfort for the Lord's people, both at that time and in times to come. Doctrine and Covenants 87, the great revelation on war, was followed by section 88, the even greater revelation on peace, comfort, and light.

The circumstances under which section 88 was received were recorded in the Kirtland Council Minute Book. A council of high priests had convened in Joseph's translating room above the Whitney store in Kirtland. "Bro Joseph arose and said, to receive revelation and the blessing of heaven it was necessary to have our minds on God and exercise faith and become of one heart and of one mind. Therefore he recommended all present to pray separately and vocally to the Lord for to reveal his will unto us concerning the upbuilding of Zion & for the benefit of the saints and for the duty and employment of the Elders. Accordingly we all bowed down before the Lord, after which each one arose and spoke in his turn his feelings, and determination to keep the commandments of God. And then proceeded to receive a revelation concerning the duty [of the Elders as] above stated. 9 o'clock P.M. the revelation not being finished the conference adjourned till tomorrow morning 9 o'clock A.M. [28th] met according to adjournment and commenced by Prayer thus proceeded to receive the residue of the above revelation."[3]

In forwarding a copy of this revelation, Doctrine and Covenants 88, to the Saints in Zion, Joseph wrote, "I send you the Olive Leaf which we have plucked from the tree of Paradise, the Lord's message of peace to us."[4] The context of this letter indicates that section 88 was not only to serve as a message of peace to all the Saints as they struggled in the world, but also as a message of peace and reconciliation from the Kirtland brethren to some of their troubled colleagues in Missouri.

Unfortunately, the historical picture concerning the dates for Doctrine and Covenants 88 is not entirely without difficulties. The Kirtland Revelation Book agrees with the Kirtland Council Minute

Book that parts of section 88 were received on each of two different days, but it gives the second date (for vv. 127–37, which deal with the School of the Prophets) as 3 January 1833—the following week rather than the following day. The Kirtland Revelation Book is supported in this dating by *The Evening and the Morning Star* (10 Mar. 1833). However, the Kirtland reprint of *The Evening and the Morning Star* (May 1836) was later corrected to give the date of 27 December. So, it remains unclear whether Doctrine and Covenants 88 was received on two days (27 and 28 December, as recorded in the Kirtland Council Minute Book and *The Evening and the Morning Star;* 27 December and 3 January, as recorded in the Kirtland Revelation Book and *The Evening and the Morning Star*), or whether it might actually have been received on three days (27 and 28 December for vv. 1–126 and 3 January for vv. 127–37). Finally, verses 138–41 were added to the end of this revelation by Joseph Smith sometime before publication of the 1835 edition of the Doctrine and Covenants. Because the Kirtland Council Minute Book refers to the instructions contained in these verses as having been given to the Prophet before 23 January 1833, they must have been received with the original revelation, but for some reason the verses were not included in written versions of Doctrine and Covenants 88 until 1835.[5]

COMMENTARY

2. The alms of your prayers. Alms are gifts of charity or sacrifices for the needy. Alms and prayers are elsewhere linked in scripture (see D&C 112:1; Acts 10:4), but in the beautiful image created here, the time and effort required to pray is equated by the Lord with acts of charity and sacrifice. Remember, the blessing of Doctrine and Covenants 88 was obtained only through fervent collective and individual prayer for a considerable period of time.

2. Lord of Sabaoth. See Commentary on Doctrine and Covenants 87:7.

2. The book of the names of the sanctified. This is apparently the same as the Lamb's Book of Life in which the names and deeds of the righteous are recorded in heaven (see D&C 132:19; Philippians 4:3; Revelation 3:5; Alma 5:58). It is not enough for individuals to have their names recorded on the membership records of the earthly Church. In order to obtain celestial glory, their names must also be recorded in this book of the sanctified (see Commentary on D&C 20:31). It should also be remembered that names once recorded in this book can also be blotted out through unfaithfulness (see Revelation 3:5; 22:19).

3. Another Comforter. Those who met in council on 27 December 1832, full of concern for the future, were mercifully given, first of all, an overwhelming blessing of divine comfort to their souls. The Comforter, or the *first* Comforter, is the Holy Ghost, which members of the Church receive as a gift at confirmation (see John 14:26). Those present during this revelation had, like all the Saints, received this first Comforter when they received the gift of the Holy Ghost. Joseph Smith taught clearly, "There are two Comforters spoken of. One is the Holy Ghost, the same as given on the day of Pentecost, and that all Saints receive after faith, repentance, and baptism."[6]

The mortal Jesus also promised his ancient disciples that he would send them *another* Comforter in addition to the first, *if* they would love him and keep his commandments (see John 14:15–16; note that Jesus' promise was conditional). This other Comforter, or the *second* Comforter, is not the Holy Ghost, but is the resurrected Christ himself appearing to a faithful disciple (see John 14:18, 21, 28). Again, Joseph Smith taught clearly, "Now what is this other Comforter? It is no more nor less than the Lord Jesus Christ Himself; and this is the sum and substance of the whole matter; that when any man obtains this last Comforter, he will have the personage of Jesus Christ to attend him, or appear unto him from time to time, and even He will manifest the Father unto him, and they will take up their abode with him, and the visions of the heavens will be opened unto him, and the Lord will teach him face to face, and he may have a perfect knowledge of the mysteries of the Kingdom of God."[7] A person who has received this other or second Comforter is said to have had his or her calling and election made sure and to be "sealed up" to eternal life.[8] Receiving the second Comforter is virtually equivalent to an unconditional promise of exaltation. Sealed by the Holy Spirit of Promise, the seal on this sure promise can be broken only by a person's committing the unpardonable sin.[9]

It is important not to confuse the two Comforters, who are two different members of the Godhead. Though neither of the terms "first Comforter" or "second Comforter" is found in scripture, they are used with some precision in the modern Church. The first Comforter, the Holy Ghost, testifies in our hearts and guarantees that our covenants are valid and that all God's promises to us will be kept *if* we will remain faithful. The second Comforter, or other Comforter, the resurrected Christ himself, testifies to us and guarantees that our probation is over, that we have been judged to be celestial in character, and that we will surely receive exaltation, with no additional conditions attached other than avoiding the sin against the Holy Ghost and the shedding of innocent blood.

3. The Holy Spirit of promise. The Holy Ghost is himself the Comforter, or the *first* Comforter received in the gospel covenant. However, there is *another* Comforter, a *second* Comforter, and the Holy Ghost has an important function in its reception as well. When we enter into the covenants of baptism and of the temple, the Holy Ghost seals the agreements and guarantees the validity of the covenants and promises. If we abide the conditions of our covenants, all God's promises *will* be kept. As Joseph Fielding Smith taught: "The Holy Spirit of Promise is *not* the Second Comforter. The Holy Spirit of Promise is the Holy Ghost who places the stamp of approval upon every ordinance that is done righteously; and when covenants are broken he removes the seal."[10]

When one receives the second Comforter, who is the risen

Christ himself, the Holy Ghost still has a role to play in this bless-ing.[11] The promise received by the faithful disciple from the risen Lord at this time is different than God's previous promises. The former promises were all conditional; this final promise, appar-ently, is not.[12] It is, rather, a declaration of what will surely hap-pen provided the disciple does not commit the unpardonable sin.[13] But this final promise of exaltation and eternal life, like any other, must also be witnessed, sealed, and guaranteed by the Holy Ghost. In his role as the one who witnesses, seals, and guarantees God's promises, the Holy Ghost is referred to as the Holy Spirit of Promise.

4. This Comforter is the promise. According to the usual contemporary usage of the terms "first Comforter" and "second Comforter," the language of verse 4 creates a slight difficulty, for the Comforter described here can be neither the person of the Holy Ghost nor the person of the Son, but, rather, is explicitly stated to be "the *promise* . . . of eternal life." It appears, therefore, that a distinction must be made between being *promised* "another Comforter," and actually *receiving* that second Comforter. On this occasion, the Kirtland council received exactly the same comfort-ing but conditional promise that the disciples of the mortal Jesus had received in John 14:15–28. Nevertheless, the risen Savior did not appear to the Kirtland brethren at this time, and ordinances and sealings necessary for their exaltation had not yet taken place. Moreover, the promised function of "[abiding] in your hearts" (v. 3) belongs exclusively to the Holy Ghost (see D&C 130:22), who is explicitly identified with this Comforter in verse 3. Therefore, verses 3 and 4 must be understood as describing a conditional promise given through the mouth of Joseph Smith and sealed by the Holy Spirit to *prepare* these brethren to receive the second Comforter—at some future time. Thus, three stages can be dis-cerned: first, one receives the first Comforter, the Holy Ghost. Second, one receives the specific promise of a second Comforter, who is the risen Lord. Third, one actually receives a guarantee of exaltation from the risen Lord. In Kirtland, receiving the promise recorded here, which was sealed by the Holy Ghost abiding in their hearts, prepared these brethren one day "to have the personage of Jesus Christ to attend [them], or appear unto [them] from time to time."[14] Receiving this promise on 27 December 1833 did not constitute the fulfillment or final realization of these blessings at that time.

5. Church of the Firstborn. See Doctrine and Covenants 76:54 and Commentary.

6. He that ascended . . . as also he descended. The personal experience of Jesus Christ spans eternity. He has personally experienced the highest degree of exaltation since he rose from the dead. But he had previously also descended from his position as God to become a mortal and to experience the worst of mortal sufferings (see Philippians 2:5–9). Then, in performing his vicarious atonement in our behalf, he further descended into the very bottom of the lowest pits of hell, "below all things." The experience of Jesus Christ in both its heights and its depths is now infinite in its scope and exceeds the combined experience or understanding of all human beings. No matter where we are, no matter what we experience, Christ has been there (see D&C 122:8; Ephesians 4:7–10). According to the apostle Paul and the prophet Alma, it is Jesus' experience of all things, either personally or vicariously, that gives him his infinite compassion upon those who suffer (see Hebrews 2:17–18; 4:15; Alma 7:11–12).

6. That he might be in all and through all things. But the omnipresence of the Son of God embraces more than just knowledge through experience. There is a further sense in which Christ has been everywhere and is "in all . . . things," both animate and inanimate. The Lord's omnipresence is spatial as well as experiential. How can a physical being with a physical body be "in all and through all things"? It is through the power and influence of his spirit which, despite what some philosophers say, is not limited to the confines of his physical body. Just as the power and influence of a light bulb can be present and can be perceived far beyond the physical bulb itself, even so the power, influence, and light of Christ extend beyond his physical body and radiate through the entire universe to be "in all and through all things."

7. The light of Christ. "The light of Christ refers to the spiritual power that emanates from God to fill the immensity of space and enlightens every man, woman, and child. Other terms sometimes used to denote this same phenomenon are holy spirit, 'Spirit of the Lord,' and 'Spirit of Truth,' but it is different from the Holy Ghost. The scriptures are not always precise in the use of such terminology, and several attempts have been made to describe the various aspects of this important manifestation of God's goodness and being."[15] The light of Christ is not a person, and it has no body, neither spiritual nor physical. It is a power, the creative power of God, which originates with the Father and has been given in its fulness to the Son. This power fills the universe, imposes laws or principles (see vv. 21–26, 36–42), and brings order out of chaos. The light of Christ is the divine energy and power of God which is employed to improve and to glorify all things. All energy, power, force, motion, heat, light, intelligence, instinct, truth, priesthood, glory, and so on, are dimensions— more or less pure and refined—of this light or power of Christ.

On the other hand, Satan has no power of his own. He has only that which has been temporarily allowed him. Thus, ultimately, his kingdom is dark, cold, and without energy, truth, or understanding.

Each person born into the world receives a portion of the light of Christ (see D&C 84:46; 93:2; John 1:9). This small portion is sufficient, in most cases, to enlighten our minds and allow the exercise of choice, or agency, for or against the light we have received. Those who love this light and seek it out, who follow their conscience, and who move toward the divine energy they sense in themselves and in the world around them will gradually be given more and more of God's light. Eventually, in this life or in the next, the faithful will receive more and more light "until the perfect day" (D&C 50:24).

7–10. The light of the sun . . . moon . . . stars . . . and

earth. Since all energy is some form of the power of God or the light of Christ, this also includes all the forces of creation and also the energy emitted by all created things. Sunlight, moonbeams, starlight, even the heat at the earth's core, are all manifestations of the light of Christ the Creator.

11. Enlighteneth your eyes . . . quickeneth your understandings. Just as the visible light of Christ makes it possible for us to perceive the physical world, so a more refined portion of the light of Christ, light from a different part of the spectrum, so to speak, makes it possible for us to perceive the intellectual and even the spiritual worlds. "God's light is also the power to understand and comprehend all things. In other words, all kinds of light are related to intelligence and truth. . . . The light of Christ therefore includes not only spiritual light but also physical light, and is a key to understanding that form of energy which is represented by the light we see all around us."[16] "Thus, the *truths* discovered by such men as Sir Isaac Newton, Thomas Edison, and Albert Einstein were actually revealed to them through the light of Christ. Such revealed truths have done much to free mankind from the slavery of ignorance and have extended the scope of our understanding of the universe. In like manner, through the power of the Holy Ghost, truths pertaining to the relationship of mankind to God and the mission of Jesus Christ have been made comprehendible."[17]

12. Proceedeth . . . to fill the immensity of space. There is not a particle of space that is not under the influence of God through the light of Christ. This light shines from the person of Christ himself and governs and controls all his creations. There is not a particle of existence that is not under his direct control. Not only is Christ the Creator of all that exists, but it is the indwelling light or power of Christ that holds things together in created form from moment to moment. This is what Paul means when he says, "And by him all things consist [or hold together]" (Colossians 1:17; see also D&C 88:41). The light of Christ is the power or the force that holds even the atoms and molecules of creation together. What scientists call the strong force, the weak force, gravity, and the electromagnetic force in physics are also manifestations of the creative power and light of Christ.

13. Which giveth life to all things. Since all energy is some form of the light of Christ, and since all living things require energy, then this light of Christ is also the source of life, breath, warmth, and so forth, for all living things. What we normally think of as the physical laws of the universe, the laws by which particles, bodies, and elements are governed and which give stability to existence and make life possible—these are also manifestations of the light of Christ and of his power displayed throughout the universe.

Elder John A. Widtsoe expressed his opinion that "associated with matter-energy was the implication in Joseph Smith's teachings that the energy in the universe is a form of intelligence; that is, in a manner not fully understood by man, some form of life resides in all matter, though of an order wholly different from the organized intelligence of men or higher living things. Hence, everything in the universe is alive. The differences among rock, plant, beast, and man are due to the amount and organization of the life element."[18]

13. The law by which all things are governed. God is a God of order and of power. Therefore everything that he creates is governed by him. He is the ultimate Law of all things and in all things. The power and influence by which he governs is the light of Christ. The Lord Jesus Christ revealed that "he is possessor of all things; for all things are subject unto him, both in heaven and on the earth, life and the light, the Spirit and the power, sent forth by the will of the Father through Jesus Christ, his Son" (D&C 50:27).

From time to time one hears the claim that God obeys laws. However, these are not the physical laws of our present world, but spiritual principles like love, justice, mercy, and so forth. God *imposes* physical laws and interrupts their operations with the application of higher laws entirely at his own will. God does not obey the universe; the universe obeys him. Neither is God like a graduate student in science, learning how things naturally work, for he tells them how they will work, and they obey him.

13. The bosom of eternity . . . the midst of all things. God rules his creation from its center, and all things revolve around him. According to Joseph Smith, this universal center of time and space, the throne of God, has a nearby star named Kolob (see Abraham 3:2–3; Facsimile 2:1–3, 7).

14. Redemption. See Commentary on Doctrine and Covenants 19:1; 45:17.

15. The spirit and the body are the soul of man. Once born into mortality to receive a physical body, we humans can never again be whole or complete without that body (see Genesis 2:7; Moses 3:7). Thus, the separation of our spirit and body at death is looked upon as "bondage" to us (D&C 45:17; 138:50) in a way we could not have comprehended as premortal spirits. In many ancient languages (including the Hebrew, *nephesh*), the words for *self* and *soul* are the same. Our whole soul must include our complete self, both our body and our spirit.

While the foregoing is technically the correct definition of the term *soul* for those who have reached mortality, not all the prophets nor all the scriptures have observed this distinction strictly but have occasionally used "soul" to equal the "spirit" alone (see, for example, Alma 36:15).

16. Resurrection . . . is the redemption of the soul. Since we cannot be complete beings without both our bodies and our spirits, the process of redemption from the powers of death and hell cannot be complete until our spirits and bodies are reunited in resurrection.[19] The earth and sea must give up our bodies, and the spirit world (Hebrew, *sheol*) must give up our spirits. Christ has done his work, and the promises made will be kept. Moreover, the spirits of the righteous may be said to be redeemed from the devil from the moment of their conversion. However, the process of redemption will not be fully completed, or the promise of redemption totally fulfilled, until our whole self, both body *and* spirit, is raised in the great resurrection of the dead. Thus, the righteous, both the celestial and the terrestrial (see D&C 45:54), will be redeemed in the first resurrection at or soon after the coming of the Lord, while the wicked will not be redeemed until the end of the Millennium (see D&C 76:84–85). At the end of the Millennium, all who have ever been born upon this earth will be redeemed from death through the power of the atonement of Christ. However, those few designated as perdition, though saved from physical death in resurrection, will not be redeemed from the second or spiritual death but will be cast into outer darkness with the devil and his angels (see D&C 76:32–39, 44–46).

17. Quickeneth. To "quicken" means to bestow life. It is only through the light of Christ that all things live.[20]

17. The poor and the meek of the earth shall inherit it. See Doctrine and Covenants 104:15–18; Matthew 5:5; Luke 6:20. The physical earth upon which we now live will, in its sanctified condition, be the celestial kingdom for all those who have lived upon it and are found worthy of that kingdom.

18–20. It must needs be sanctified. In its present state, however, this physical earth is in a fallen, telestial condition. Although the earth itself obeys the laws given unto it, it is limited by the wickedness and pollutions of her "children" (Moses 7:48). In order to become a celestial sphere, it must first be sanctified (or made holy; see D&C 20:30 and Commentary). This will be accomplished in stages. The earth has already experienced the Creation and the Fall, and it was baptized by water at the time of Noah. At the second coming of Christ, the earth will be baptized with fire and with the Holy Ghost, and all things that cannot abide a terrestrial glory will be burned away. The earth will be raised from its present telestial state to a terrestrial state for the period of the Millennium. At the end of the Millennium, the earth will go through a change analogous to death and resurrection and will be raised from a terrestrial state to celestial glory (see v. 26). From the beginning, it was intended that this earth would become a celestial world. The earth obeys that natural law which God has imposed upon it, and as a result of filling "the measure of its creation," it will ultimately be sanctified and glorified (v. 25).

21. Sanctified through the law . . . of Christ. See Doctrine and Covenants 76:70. The law which sanctifies those who are to receive celestial glory, and thus inherit the earth, is the "law of Christ." This law includes provision for repentance and forgiveness through the atonement of Christ by our faith in him. It is important not to become too legalistic here and forget that the law which sanctifies us includes provision for our human sins and weaknesses, if we will only repent and come unto Christ. The law of Christ (faith, repentance, baptism, receiving the Holy Ghost, and enduring to the end) will sanctify or *make* holy those who cannot make themselves holy (and no one can; see Alma 22:14; Romans 3:23), but who have come to Christ in faith (anyone can, but not everyone does; see 3 Nephi 27:16). Thus, those who have accepted the gospel and come to Christ can expect to be *made* holy (that is, be sanctified) and to inherit the celestialized earth.[21] All others, those who either would not accept the gospel or who would not live its principles, will eventually be forced to leave this earth and live somewhere else in eternity.

22–24. Who is not able to abide the law . . . cannot abide [the] glory. Each kingdom has its own system or law; the higher the law, the higher the glory. That law by which we attempt to govern ourselves here in mortality, even though we succeed at it only imperfectly (see vv. 29–31), determines the glory we will ultimately receive in the resurrection. The resurrection and final judgment will employ a process of segregating like with like. The celestial kingdom will be celestial, in part, because noncelestial individuals will simply be removed and will be put somewhere else with people who are just like themselves. This is not only just; it is also merciful. For, on the one hand, we will all receive in eternity what we sought to achieve in mortality (thus satisfying justice), while, on the other hand, we will not be forced to live forever under conditions or laws we cannot abide (thus allowing mercy).

24. Not a kingdom of glory. Those who will not abide any law but insist on being a law unto themselves cannot receive any portion of the commensurate glory or power of God.

25–27. See Commentary on verses 17–21.

27. A spiritual body. As used in the scriptures, the word *spiritual* often does not mean "immaterial" but rather refers to matter which has been infused with spirit. A spiritual body in this sense is not an immaterial or nonphysical body but rather a resurrected body into which both the spirit of the individual and the glory of God have been infused and joined together forever and ever. This is the sense in which Paul uses the term "spiritual body" of the resurrection in 1 Corinthians 15:44. Even today, when we speak of a spiritual person, we do not mean someone who is nonphysical. Rather, we mean someone physical in whom the power of the Spirit is particularly evident.

There is such a thing as a spirit body, or a body composed only of spirit, and before mortality all human beings possessed such spirit bodies. But this is not the same as the "spiritual body" of the resurrection, for once we obtain a physical body in mortality, it is our privilege in the resurrection to receive that same material body back again as a "spiritual body," that is, one united with our spirits inseparably and forever and infused also with some measure of the glory of God (v. 27; see also 1 Corinthians 15:44, 53–55; 2 Corinthians 5:4).

28. The same body which was a natural body. The "natural" body is our mortal, physical body in its present fallen state. According to Joseph Smith, "There is no fundamental principle belonging to a human system that ever goes into another in this world or in the world to come. . . . If anyone supposes that any part of our bodies, that is, the fundamental parts thereof, ever goes into another body, he is mistaken."[22]

28–31. Your glory shall be that glory by which your bodies are quickened. See Commentary on verses 22–24.

32. They who remain. These are the sons of perdition, who will be resurrected ("quickened"), but who will not progress in glory from that time on. Rather, they will regress, having lost their second estate (see Abraham 3:26), and will be consigned after judgment to their own place or condition—but apparently one totally without glory (see D&C 76:44–48).

32. That which they are willing to receive. Those who are consigned to perdition are perdition by choice. Throughout their mortal lives, then throughout their sufferings in hell before their resurrection, these individuals will not repent, will not bend, will not yield to God nor respond to his love and mercy. Thus, perdition is the ultimate expression of individual selfishness and pride: "I will have my way; I will not yield; I will not bend; I will not obey—no matter how terrible the cost—worlds without end." God's desire, his work and his glory, would be to exalt these sons of perdition, but he cannot, for they will not allow it. As free agents, they choose their fate with full knowledge of the consequences. They knowingly reject God and his plans and desires for their salvation.[23]

33. A gift. We sometimes forget that salvation in any degree of glory is a gift, indeed, the greatest of all God's many gifts (see D&C 6:13; 84:54–57; see also Alma 33:16). God seeks to give all his children the gift of salvation, but some just won't accept it. Similarly, in human relationships some people are too proud or too independent to accept gifts from others, and consequently they lose both the rejected gift and also the opportunity to strengthen their relationship with the rejected giver.

34–40. That which is governed . . . is also preserved. Nowhere is the link between agency, governance, and glory so well defined in scripture as in these verses. We are saved ("preserved"), perfected, and sanctified by that which we choose to obey. God does not, will not, cannot, force his laws upon us. Rather, he teaches us, through the light of Christ in its varying intensities, the consequences of obedience and disobedience to the varieties of law in the universe. We then choose what we are willing to obey and, consequently, what we are willing to be blessed by. Obedience to law enlarges, enables, and empowers us.

We are not restricted or limited by law, but are set free and propelled forward by our obedience to it. The greater our obedience, the greater our safety, perfection, sanctification, and glory (see vv. 29–31, 34).

Note that while we normally think of the wicked who ultimately receive telestial glory as *disobedient* souls (compare, for example, D&C 76:84, 103–5), Doctrine and Covenants 88 describes such souls as obedient, but as obedient to a lesser law (see vv. 24, 31, 38). While these individuals may not have abided a celestial or even a terrestrial law during the period of their probation, they did of their own free will choose to abide at least a telestial law (see D&C 76:81–89) and so are saved and glorified by telestial law on a telestial level.

In the scriptures, there is usually a difference between a *rule* and a *law*. For example, according to the rabbis, there are 613 rules (do's and don'ts) that make up the single law of Moses. The term *law*, then, often refers to a whole system or plan made up of many rules. As we choose to live by the law of Christ or the law of Moses, we may not succeed in keeping all the rules incorporated therein, or perhaps we may not succeed in keeping them all perfectly. Nevertheless, as we choose to govern ourselves (albeit imperfectly) according to one law or another in this life, we will eventually receive the fulness of that law's glory and blessings in the resurrection (see vv. 22–24, 28–32 and Commentary). The law we accept and live *here* (though somewhat imperfectly) in turn exalts us *there*, and those who reject all law in this life (perdition) will have no law to protect or preserve them in eternity.

35. That which breaketh a law. The reference here is to perdition, that which refuses to abide any law outside itself. Since perdition refuses to abide any law, there are no conditions under which they can be saved, for all things that are preserved in eternity are preserved by obedience to law. Obedience *enables*; disobedience *disables*. There is no other way. Further, since perdition seeks to abide totally in sin and refuses to abide any law, there can be no atonement made in their behalf to rescue them from spiritual death. Thus, at the resurrection, those who inherit perdition are raised up with all others who have lived upon the earth, but unlike those who inherit some degree of glory, these are raised up "filthy still" (2 Nephi 9:16), having refused all cleansing, mercy, and atonement.

36–39. All kingdoms have a law. All creation has been organized by God and placed under certain laws and conditions. However, not all kingdoms and laws are the same. That which does not have agency obeys the physical laws imposed upon it, and will receive the glory intended for it, by God. However, that which enjoys the priceless gift of agency must be allowed to find its own level and to live the law of its own choosing. The period between our mortal birth and our resurrection provides the time and means for accomplishing this. This "day of our probation" is a full twenty-four hour day and includes both the hours of sunlight (our mortality when progress is easiest) and also the hours of the night (our time in the world of spirits, when progress, for the wicked, is more difficult). In this brief period of probation, God allows that which has agency to sort itself out, to find its own level, and to choose its own law. In the long run, like will find like. The Saints will gather with the Saints, and the wicked will gather with the wicked.

39. Justified. See Commentary on Doctrine and Covenants 20:30.

40. Intelligence cleaveth unto intelligence. "Cleaveth unto" here means to be joined together with. In eternity, like will be joined to like. The laws of God will sort us out, or perhaps it would be more correct to say that by the laws of God we will sort ourselves out. The merciful will receive mercy (see Matthew 5:7). The loving will be loved (see Matthew 5:43–45). Those who seek for light will find light, and all things will be drawn to their own proper place to be surrounded by beings with the same virtues and the same values.

41. He comprehendeth all things. See verses 6–13 and Commentary; Doctrine and Covenants 38:2; 76:24 and

Commentary; see also John 1:3; Colossians 1:16–17. Although darkness does not comprehend the light (see vv. 48–49; D&C 45:29; John 1:5), the light of Christ comprehends all things. *Comprehend* in this instance can mean both "to understand" and also "to encompass, to include, or to be larger than" something else. This verse describes the relationship and influence of Christ on all of creation, or the role of the light of Christ which permeates all things. Since the light of Christ is in all things and is the force that holds them together, Christ himself must comprehend all these things (in both senses of the term) in all their aspects and in all their functions. From the center of eternity, Christ governs all creation and administers all the laws of all the kingdoms (some personally, and some through the Holy Spirit and other intermediaries; see D&C 76:86–88). In his administration of all existence, there is no guesswork. The Creator is larger and greater than his creation, and he understands the whole of it as well as each of its individual parts (see Commentary on v. 6; see also 2 Nephi 9:20).

42. He hath given a law . . . by which they move. This passage explicitly declares that the laws of physical motion, the physics of our universe, are decreed and imposed upon all the heavenly bodies by God through the light and power of Christ. Thus, the orbits of the moon around the earth, the earth around the sun, the sun around our galaxy (the Milky Way), and our galaxy around its center are all functions of the governance and power of God through the light of Christ.

44. All these are one year with God. This seems to be a different—though not necessarily contradictory—formula than that found in Abraham 3:4, Facsimile 2:1 (see Moses 3:17; Abraham 5:13; Psalm 90:4, 2 Peter 3:8).[24] However, the scriptures are unanimous in declaring that time is not reckoned the same with God as it is with human beings (see, for example, D&C 38:1; 130:4–7; Revelation 10:6). Since Alma teaches that "all is as one *day* with God, and time only is measured unto men" (Alma 40:8; emphasis added), it would seem to caution us against taking any formula too literally.

45–47. These verses seem to endorse what theologians call the teleological argument for the existence of God. Basically, this argument states that the existence of a glorious creation indicates or implies the existence of a glorious creator. All who have perceived the order and glory of creation or the orderly operation of natural laws have perceived the influence of God in the universe—whether or not they choose to accept this testimony borne by creation concerning its Creator.

48. Hath seen him. Whoever has perceived the order, power, and majesty of creation has also thereby received physical, empirical evidence for the Creator. Yet even so, when Jesus Christ, the Creator himself, appeared in the flesh to human beings upon the earth, with all the signs and miracles indicating his identity as God, he was not understood, nor perceived to be what he really was (see John 1:5).

49. You shall comprehend even God. To some this claim sounds almost blasphemous, yet it is also the testimony of the beloved apostle John, who wrote that "this is life eternal, that they might know thee the only true God, and Jesus Christ, whom thou hast sent" (John 17:3). Since the Saints are promised eternal life through the gospel covenant, it follows that they *must* come to know not only Jesus Christ, the creator of all things, but also the very Eternal Father who sent him.

The Prophet Joseph Smith taught, "We consider that God has created man with a mind capable of instruction, and a faculty which may be enlarged in proportion to the heed and diligence given to the light communicated from heaven to the intellect; and that the nearer man approaches perfection, the clearer are his views, and the greater his enjoyments, till he has overcome the evils of his life and lost every desire for sin; and like the ancients, arrives at that point of faith where he is wrapped in the power and glory of his Maker, and is caught up to dwell with Him. But we consider that this is a station to which no man ever arrived in a moment; he must have been instructed in the government and laws of that kingdom by proper degrees, until his mind is capable in some measure of comprehending the propriety, justice, equality, and consistency of the same."[25]

49. Being quickened in him and by him. As we ponder something as overwhelming as coming to know God, we must remember that it is only through his power that we shall someday accomplish this and not through our own power. Our boasting should not be that we are smart enough to comprehend God, but that God is smart enough—and merciful enough—to teach and enlighten us and eventually bring us into his presence to "know as [we] are known" (D&C 76:94).

50. Then shall ye know. When we have been quickened or raised up in the resurrection, we will be better able to perceive the light of Christ for what it is. We will then appreciate all the testimonies born by the physical universe of its Creator, and we shall know that the light of Christ has been in all things and through all things—including ourselves. All progress, enlargement, or improvement ("abound[ing]") for any being on any level comes only through the influence or with the aid of the light of Christ.

51–61. The parable of the multitude of kingdoms. According to Moses (see Moses 1:27–29) and to the Prophet Joseph Smith (see D&C 76:21, 24 and Commentary), there are countless inhabited worlds like this one among the creations of God. As these worlds go through the process of creation, cleansing, sanctification, and so forth that leads to their becoming celestial spheres (while they are still "under construction," so to speak), there is a time when each will enjoy the actual, physical presence of its Creator, the Lord Jesus Christ. In our case, the Lord will personally visit this earth during the Millennium, though he will likely not dwell here, and during that time all those raised in the first resurrection (that is, with celestial or terrestrial glory; see D&C 45:54; 76:17, 50 and Commentary) will at some time enjoy his personal presence.[26] However, when our millennial day is over, the Lord will leave this earth to visit yet other worlds in their proper turn as they approach completion of their celestial natures.

Thus, one by one the Lord personally visits each of his created worlds and all of his righteous servants.

In addition to this, according to Elder Orson Pratt, as each world passes through its terrestrial millennium to be recreated a glorious, celestial sphere, "then, from that time henceforth and for ever, there will be no intervening veil between God and his people who are sanctified and glorified, and he will not be under the necessity of withdrawing from one to go and visit another, because they will all be in his presence."[27] Thus, it would seem that regardless of where the Savior might be located physically in the universe as he travels from one kingdom to another, all celestial beings will enjoy a relationship with him as close as if they were physically present with him, and, indeed, can be said to be "in his presence."

64–65. That is expedient for you. The 1828 edition of Webster's *American Dictionary of the English Language* defines *expedient* as "that which serves to promote or advance." When we seek what is right and what will move us toward our Heavenly Father or aid the cause of Zion, the Lord will answer our prayers positively. But should we attempt using the power of prayer for selfish or unrighteous goals, we will find ourselves condemned for it. President Joseph Fielding Smith taught that "too many times in prayers things may be asked for which are not expedient but to gratify our vanity or foolish desires, and then if answered the prayer could be to our hurt. We have a wonderful example of this in the case of Martin Harris, when he persisted, after the Lord had refused his request and on his repeated seeking the request was granted." President Smith also said that "the promise is sure that the Lord will not deny the humble petition which is offered, and it may not be expedient in some prayers that the answer be given as requested. Moreover, it is true that the Lord is not always near. The man who has ignored the Lord, who has not kept his commandments, and who does not pray, may find it a very difficult thing to obtain an answer to his earnest prayer when in distress, and the answer is sorely needed."[28]

66. The voice of one crying in the wilderness. This phrase is usually associated with the person of John the Baptist, who literally called out to Israel from the wilderness outside her towns and cities (see Mark 1:3–4). However, John's voice cried out the words of Jehovah that prepared Israel for his coming, and so ultimately this phrase refers equally well to the voice of God himself (see D&C 1:38). The settled towns of Israel were associated with the world of men, while the wilderness symbolically represented a different plain from which God often spoke through his prophets.[29] Those present when Doctrine and Covenants 88 was given were privileged to hear word of Christ's coming communicated through the Spirit and spoken by a prophet of God just as ancient disciples heard that preparatory word through the Baptist.

67. If your eye be single. See Commentary on Doctrine and Covenants 4:5. President Gordon B. Hinckley has taught: "As we look with love and gratitude to God, as we serve him with an eye single to his glory, there goes from us the darkness of sin, the darkness of selfishness, the darkness of pride. There will come an increased love for our Eternal Father and for his Beloved Son, our Savior and our Redeemer. There will come a greater sense of service toward our fellow men, less of thinking of self and more of reaching out to others."[30]

68. And the days will come that you shall see him. This passage is a repetition of the promise made to some of these same individuals the preceding year.[31]

69. The great and last promise. That is, "last" in the sense of the most recent. That promise—made in the preceding verses—was that the brethren present would be privileged to see the Lord if they remained faithful. "Certainly the meaning is not that this was the final (or chronologically last) promise [God] would make to his servants. The meaning therefore seems to be that this was the *ultimate* promise—that is, that when they were ready, they would see his face and stand in his presence. The feeling is also contained in the passage that this was the last promise until they had accomplished the preparation needed to obtain the promise the Lord had given them."[32]

69. Cast away your idle thoughts and your excess of laughter. In the context of this verse, the Lord reminds the brethren that his work is serious business and should be viewed as such, though this is neither a condemnation of humor nor of pondering secular subjects. Note particularly that it is not laughter that is condemned here, but *excess* of laughter. The issue is one of focus. Idle thoughts (empty and purposeless) and excess of laughter might indicate one has lost focus on the real purposes of life and is looking elsewhere for immediate, temporal satisfaction (see D&C 59:15 and Commentary).

70. Tarry ye . . . and call a solemn assembly. The leadership of the Church, at least as represented by those present when Doctrine and Covenants 88 was received, were not to go to Missouri, but were to remain in Kirtland until the Lord prepared them for the full blessings they were yet to receive. One preparatory step would be the construction of the Kirtland Temple and the reception by some members of keys and ordinances associated with the temple (see vv. 118–26). Within two weeks of receiving Doctrine and Covenants 88 (on 11 January 1833), Joseph Smith wrote to the Saints in Missouri informing them of the Lord's instructions that a temple be built in Kirtland.[33] He further clarified the promise of the Lord that the faithful would by obedience to these instructions be blessed with an appearance of the Lord himself.[34] On a later occasion, the Prophet taught the Twelve, "We must have all things prepared, and call our solemn assembly as the Lord has commanded us [in D&C 88:70], that we may be able to accomplish His great work, and it must be done in God's own way. The house of the Lord must be prepared, and the solemn assembly called and organized in it, according to the order of the house of God; and in it we must attend to the ordinance of washing of feet. . . . The endowment you are so anxious about, you cannot comprehend now. . . . You need an endowment, brethren, in order that you may be prepared and able to overcome all things. . . . All who are prepared, and are sufficiently pure to abide the presence of the Savior will see him in the solemn assembly."[35]

Between 21 January and 1 May 1836, a number of meetings and assemblies were held in Kirtland in which there was a remarkable outpouring of spiritual gifts.[36] During the week of 27 March 1836, solemn assemblies were held at the dedication of the Kirtland Temple and were accompanied by a spiritual outpouring akin to that experienced by the New Testament Saints on the day of Pentecost (see Acts 2). According to accounts of many of those present at that dedication and other meetings during the week following, including a second dedication session, the gifts of the Spirit were manifested, and "the Savior made His appearance to some, while angels ministered to others."[37] Another solemn assembly was also held the following year on 6 April 1837. Elders who had not attended the earlier assembly were washed and anointed at that time.[38]

70. The first laborers in this last kingdom. This probably refers to the early leadership of the Church restored in this, the last dispensation of earthly time.

72. I will take care of your flocks. The reference is to the converts made by traveling missionaries and to branches of the Church established in distant areas. The Lord will provide leadership (elders) according to the needs and the faithfulness of his Saints.

73. I will hasten my work in its time. The Lord himself will do what is necessary at the appropriate times to move his work forward—as long as his Saints are obedient and keep their covenants. We don't need to worry about how the gospel will finally be made available in this country or in that area. The Lord's plans are already made and merely await the right time and obedient servants to carry them out.

74. And I give unto you . . . a commandment. The leaders of the Church are here commanded to prepare themselves for the blessings of the temple, which will in turn prepare them to receive the fulness of his "great and last promise" (v. 75), that they will be clean and worthy of his personal appearance to them.

74. Cleanse your hands and your feet. A reference to some of the ordinances soon to be received in the house of the Lord. The brethren are to prepare themselves for the ordinances of the temple by sanctifying their own lives individually and by collectively constructing the necessary edifice, the Kirtland Temple. These ordinances performed in a house of God constructed for the purpose would in turn make it possible for the Lord to keep his promise to the faithful to appear unto them (see vv. 68–69, 75).

75. That I may testify unto your Father. The Father has committed all judgment into the hands of the Son (see John 5:22–23) and will accept the testimony or the advocacy of the Son in regard to each and every individual (see D&C 29:27–28; 45:3–5; Matthew 10:32–33; 3 Nephi 27:16).

75. Clean from the blood of this wicked generation. Naturally, the cleansing agent here is the atonement of Christ. However, each member of the Church is under covenant to serve the Lord and to keep his commandments. Therefore, we have an obligation to preach the gospel to those who have not been warned so that their fate, should they refuse to repent, cannot be charged to our negligence. Refusal to separate ourselves from the world, or refusal to warn the world of its peril in some form of missionary service as prescribed by the Lord, leaves members guilty in some degree of the blood and wickedness of their generation.

76. Continue in prayer and fasting. That is, continue in the regular practice of prayer and fasting.

77. Teach one another the doctrine. Given originally here to the leading elders of the Church, this commandment has now been extended to the whole Church. Our efforts in all our classes, lessons, and sermons should be directed at teaching the doctrine of the kingdom to those who are less knowledgeable than ourselves. In the wards and branches of the Church, this is done through calling teachers and speakers who serve for a period of time and who then resume their place in the congregation or class to be taught in turn by others.

78–84. Teach ye diligently. These verses originally applied to the leading elders of the Church and referred to the School of the Prophets (see vv. 127–38) which would prepare leaders of the Church for their service, not just in frontier America, but throughout the world. The Lord needs informed, educated, knowledgeable, and intelligent people to lead his Church. Such qualifications are needed not to impress the world but to better serve the Lord and his Saints. To be as effective as possible in the Lord's service, Church leaders and others must generally have some knowledge of the language and culture of the people whom they serve. In 1832 the instructions given here to establish a School of the Prophets were likely in part at least to prepare Church leaders for the foreign missions to which they would soon be called (see v. 84). At a time before there was a Quorum of the Twelve, the Kirtland School of the Prophets served to train those likely to be called into that quorum in the future.

78. And my grace shall attend you. The promise is made that if the brethren will study diligently and teach one another what they know, the grace of God will add to what they learn, and the whole will be greater than the sum of its parts (on "grace," see Commentary on D&C 20:30–32; 84:99).

78. In theory, in principle, in doctrine. See Commentary on Doctrine and Covenants 97:14.

78. The law of the gospel. This phrase is a reference to all the principles that together constitute the gospel (see also v. 123 and Commentary on D&C 104:18).

84. To go forth among the Gentiles. See Doctrine and Covenants 109:60 and the title page of the Book of Mormon. The term *Gentiles* here refers to those of every nation, kindred, tongue, and people, who are to receive their opportunity to hear the gospel in this dispensation of the restored gospel.[39]

84. To bind up the law and seal up the testimony. To "bind up the law" is to impose the law decreed by God upon those who are to receive it. To "seal up the testimony" is to make sure that a knowledge of the gospel and a warning of the fate that awaits the wicked have been given. Those to whom testimony has been born and to whom the law of the Lord has been revealed may then either accept or reject them. But the garments of the Saints who have warned them are free of their blood and sins either way.

Joseph Smith later reflected upon this passage, saying that "when you are endowed and prepared to preach the Gospel to all nations, kindred, and tongues, in their own languages, you must faithfully warn all, and bind up the testimony, and seal up the law, and the destroying angel will follow close at your heels, and exercise his tremendous mission upon the children of disobedience; and destroy the workers of iniquity, while the Saints will be gathered out from among them, and stand in holy places ready to meet the Bridegroom when he comes."[40]

85. The desolation of abomination. See Commentary on Doctrine and Covenants 84:117. This passage informs us that for those who will not repent, the desolation they experience here continues into the next life, the spirit world. For those who will not repent even in the spirit world, the abomination of total desolation continues as "outer darkness," a place reserved for perdition that is outside the created order and is desolate of the light and power of Christ.[41]

85. Let those who are not the first elders continue in the vineyard. See Commentary on verse 75.

86. Abide ye in the liberty wherewith ye are made free. The principles of the gospel of Jesus Christ fulfill, supersede, and render obsolete the rules of the law of Moses, just as redemption in Christ supersedes the conditions of the Fall. Therefore, knowledge of and obedience to the law of Christ set his Saints free from all other requirements and considerations—including the demands of the law of Moses. This "Christian liberty" was a frequent subject of Paul's epistles to the Saints in the New Testament (see, for example, 1 Corinthians 8:8–9; 10:29; 2 Corinthians 3:17; Galatians 5:1, 13). The apostle James spoke of the gospel as another law, "the perfect law of liberty" (James 1:25), by which the Saints were set free from their sins under the rules of the law of Moses (see also James 2:10–13), or any other rules not of the gospel.

On the other hand, those who have been set free from sin and error through the atonement of Christ cannot use his sacrifice as an excuse to continue wilfully in their sins (compare Romans 6:16). The gospel frees us from sin; it does not sustain us in the continued pursuit of sin. It is a matter of loyalty, of whom we ultimately serve. If Christ is truly our Lord, then we are freed from the demands of strict justice (that is, we are "justified" by his atonement) even though we may serve him imperfectly. But if our highest loyalty is freely given to anything or anyone else, then we are on our own before the judgment of God. The liberty of the gospel frees us *from* sin; it does not free us *to* sin. The term *abide* is important here as descriptive of our location, of our orientation, and, therefore, of our loyalty. Granted that we are all imperfect in our performance, do we "abide" in Christ, giving him our loyalty, while making occasional mistakes? Or do we "abide" in anything else, bestowing upon that our ultimate loyalty, though often performing good deeds? The former is justified by the power of the Atonement, but the latter is not and must be judged on its own merits.

87–95. Parallel passages concerning the signs of the end time as recorded in verses 87–95 may also be seen in Doctrine and Covenants 29:14; 43:18–25; 45:26, 42, 48; and 133:22, 49 and Commentary. See also Joel 2:10, 31; 3:15–16; Matthew 24:29–31; Joseph Smith–Matthew 1:23–37; Revelation 11:13. Doctrine and Covenants 133, received before section 88, explains that the sun and moon shall hide their light and the stars be hurled from their places out of shame when confronted by the incomparable glory of the Lord's presence (see D&C 133:49).

88. After your testimony. See Doctrine and Covenants 43:25, 33 and Commentary.

92. And angels shall fly . . . sounding the trump of God.

This verse describes collectively the activity of all the angels of God from the Restoration to the second coming of Christ, including the seven angels which will be enumerated in verses 94–106 (see D&C 77:12; 29:13 and Commentary; 1 Thessalonians 4:15–16). According to Smith and Sjodahl, "These angels are mighty men of God, messengers of the Almighty, who shall call upon the inhabitants of the Earth to prepare themselves for the coming of the Bridegroom. Moroni was such an angel [Revelation 14:6]."[42]

92. The judgment of our God. The blowing of God's trumpet announces the return of the Risen Lord and the beginning of his judgment. As each of seven blasts is heard, a different category of people is addressed, from the celestial at the first trump (see vv. 96–98), to the terrestrial (see v. 99), the telestial (see vv. 100–101), and perdition (see v. 102). Then Zion is established (see vv. 103–4), Babylon falls (see v. 105; see also Revelation 8:2–11:15), and the Saints receive their inheritances (see vv. 106–7). A second series of trumpet blasts (see vv. 108–10) will herald a review of earth's history and announce the finishing of God's millennial works. This passage agrees with Doctrine and Covenants 77:12, which states that the two series of blasts mark the preparing and finishing of the Lord's work, respectively ("the sounding of the trumpets of the seven angels are the *preparing* and the *finishing* of his work"; emphasis added).

92. Lo, the Bridegroom cometh. See Doctrine and Covenants 33:17–18; 65:3–5 and Commentary; see also Isaiah 62:5. The second coming of Jesus Christ will fulfill the prophecy implicit in the parable of the ten virgins (see Matthew 25:1–13).

93. There shall appear a great sign in heaven. See Doctrine and Covenants 45:40; Matthew 24:30; Joseph Smith–Matthew 1:36. This "great sign" will be seen by all people at one time. However, it has not been revealed exactly what this sign will be.[43] The Prophet Joseph Smith observed that following the many signs of wars and physical destruction, "then will appear one grand sign of the Son of Man in heaven. But what will the world do? They will say it is a planet, a comet, &c. But the Son of Man will come as the sign of the coming of the Son of Man, which will be as the light of the morning cometh out of the east."[44]

94. And another angel shall sound his trump. This is not the first of all the many trumpets of God, for there have been many since the beginning of the Restoration to prepare for the actual second coming of the Lord (see v. 92 and Commentary; D&C 77:12). However, this trump is the first of the enumerated series of trumpet blasts associated specifically with the end time. The sounding of this first trumpet heralds the destruction of the great and abominable church (see v. 94). It is followed by a period of silence (see v. 95) and then the face of the Lord is revealed (see v. 95). The sounding of this first trump also brings about the resurrection of the celestial dead and the raising up of the celestial living to meet the Lord in the air (see vv. 96–98; 1 Thessalonians 4:15–17).

94. That great church, the mother of abominations. See Doctrine and Covenants 29:21; 77:12; 86:3 and Commentary; see also 1 Nephi 13–14; Revelation 17–18. This does not refer to a particular church or religious philosophy, but rather to all that opposes the truth of the living God or all that is of a telestial nature upon the earth (see 1 Nephi 22:23; 2 Nephi 10:16).

94. That made all nations drink. See Doctrine and Covenants 35:11 and Commentary.

95. Silence in heaven for the space of half an hour. See Doctrine and Covenants 38:11–12; Revelation 8:1. Orson Pratt pointed out that "whether the half hour here spoken of is according to our reckoning—thirty minutes, or whether it be according to the reckoning of the Lord we do not know. We know that the word hour is used in some portions of the Scriptures to represent quite a lengthy period of time. . . . During the period of silence all things are perfectly still; no angels flying during that half hour; no trumpets sounding; no noise in the heavens above; but immediately after this great silence the curtain of heaven shall be unfolded

through the Prophet Joseph Smith, particularly with the translation of the Book of Mormon. This is entirely correct, but Moroni is one of the many angels who figuratively sound the trump of God before the seven trumpets of the end time enumerated here (see v. 92 and Commentary). Moreover, it may be that Moroni is the fifth angel of the end time in addition to being the herald of the Restoration. In the context of these verses, the sound of the fifth trump announces the victory of the gospel of Jesus Christ in all the world, for the wicked will have been destroyed and removed, the earth will be cleansed, and the remaining mortals, both celestial and terrestrial, will belong to Christ. Therefore, every knee that remains upon the earth will bow before him and every tongue will confess that he is the Lord Jesus Christ.

This does not mean that everyone upon the earth at the beginning of the Millennium will accept the fulness of the gospel and its ordinances, however. Other Christian churches will remain upon the earth during the millennial period. All human beings will be just; all will belong to Christ; but not all will accept the fulness of his gospel and its ordinances in order to receive "the fulness of the Father" (D&C 76:77). Thus, there will be both celestial and terrestrial beings upon the earth during the Millennium.

105. The sixth trump. The sixth trump announces the total destruction of Babylon. With the destruction of the wicked at the Lord's coming, Babylon will have no more inhabitants. Babylon, the great and abominable church, is telestial at its best (see D&C 133:5, 14), and after the coming of the Savior to the earth, nothing telestial will remain here. Babylon will truly and utterly be fallen.

106. The seventh trump. In scriptural symbolism, the number seven often stands for completion or perfection. Thus, the sounding of the seventh trumpet announces the complete victory of Jesus over his enemies and the completion or perfection of his work: "It is finished!"

106. Trodden the wine-press alone. See Doctrine and

Covenants 19:16–18; 29:17; 43:26; 76:107 and Commentary; see also Revelation 14:10.

107. And be made equal with him. The celestial law of consecration requires that we be willing to sacrifice all that we have in order to be equal one with another and that there be no poor among us (see D&C 51:3; 70:14; 78:5–6; Moses 7:18). Will Jesus Christ obey the law of consecration? Yes, just as he has obeyed all other laws of the kingdom of God. And what will Jesus' sacrifice and consecration be? It will be his perfection, his righteousness, and his glory! As we are willing to be made equal with one another, for better or worse, in temporal things in obedience to the celestial law, so Christ is willing to be made equal with us in all things in obedience to the same celestial law. It is not blasphemy to assert that we shall in some sense become equal with the Savior in the celestial kingdom; rather, it is a tribute to his perfect righteousness, obedience, and love for us. It is a measure of his perfect grace that he desires to share all things equally with us, and it is a tribute to his power that he can accomplish this if we are willing. Thus, through his gospel and his grace, we can truly become "joint-heirs with Christ" (Romans 8:17). It is common for some to think of the Church as a collection of individuals all competing with one another for greater or lesser eternal rewards or glory. Perhaps the clear teachings of the law of consecration, the concept of Zion, and the promise of this verse ought to give us pause before accepting such a highly competitive view of the eternities.

108–10. Again sound his trump. A *second* series of seven soundings of the trumpet (see vv. 108–10) will mark the completion of Christ's works and herald a review of the true history of the world from the beginning to the end. This revelation will announce to all what really happened historically, including all previously unknown plans, intents, and acts of human beings and all the workings of God throughout the dispensations of time.

110. There shall be time no longer. See verse 44; D&C 84:100 and Commentary. The reference is probably to telestial

dwelling. Establishing the household or the exalted family of God is the very heart and soul of what temples are about.

120. With uplifted hands. The ancient pattern of Jewish prayer was not on the knees with hands or arms folded but standing, with the hands lifted to heaven (see Psalm 44:20; 88:9; Isaiah 1:15; Romans 10:21). This is also, approximately, the position of a body on a cross and may be the symbol or type behind Moses on the hill with uplifted hands and a man on either side of him winning victory for Israel at Rephidim (see Exodus 17:10–12).

121. Cease from all your light speeches. See Commentary on verse 69 and on Doctrine and Covenants 59:15. We must be wise in preventing behavior offensive to the Spirit or that diverts our attention from the purpose of our existence upon this earth. From Liberty Jail, the Prophet Joseph Smith warned: "The things of God are of deep import; and time, and experience, and careful and ponderous and solemn thoughts can only find them out. Thy mind, O man! if thou wilt lead a soul unto salvation, must stretch as high as the utmost heavens, and search into and contemplate the darkest abyss, and the broad expanse of eternity—thou must commune with God. How much more dignified and noble are the thoughts of God, than the vain imaginations of the human heart! None but fools will trifle with the souls of men.

"How vain and trifling have been our spirits, our conferences, our councils, our meetings, our private as well as public conversations—too low, too mean, too vulgar, too condescending for the dignified characters of the called and chosen of God, according to the purposes of His will, from before the foundation of the world!"[47]

121. From all laughter. In Doctrine and Covenants 59:15, the command was that we not have "much laughter." In Doctrine and Covenants 88:69 we are told not to have an "excess of laughter." Yet in this verse the wording is "all laughter." Does this mean we are not to laugh at all? No, for the context is different in each case. Section 88 counsels us to avoid "an excess of laughter" in our daily lives. Section 59 counsels us to avoid "much laughter" on the Sabbath day, and this verse counsels avoiding "all laughter" while engaged in the solemn activities of the temple. While there was yet no Quorum of the Twelve, the School of the Prophets was designed in part to train those who might be called to that quorum and to give them some of the initiatory rites for that calling (see vv. 138–41). They are to attend with all proper decorum to their temple activities, including the School of the Prophets, which was intended eventually to meet there. Outside the temple, the less stringent instructions of Doctrine and Covenants 59:15 would more aptly apply.

Elder Joseph Fielding Smith once observed: "I believe that it is necessary for the Saints to have amusement, but it must be of the proper kind. I do not believe the Lord intends and desires that we should pull a long face and look sanctimonious and hypocritical. I think he expects us to be happy and of a cheerful countenance, but he does not expect of us the indulgence in boisterous and unseemly conduct and the seeking after the vain and foolish things which amuse and entertain the world."[48]

122. Let one speak at a time. See 1 Corinthians 14:29–31.

123. See that ye love one another. This is the "royal law" of James 2:8 and "the more excellent way" of 1 Corinthians 12:31 (see also John 13:34; 15:12, 17).[49]

123. Impart one to another as the gospel requires. See v. 78 and Commentary on Doctrine and Covenants 104:18.

124. Cease to sleep longer than is needful. Note that the commandment is not to sleep *less* than necessary, either. Take what time your body needs to really refresh itself, and then don't waste any more time lying in bed, for time is also a stewardship.

124. Arise early. Elder Russell M. Nelson has suggested that "those who feel defeated and downtrodden, look to the early hours of the day for your rescue. The Lord tells us, 'Cease to sleep longer than is needful; retire to thy bed early, that ye may not be weary; arise early, that your bodies and your minds may be invigorated' (D&C 88:124).

Naturally, this kind of oneness and fellowship is difficult and so requires "the grace of God."

134. He that is found unworthy. The highest school in the Church, the School of the Prophets (which was intended to prepare the first elders of the Church for missionary work and Church service) required a level of righteousness consistent with the fellowship of the temple. Should an individual not be worthy of the salutation described in verse 133, he would be unworthy of entry into the school just as much as he would be unworthy to enter into the temple if it had then been completed and dedicated.

138. The blood of this generation. See Commentary on verses 75 and 85. In the setting of the first School of the Prophets, the ordinance of washing of the feet signified, among other things, that an individual had performed his duty to call the world to repentance and warn of the wrath to come and was therefore clean of the blood of this generation.

139. The ordinance of the washing of feet. In the institution of the sacrament of the Lord's supper, Jesus took an existing practice of the law of Moses and gave it a new, fuller meaning in the context of the gospel covenant. Jesus did the same thing with the Jewish custom under the law of Moses of washing the feet (see JST John 13:10; see also Genesis 24:32; Luke 7:44). Moreover, the priests, the sons of Moses and of Aaron (see D&C 84:34), were *required*, not by custom but by the law, to wash their feet before entering the temple and participating in its ordinances (see Exodus 30:18–21; 40:30–31). Therefore, the first School of the Prophets met in a large upper room (see Luke 22:12; the term is sometimes related to temple activities), and because, as sons of Moses and Aaron, they were being prepared for the endowment that would come with the building of the Kirtland Temple, their feet were also washed.

However, one change instituted by Jesus in the washing of feet was that Jesus himself, in an act of humility and service, washed the feet of the disciples, rather than allowing them to wash their own feet. Joseph Smith described the washing of feet which occurred on 23 January 1833, as recorded in *History of the Church,* 1:323: "We again assembled in conference; when, after much speaking, singing, praying, and praising God, all in tongues, we proceeded to the washing of feet (according to the practice recorded in the 13th chapter of John's Gospel), as commanded of the Lord. Each elder washed his own feet first, after which I girded myself with a towel and washed the feet of all of them, wiping them with the towel with which I was girded. Among the number, my father presented himself, but before I washed his feet, I asked of him a father's blessing, which he granted by laying his hands upon my head, in the name of Jesus Christ, and declaring that I should continue in the Priest's office until Christ comes. At the close of the scene, Brother Frederick G. Williams, being moved upon by the Holy Ghost, washed my feet in token of his fixed determination to be with me in suffering or in journeying, in life or in death, and to be continually on my right hand; in which I accepted him in the name of the Lord."

Although various washings continue in the restored Church, the practice described in verses 139–41 was limited at that time to the first elders of the Church who were being trained and disciplined for leadership in the first School of the Prophets. The initiatory washing of feet and the salutation (see v. 133) were not practiced in the subsequent schools in Kirtland or in Missouri, which were open to a broader number of the Saints. After the Kirtland Temple was completed, the practices described in verses 139–41 were continued by the First Presidency and Quorum of the Twelve, the successors to the original School of the Prophets.

1. See Background to D&C 86–87.
2. Grant, *Journal of Discourses,* 2:147.
3. Cited in Cook, *Revelations of the Prophet Joseph Smith,* 181; spelling, punctuation, and grammar standardized.
4. Joseph Smith to W. W. Phelps, 11 Jan. 1833; spelling, punctuation, and grammar standardized; see Jessee, *Personal Writings,* 262.
5. See Collier and Harwell, eds., *Kirtland Council Minute Book,* 6–7.
6. Smith, *History of the Church,* 3:380.

89

BACKGROUND

In the United States of the 1830s, the same refreshing spirit of reform and revival that had prepared the way for the restoration of the gospel continued to play a part in American society in crusades for religious revival, for the abolition of slavery, and, in particular, for the temperance movement against the use of alcohol. It has been estimated that between the years 1792 and 1823, the per capita consumption of alcohol in the United States tripled, from two and one-half to seven and one-half gallons per year.[1] To combat this increase and its attendant evils, the American Temperance Society was formed in 1826. By 1831 there were more than two thousand local temperance societies in the United States, with over 150,000 members nationally.[2] Thirty of these societies were located in Ohio, with the largest in Kirtland, where virtually all the Christian churches supported the temperance movement.[3] Merely two years later, in 1833, there were five thousand local temperance societies nationally with a combined membership of one and one quarter million persons. One result of the temperance movement in eastern Ohio was the closing of a distillery at Kirtland and of two more in nearby Mentor "for want of patronage."[4] Just as the Spirit of the Lord had prepared the ground for the Restoration in so many other ways, it was also preparing the ground for a remarkable change in American frontier culture, and in the cultural beliefs and habits of Church members in particular, in matters of temperance. The soil was ready for planting. The revelation known as the Word of Wisdom was about to be given to the Saints.

Since September 1832, after moving from the Johnson farm in Hiram, Ohio, Joseph and Emma had been living in quarters above Newel K. Whitney's store in Kirtland. Their first child to survive infancy, Joseph Smith III, was born there on 6 November, the day the Prophet returned from a short mission to the East with Bishop Whitney.[5] Above Emma's kitchen, which was located on the ground floor, Levi Hancock had created a small schoolroom by remodeling a former porch. This room measured roughly eleven by fourteen feet and served as a meeting place for the School of the Prophets between January and April 1833 (see D&C 88:118–41 and Commentary).[6]

Although Brigham Young was not a member of the school in 1833 and was not present on the day the Word of Wisdom was actually received, he was a member of the 1835 school and was familiar with conditions at the earlier meetings, which he described as follows: "When they [the brethren] assembled together in this room after breakfast, the first they did was to light their pipes, and, while smoking, talk about the great things of the kingdom, and spit all over the room, and as soon as the pipe was out of their mouths a large chew of tobacco would then be taken. Often when the Prophet entered the room to give the school instructions he would find himself in a cloud of tobacco smoke. This, and the complaints of his wife at having to clean so filthy a floor, made the Prophet think upon the matter, and he inquired of the Lord relating to the conduct of the Elders in using tobacco, and the revelation known as the Word of Wisdom was the result of his inquiry."[7] Reports from others who were present at the School of the Prophets on 27 February 1833 indicate that Joseph received the revelation (D&C 89) on that date in the presence of two or three others, in an adjoining room in which the Prophet received revelations, and then brought the written revelation into

sickness, fatigue, and depression was not in violation of the Word of Wisdom. Subsequently, there are many casual references in Joseph Smith's history of Church members drinking wine."[12] We must remember, however, that in the nineteenth century, without today's sophisticated pharmaceuticals, alcohol, nicotine, and caffeine of necessity played a much larger role in the relief of pain, fatigue, and depression than they do today, but their imputed efficacy usually exceeded their actual benefits. The supposed medicinal use of these substances was part of the cultural heritage of early Church members. In his great mercy, the Lord did not give the Word of Wisdom as a commandment to this first generation of Saints who were, by and large, already addicted to one or more of the forbidden substances and who were already culturally conditioned to accept their use both medicinally and socially. A significant difference between nineteenth and twentieth century observance of the Word of Wisdom is that twentieth century Saints understood "observance" to require complete abstinence, whereas nineteenth century Saints tended to interpret "observance" as moderation in the use of prohibited items.

Neither Joseph Smith nor Brigham Young nor any of their successors to date have sought to make observance of the Word of Wisdom a test for continuing membership in the LDS Church. Though Church leaders have counseled observance of the Word of Wisdom from the beginning, and frequent attempts were made to impress its importance upon the Saints, *total* abstinence from coffee, tea, alcohol, and tobacco was seldom preached or practiced in the first thirty years after the revelation was received.[13] President Joseph F. Smith explained, "The reason undoubtedly why the Word of Wisdom was given—as not by 'commandment or restraint' was that at that time, at least, if it had been given as a commandment it would have brought every man, addicted to the use of these noxious things, under condemnation; so the Lord was merciful and gave them a chance to overcome, before He brought them under the law."[14] It might be added that between 1833 and the 1860s, the Church had many other grave issues to occupy its collective attention—that is, mobs and persecution, emigration to Utah, and survival in a harsh environment.

However, as time has passed, as older generations have given way to new ones, and as more effective medical alternatives have become available to the so-called stimulants of the nineteenth century, the Lord has through his prophets gradually required increasingly strict adherence to his will as expressed in 1833. By the 1860s, it could be said that "Mormons were temperate and moderate but not abstinent."[15] Many Church leaders did not begin completely to live the Word of Wisdom until several decades after it was received. On 13 October 1882, the Lord revealed to John Taylor that the Word of Wisdom should henceforth be considered a commandment to the Church. Soon thereafter, on 28 September 1883, the Quorum of the Twelve collectively resolved to observe the Word of Wisdom in its entirety, and on 11 October 1883 observance of the Word of Wisdom was made a condition for attending the recently revived Schools of the Prophets.[16] (These later schools were not the same as the 1833 school but were perhaps more like predecessors of today's priesthood leadership training meetings.)

During October conference in 1908, President Anthon H. Lund of the First Presidency announced that individuals violating the Word of Wisdom should not be called to leadership positions in local units and quorums of the Church.[17] In 1913 the First Presidency instructed the president of the Salt Lake Stake not to recommend young men for missionary service unless they were observing the Word of Wisdom.[18] And finally, in 1919, the First Presidency under Heber J. Grant began to make observance of the Word of Wisdom a condition for receiving a temple recommend.[19]

It must be noted that the history of Word of Wisdom observance in the Church does not indicate any change in "the will of God" (v. 2) from earlier times. It has been the Lord's will since at least 27 February 1833 that the Saints observe the Word of Wisdom. The Lord has been merciful, however, in allowing us collectively to change our culture and our habits over time, rather

possible that the first warning is directed at those things specified in 1833 (that is, alcohol, coffee, tea, and tobacco), while the Lord's forewarning is directed at future hazards like the scourge of narcotics and other harmful drugs now ravaging our society but not readily available in 1833.

5. Wine or strong drink. The Lord counsels the Saints of 1833 against the use of wine except in the sacrament (see D&C 20:75; 27:4 and Commentary). That counsel has since been changed to a commandment. "Strong drinks" (v. 7) are those containing alcohol, as opposed to "soft drinks," which contain no alcohol.

6. Pure wine of the grape. This does not indicate that the wine used in the sacrament was merely fresh grape juice. The wine commonly used for the sacrament in the nineteenth century Church was fermented and contained alcohol (see D&C 20:75; 27:4 and Commentary). If the reference to wine here, or "pure wine of the grape," were understood to mean unfermented wine, then verses 5–6 would constitute a prohibition against the use of grape juice, except for the sacrament—and this is clearly not the case. Since the beginning of the twentieth century, the uniform practice of the Church has been to use water for the sacrament.

7. For the washing of your bodies. Disinfectant purposes are still a major medicinal use of distilled alcohol today.

9. Hot drinks. There is ample journal evidence that the Saints in Kirtland understood "hot drinks" to mean tea and coffee without having the term defined for them.[22] However, in case anyone was in doubt, Joseph Smith stated in July 1833 that "tea and coffee . . . are what the Lord meant when He said 'hot drinks.'"[23] Hyrum Smith and Brigham Young both publicly defined "hot drinks" for the Saints as referring specifically to tea and coffee.[24] Zebedee Coltrin reported that in the early Church "there was no easing off on Tea and Coffee; these they had to give up straight or their fellowship was jeopardi[z]ed."[25] Though the term "hot drinks" might seem ambiguous to some today, it was understood by the Saints in the 1830s, and it has been defined for subsequent generations of Saints again and again to mean tea and coffee.[26] Moreover, it would be absurd to affirm that the Prophet Joseph Smith had authority to receive a revelation forbidding the use of "hot drinks" but that neither he nor his successors had authority to define for the Saints what that term might include, that is, coffee and tea.

Speculation by members that the drug caffeine might be the cause of the Lord's prohibition against tea and coffee has led some to avoid all forms of caffeine in addition to tea and coffee, even that found in chocolate and so forth, but this is neither the policy of the Church nor its collective practice (see Jacob 4:14 for the blindness that comes from "looking beyond the mark"). Concerning cola drinks containing caffeine, the First Presidency has issued the following statement: "With reference to cola drinks, the Church has never officially taken a position on this matter, but the leaders of the Church have advised, and we do now specifically advise, against the use of any drink containing harmful habit-forming drugs under circumstances that would result in acquiring the habit. Any beverage that contains ingredients harmful to the body should be avoided."[27] "The official interpretation of hot drinks (D&C 89:9) is that it means tea and coffee."[28]

10. All wholesome herbs. "The word *herb* refers to vegetables and plants that are nourishing and healthful for man. Whereas verses 5 through 9 of Doctrine and Covenants 89 contain warnings against things not good for man, verses 10 through 17 list the things that should be used to maintain good health."[29] Unfortunately, the Lord has left it to us to learn for ourselves which herbs or plants are wholesome, and therefore useful, and which plants are not wholesome. No one in the Church except the prophet has the right to make this determination for others. Neither should anyone interpret this verse as an endorsement of herbal medicine instead of mainstream medicines and doctors. There is no implication here that herbs and herbalists are to be preferred to modern doctors.

11. In the season thereof. This phrase does not prohibit the

(not just wheat). A staff is a support, and the staff of life is a support or aid that gives life to human beings.

15. And these hath God made. There is an ambiguity here involving the word "these." The pronoun can be understood inclusively as referring back to *all* the beasts, the fowls, and the wild animals mentioned in verse 14, or it can be understood as referring to the wild animals alone, since these are mentioned last in the series. Since the latter interpretation does not require the revision of previous verses and more closely approximates the actual practice of the present-day Church, it would seem to be the more reasonable understanding.

17. Wheat for man. While all grains, fruits, and vegetables are given as food for man (see vv. 10–11, 16–17), in frontier America wheat was the most nourishing grain readily available for human beings. Some species are better adapted for the use of some grains than others. This does not mean that a species cannot eat other grains, only that there are some grains more nourishing to it naturally than others.

17. Mild drinks. Among the several nonalcoholic drinks made with barley in the nineteenth century was barley-water, which was made by soaking barley in warm water and saving the broth, "which is reputed soft and lubricating, and much used in medicine."[33] A similar mild drink was made from boiling roasted barleycorns into a stronger flavored drink.

18. Walking in obedience to the commandments. The promises of verses 18–21 are based not solely upon living the Word of Wisdom but also upon keeping all of God's commandments. Keeping the principles of the Word of Wisdom while disobeying the other commandments of God would not entitle an individual to the promised blessings. Thus, it will be seen that the promises made in verses 18–21 do not refer merely to the physical results of healthy living, which results are as readily available to the wicked as to the righteous. Observance of the Word of Wisdom may involve our temporal behavior, but its promises are primarily spiritual blessings for obedient Saints.[34]

Elder Harold B. Lee taught: "If you would escape from the devastations when God's judgments descend upon the wicked, as in the days of the children of Israel, you must remember and do what the Lord commands: ' . . . all saints who remember to keep and do these sayings,' meaning keep this great law of health, known as the Word of Wisdom to you Latter-day Saints, and in addition thereto 'walk in obedience' to the commandments, which would include honesty, moral purity, together with all the laws of the celestial kingdom, then 'the destroying angel shall pass by them, as the children of Israel, and not slay them."[35]

18. Health in their navel. Anciently, the navel was considered to be the cosmic center of a human being, since it indicated an individual's origins and his or her link with eternity past and future. Many ancient peoples and traditions referred to their temples as "the navel of the universe." For example, both the pagan Greek shrine at Delphi and the Christian Church of the Holy Sepulcher in Jerusalem displayed to visitors stones considered to be the *"omphalos ges"* (Greek for "navel of the world"). Perhaps it is this kind of symbolic link with eternity and with one's ancestors and posterity—represented by one's navel—which must be healthy and which *will* be healthy for those who observe the Word of Wisdom, if they also keep the commandments of God.

19. And shall find wisdom. The revelation is, after all, a word of *wisdom*. Wisdom is not a physical but a spiritual blessing, bestowed on those who keep the commandment. Once again, this is much more than just a blessing of health to those who live a healthy lifestyle.

20. And shall run and not be weary. Many people who live the Word of Wisdom do get weary, and eventually even the healthiest among us faint or cannot continue their physical exertions. Some who scrupulously observe the Word of Wisdom cannot walk at all. So, what shall we say, that God only keeps his promise in Doctrine and Covenants 89 *most* of the time? Of course not. But we must understand that the promises here are spiritual

DOCTRINE AND COVENANTS

90

BACKGROUND

Because Joseph Smith gave no background information concerning Doctrine and Covenants 90 in *History of the Church,* a brief review of the leadership offices of the Church might be helpful at this point. The reader will recall that Joseph Smith and Oliver Cowdery received the Aaronic Priesthood from John the Baptist, and Peter, James and John conferred the Melchizedek Priesthood on Joseph and Oliver in the spring of 1829. At that time, they also received the apostleship and those keys of the priesthood necessary to restore and preside over the Church of Jesus Christ. From that time onward, regardless of how the Church might be organized administratively, the necessary keys and powers for preaching the first principles of the gospel and performing the ordinances thereof were present in its leaders (but see D&C 110), and their righteous actions in these functions were valid before God just as in the primitive Church.

In April 1830, the "Articles and Covenants of the Church" (see Background to D&C 20) affirmed that Joseph Smith and Oliver Cowdery were called of God and ordained apostles and elders of the Church. They were also designated first and second elders of the Church, respectively (see D&C 20:2–3). These callings and ordinations did not give Joseph and Oliver any additional priesthood authority that they did not already possess, but they did provide a temporary structure through which their authority was administered to the Church and by which the Church could sustain its leaders. This temporary administrative arrangement, with a first and second elder, remained in place until 25 January 1832, by which time a number of high priests had been ordained. At that time, at the Lord's direction, Joseph Smith was sustained and ordained President of the High Priesthood of the Church (see note to *History of the Church,* 1:243). Six weeks later, on 8 March 1832, Sidney Rigdon and Jesse Gause were also called and ordained as counselors to Joseph Smith in the Presidency of the High Priesthood (see D&C 107:9, 21–22, 65–67, 91–92). The Kirtland Revelation Book (10–11) contains the following brief statement of these events: "March 8, 1832: Chose this day and ordained brother Jesse Gause and Brother Sidney to be my counselors of the ministry of the presidency of the high Priesthood."

President Jesse Gause was excommunicated from the Church on 3 December 1832.[1] Consequently, on 5 January 1833, Frederick G. Williams, who had served as a clerk to the Presidency since 20 July 1832, was called to replace Brother Gause as a counselor.[2] However, it does not appear that the Presidency was officially reorganized in the modern sense at that time. Exactly one year after Joseph had chosen his original counselors in the Presidency of the High Priesthood, he received on 8 March 1833 at Kirtland Doctrine and Covenants 90, which revelation confirmed the callings of Sidney Rigdon and Frederick G. Williams as counselors in the Presidency. Doctrine and Covenants 90 also further defined their duties as counselors to Joseph Smith and for the first time declared that the President's counselors were to be "accounted as equal with [him] in holding the keys of this last kingdom" (v. 6). Ten days later, on 18 March 1833, Sidney Rigdon and Frederick G. Williams were ordained counselors to Joseph Smith in the Presidency of the High Priesthood as defined in Doctrine and Covenants 90. Of this occasion, Joseph wrote, "Elder Rigdon expressed a desire that himself and Brother Frederick G. Williams should be ordained to the offices to which they had been called, viz., those of Presidents of the High Priesthood, and to be equal in holding the keys of the kingdom with Brother Joseph Smith, Jun., according to the revelation given on the 8th of March, 1833."[3]

This new Presidency of the High Priesthood, or First Presidency, as it later came to be known, was different from the previous Presidency in that it was organized as a quorum with Joseph's counselors "accounted as equal with [him] in holding the keys" (v. 6) while the President lived and while they were in harmony with him. Since 1833, the term "Presidency of the High Priesthood" has been used synonymously with the term "First Presidency of the Church."[4]

Similarly, though the apostleship had been restored and held by men upon the earth since the spring of 1829 (cf. Background to D&C 18, also D&C 20:2–3), the second leading quorum of the Church, the Quorum of the Twelve Apostles, would not be officially organized as a quorum until 14 and 15 February 1835, also in a manner directed by the Lord (see D&C 18:26–38).[5] As long as the keys were held by living leaders, it did not really matter at that time, when the Church was small, how the lines of administration were drawn. Brigham Young waited three years after the death of Joseph Smith to reorganize the First Presidency. However, since the administration of Lorenzo Snow, it has been the custom to reorganize the Quorum of the First Presidency soon after the funeral of the previous President.

COMMENTARY

1. Thy sins are forgiven thee. Once again notice the human failures of Church leaders and the Lord's willingness to forgive them upon proper repentance.

1. According to thy petitions. It would appear that Doctrine and Covenants 90 may have been received in response to the prayers of the Prophet and his associated brethren for divine guidance.

2. The keys of the kingdom. See Commentary on Doctrine and Covenants 65:2.

2. Which kingdom is coming forth for the last time. The concept of "the last days" already contains the implication that this restoration of the gospel will be the last in the world's history, but see Commentary on Doctrine and Covenants 24:19; 27:13; 33:3; 88:84.

3. Shall never be taken from you. In Doctrine and Covenants 43:3, the Prophet was told that as long as he remained faithful he would hold the keys of the kingdom but that if he fell from faithfulness, those keys would be given to another. A similar promise to Joseph was repeated in Doctrine and Covenants 64:5. However, in this verse the Prophet was told, unconditionally, that he would never lose the keys of the kingdom and that they would remain with him not only in this world but in the world to come. This progression may indicate that sometime between September 1831 (see D&C 64) and March 1833 (see D&C 90), the nature of the Lord's promises to the Prophet Joseph Smith had changed—amounting to a much stronger assurance that his exaltation was secure (see, for example, D&C 132:49).

3. Neither in the world to come. Joseph Smith still holds the keys of this dispensation of the gospel, and he still presides over the work of the Church in the spirit world. In eternity Joseph will continue to preside in the priesthood order over Brigham Young, John Taylor, and so forth, and ultimately over all others who have received their priesthood and keys through the Restoration in the latter days.

4. Through you shall the oracles of God be given to another. The "oracles," as the term is used here, mean the divine revelations (as in v. 5). The process of how Joseph's revelations will be disseminated through his counselors and others is further clarified in verses 6–11 (especially v. 9). The Prophet Joseph will receive the word of God and will then share it with his counselors in the Presidency. Through the First Presidency, the word will then be delivered to the Church (see v. 4) and through the Church to the world (see v. 9). "Whenever new doctrines are to be introduced, they are first presented by the President to his counselors and then to the Quorum of the Twelve Apostles in a meeting of the council of the first presidency and the quorum of the twelve apostles. If unanimously approved [D&C 107:27], they are then presented to the membership of the Church at a general conference for a sustaining vote."[6] New doctrine (that is, new divine information as opposed merely to policy changes or to clarification of existing doctrine) comes to the Church *collectively* in no other way.

5. Let them beware . . . condemnation. Compare Doctrine and Covenants 84:54–59 and Commentary. The imagery of this verse recalls Matthew 7:24–27.

6. They are accounted as equal with thee. Compare Doctrine and Covenants 107:22. As long as the President of the Church is alive, and as long as his counselors are in harmony with his leadership, they share the keys of the kingdom with him and through him to a wide degree. However, there are some powers that are conferred upon only one man on the earth at one time, and these the prophet holds alone (see D&C 132:7). All other keys and powers are held jointly by the Presidency, who are accounted equal with him in these areas. Thus, the First Presidency does not consist merely of a single authorized individual plus his assistants, but is rather a quorum of three or more individuals who share jointly the vast majority of the powers of the kingdom. Naturally, the President *presides* over this quorum, and his counselors defer to his leadership (but see D&C 107:27). However, administratively, it would be correct to say that the Church is governed by quorums rather than by individuals. The Prophet Joseph Smith declared concerning the authority of the Twelve, "The Twelve are not subject to any other than the first Presidency . . . and where I am not, there is no First Presidency over the Twelve."[7] Thus, when the prophet dies, the Quorum of the First Presidency is temporarily dissolved, and his counselors resume their former positions in the Church and its existing quorums. Until the Quorum of the First Presidency is reorganized, the presiding authority over the Church rests upon the second standing quorum of the Church, the Quorum of the Twelve Apostles, led by its presiding officer, until such time as the First Presidency is reorganized (see D&C 107:23–24).

7. The school of the prophets. See Doctrine and Covenants 88:77–80, 118–41 and Commentary.

8. That thereby they may be perfected in their ministry. The antecedents of the pronouns "they" and "their" appear to be Joseph's new counselors in the First Presidency, who will in turn train the leadership of the Church to minister salvation to the Church and the world. The pronouns might also be taken here to apply to the School of the Prophets as a whole, who would serve the same function in their ministries throughout the Church in training leaders at intermediate and local levels.

9. Unto the Gentiles first. By covenant and promise, when the fulness of the gospel was restored at the time of Christ, it was taken first to the physical and literal descendants of the patriarchs Abraham, Isaac, and Jacob. In that same dispensation, in the meridian of time, the majority of the children of Israel rejected the gospel. As a result, in this last dispensation the gospel is by and large to be taken first to the Gentiles, that is, to every *other* nation, kindred, tongue, and people besides the Jews (see D&C 45:9, 25, 28–31 and Commentary). Collectively and as a people, the Jews will be the last to receive the gospel in this dispensation.

10. The heathen nations, the house of Joseph. In the Old Testament, the term "house of Joseph" is sometimes used to describe Ephraim and Manasseh specifically (for example, see Joshua 17:17), and sometimes to describe all ten tribes of the northern kingdom collectively (for example, see Zechariah 10:6). Since Ephraim, Manasseh, and the other ten tribes were eventually scattered among and grafted into every nation, kindred, tongue, and people, the house of Joseph now includes branches (see Genesis 50:22) among all the nations of the earth, including the "heathen," or non-Christian, nations of the world. The Nephites and Lamanites were "a remnant of the house of Joseph" (3 Nephi 15:12), but other remnants of Joseph can be found and are now being sought out by missionaries among all the nations of the earth.[8] It is probably not a coincidence that the Prophet of the last dispensation—the dispensation of the times of the Gentiles when the house of Joseph will be reclaimed from all the world—was named Joseph (see D&C 113:4; Ezekiel 36:24; 37:21; 39:28; 2 Nephi 3).

11. In that day. This is the day referred to in verse 10 when the arm of the Lord shall be revealed in power. It is probably to be understood as the "day" of his coming to earth to establish his millennial kingdom. While the great missionary work of the present-day Church begins to fulfill this prophecy, only after the return of the Savior in power will the promise of everyone hearing the fulness of the gospel in his or her own language be entirely fulfilled. Until that time, many people will continue to die in ignorance of the gospel. According to Joseph Smith, however, after the Second Coming, all the heathen nations will be taught the gospel, and those who will not accept it "must eventually be destroyed from the earth."[9]

13. The translation of the prophets. The term "the prophets" is here used to mean the books of the Old Testament. Joseph Smith finished his translation of the New Testament (see D&C 45:60) on 2 February 1833, more than a month before Doctrine and Covenants 90 was received. Since Joseph had already spent considerable time on the Old Testament before beginning the New, the expectation seems to be that his translation of the Old Testament Prophets would also soon be completed.

13. The church and the school. That is, the Church of Jesus Christ and the School of the Prophets.

15. And study and learn. One purpose of the School of the Prophets was to teach the first elders of this dispensation what they would need to know in order to take the gospel to the peoples of the world, including their languages, literature, and cultures.

16. In all your lives. Absent cases of serious sin or unworthiness, members of the First Presidency are called to serve for life—even when they may be suffering from the effects of extreme age or poor health.

19. Let a place be provided. It will be remembered that Frederick G. Williams was a resident of Kirtland before joining the Church and that he owned a large farm there. However, when Brother Williams accompanied Oliver Cowdery and the Lamanite missionaries to Missouri, his farm of necessity was parceled out to other Latter-day Saint families moving into the Kirtland area from New York, including those of Joseph Smith Senior and Ezra Thayre.[10] In accordance with these instructions in Doctrine and Covenants 90, other accommodations were now provided for the Williams family, and the following year Frederick G. Williams consecrated his entire farm to the Church without remuneration. The Williams farm eventually made up part of the parcel of land that provided grounds around the Kirtland Temple.[11]

22–23. Let the bishop . . . obtain an agent. Bishop Newel K. Whitney had previously been instructed (see D&C 84:113) to employ an agent to help him with the duties of administering the bishop's storehouse in Kirtland but had apparently not yet done so. These instructions made it clear that the prospective agent would not simply be an employee, but would consecrate his own time and wealth to the building up of Zion as was expected of other Church leaders. There is no historical evidence that Bishop Whitney ever did employ an agent to help him.

24. The covenant with which ye have covenanted one with another. This passage referred originally to the covenant entered into by the leaders of the Church and others who attended the School of the Prophets. It is described more fully in Doctrine and Covenants 88:130–36. However, by extension this would also apply to those who later made similar covenants in the Kirtland Temple or in any of its many successors.

25–27. Let your families be small. This commandment should not be construed as applying to the number of children Saints ought to have. Rather, it applied initially to the extended social obligations of the Saints. In the spirit of Christian charity, it was the practice of the Prophet and other Church leaders to open up their homes and share their resources with those Saints and others who came to Kirtland in need. At other times, members like Newel Whitney or John Johnson were in turn called upon to share their resources with the Prophet in his need.

Eventually, as Church leaders, particularly Father and Mother Smith, continued to open their homes to the Saints who were moving into the Kirtland area from the East, certain problems arose. Some members took advantage of the kindness of their hosts. Other members who were unworthy avoided the responsibilities of consecration but still received its blessings by attaching themselves to more faithful families. In addition, the sheer burden of housing so many individuals in their comparatively small homes became very taxing on them, but it was hard to say no to anyone who claimed to be in need. Thus, the Lord here counsels his leaders, and particularly Father and Mother Smith, who were generous to a fault, to use wisdom and where possible to reduce the number of their dependents who were not actually blood relatives or who were not personally worthy of receiving the blessings of consecration on their own.

28. Vienna Jaques. Forty-five-year-old Sister Vienna Jaques had joined the Church sometime in 1832. Though she lived in Boston, and apparently supported herself there as a nurse, she was converted by the Book of Mormon and visited Joseph Smith in Kirtland, being baptized while she was there. After returning briefly to Boston, Sister Jaques moved to Kirtland sometime before March 1833 and was instructed to consecrate her wealth, including fourteen hundred dollars cash, to the Lord. This she did without hesitation. Doctrine and Covenants 90 here directs that her expenses of moving to Missouri be paid by the Church and that she receive an inheritance in Zion. Sister Jaques arrived in Independence in the summer of 1833 but lost her temporal inheritance when the Saints were driven from Jackson County. However, she remained faithful and steadfast for more than fifty years thereafter, moving with the Saints in all their wanderings, and finally dying in Salt Lake City in 1884, at the age of ninety-six.[12]

32–35. I have called you also to preside over Zion. In the early days of the Church there were sometimes administrative questions of exactly who presided over whom and in what circumstances. Despite such revelations as Doctrine and Covenants 43:3–5 or 64:5, some in Missouri believed that they presided there independently of the Prophet Joseph Smith. Doctrine and Covenants 90 settles this argument and clarifies the administrative situation (see vv. 2–5). Though Bishop Partridge was the bishop in Missouri and really the presiding bishop in the Church, he was subordinate to Joseph and the other members of the First Presidency (see vv. 6, 13, 16). Among other faults, Partridge's resistance to Joseph's leadership, as well as the resistance of others in Missouri, did not please the Lord (see v. 35).[13]

35. William E. McLellin. See Background to Doctrine and Covenants 66; Commentary on Doctrine and Covenants 75:6–7. Brother McLellin was out of favor at this time for at least two reasons. First, he had returned prematurely from two missions in a row, one to the East and one south of Kirtland. Second, he had organized a party of emigrants and led them to Missouri in direct violation of the rules and procedures established by the Lord through the Prophet Joseph Smith, thereby adding to the difficulties of the Saints there.[14]

36. I, the Lord, will contend with Zion. The Lord announces his intention of chastening the Saints in Missouri for their sins and their rebellion. He will not shirk the unpleasant duty of disciplining his own people when necessary (see D&C 97:25–26; 100:13; 101:2–10).

37. For [Zion] shall not be removed. At first, this

declaration might seem to contradict the historical facts, since the Saints were forcibly removed not only from Jackson County but eventually from all of Missouri. However, the meaning here is that Jackson County, Missouri, is and always will be the location of the center place of Zion (see D&C 57:3). All the prophecies about the physical Zion will be literally fulfilled, though not in the time frame the early Saints envisioned. According to Doctrine and Covenants 101:17–20, "Zion shall not be moved out of her place, notwithstanding her children are scattered. . . . And, behold, there is none other place appointed than that which I have appointed; neither shall there be any other place appointed than that which I have appointed, for the work of the gathering of my saints." In the Lord's own due time, Zion will be redeemed and established where and how he has declared it.

1. See Background to D&C 81; Jessee, *Papers,* 2:4.
2. See Cook, *Revelations of the Prophet Joseph Smith,* 192.
3. Smith, *History of the Church,* 1:334.
4. Compare D&C 68:15 and 19 with D&C 68:22; see also Ludlow, ed., *Encyclopedia of Mormonism,* 2:512–13, where the latter is said to have been organized in 1832, although the former title is used in the contemporary documents.
5. See Smith, *History of the Church,* 2:186–98.
6. Ludlow, ed., *Encyclopedia of Mormonism,* 3:1127.
7. Smith, *History of the Church,* 2:374.
8. See Commentary on D&C 19:27 and 64:36.
9. Smith, *History of the Church,* 5:212.
10. See Background to D&C 32; 56; 64:21; and Commentary.
11. See Backman, *Heavens Resound,* 73, 144.
12. See Black, *Who's Who in the Doctrine and Covenants,* 145–47.
13. See also Commentary on D&C 81:1; 84:56.
14. See Shipps and Welch, *Journal of William E. McLellin,* 303–5.

91

BACKGROUND

On 8 March 1833, Joseph Smith received a revelation (D&C 90) concerning the First Presidency of the Church and its role in taking the gospel to the world. In that revelation, it was also indicated to Joseph that he was to continue his work on the Joseph Smith Translation by completing his inspired revision "of the prophets" (D&C 90:13), that is, the Old Testament books. Accordingly, on the very next day, 9 March 1833, Joseph resumed work on the Joseph Smith Translation in his quarters above Newel Whitney's store. It appears, however, that a question soon arose concerning the exact definition of "the prophets." The Roman Catholic and Eastern Orthodox churches include in their Old Testament a dozen or so books known as "the Apocrypha," which they consider to be inspired scripture and the word of God. Unfortunately, ancient Hebrew manuscripts of the Bible do not include these books, so Protestants, following the example of Martin Luther, have generally excluded the Apocrypha from their bibles. However, the copy of the King James Bible that Joseph Smith used in his work on the Joseph Smith Translation did contain the Apocrypha at the end of the Old Testament, so naturally the question arose: Exactly which books belong in the Old Testament? Were the Apocrypha part of "the prophets" and therefore part of Joseph's translation obligation according to the instructions in Doctrine and Covenants 90:13, or were they later additions to the Bible and therefore beyond the scope of his translation of the biblical scriptures?

In approximately the second century before Christ, a Greek translation of the Hebrew Old Testament called the Septuagint (or LXX) began to circulate in the ancient world. This Greek version of the Old Testament contained more books in it than the Hebrew Bible it supposedly translated. So, there are two possibilities: (1) either the Greek translators in 200 B.C. added material to their Bible which was not found in the original Hebrew, or (2) the rabbis of the first centuries after Christ removed some books from the Hebrew Bible of which the Septuagint translation, made earlier, still bears witness. Most contemporary biblical scholars favor the first option.[1]

This extra material found in the Septuagint Greek translation but not in the Hebrew Bible has come to be called the Apocrypha, from the Greek word meaning "hidden." The Apocrypha consist of twelve to fifteen compositions (depending on how one divides them up), including 1 and 2 Maccabees, 1 and 2 Esdras, Judith, Tobit, Susannah and the Elders, Wisdom of Solomon, Baruch, Ecclesiasticus or Sirach, the Prayer of Manasseh, and additions to the books of Daniel and Esther. These books are accepted by Catholics and by Eastern Orthodox churches generally as inspired scripture (though sometimes called "deuterocanonical"), but they are considered nonscriptural by most Protestants. Hence, there is not one Christian Bible but at least two, depending upon whether and to what extent the Christians in question accept the Apocrypha as scripture.

Because different churches hold different views on the inspiration of the Apocrypha, and because the Apocrypha was found in the Bible with which he was working, Joseph inquired of the Lord for a clarification of its status. In answer to his questions, Joseph Smith received Doctrine and Covenants 91, which defines for Latter-day Saints the place of the Apocrypha in relation to the scriptures. Joseph noted briefly, "March 9—Having come to that portion of the ancient writings called the Apocrypha, I received the following."[2]

COMMENTARY

1. Concerning the Apocrypha. It is crucial to understand this term correctly. As a proper noun, *the Apocrypha* (with the definite article and an uppercase *A*), refers specifically and exclusively to the extra books of the Old Testament found in the Greek Septuagint but not in the Hebrew Bible. Thus, the divine information given in Doctrine and Covenants 91 about "the Apocrypha" cannot be legitimately applied to any other category of ancient literature.

Unfortunately, the adjective *apocryphal* (with a lowercase *a*) is a confusingly similar term which has often been applied to many other bodies of ancient literature such as the Dead Sea Scrolls, the Nag Hammadi codices, or the "apocryphal" books of the New Testament. Careless or uninformed writers have confused "the Apocrypha" with other ancient writings called "apocryphal" only because they were considered spurious or of questionable authenticity. Such an equation simply must not be made; the similar terms *the Apocrypha* and *apocryphal* are decidedly *not* equivalent. Joseph's question on 9 March 1833 concerned "the Apocrypha"— those dozen or so books found in the Greek Septuagint but not in the Hebrew Bible and accepted as scripture by Catholics but not by most Protestants. The Lord's answer to Joseph's question addressed those books specifically, and the information contained in Doctrine and Covenants 91 cannot legitimately be applied to other classes of literature simply because the latter are sometimes called apocryphal. For example, the modern forgeries and so-called revelations of LDS dissidents would rightly be described as apocryphal (meaning "spurious") by Latter-day Saints, but they are certainly not to be considered among the Apocrypha of the Greek Old Testament, nor are they entitled to the limited endorsement found in Doctrine and Covenants 91. By the same token, the relatively positive evaluation of the Apocrypha in verses 1 and 5 cannot properly be applied to the Dead Sea Scrolls, the Nag Hammadi codices, or any other body of ancient apocryphal literature.

1. Many things contained therein . . . are true. Several books of the Apocrypha are true historically or contain spiritually inspiring material. For example, much of our knowledge of Jewish history between the Old and New Testaments comes from 1 and 2 Maccabees and the Wisdom of Solomon, while the Prayer of Manasseh is a moving example of the broken heart of a repentant sinner (though probably not really written by the evil king Manasseh).

1. It is mostly translated correctly. The problem with the Apocrypha is not the translation, but the nature of the documents themselves. Being historically true is not exactly the same thing as being divinely inspired.

2. Many things contained therein . . . are not true. For example, it is easy to see the popular folklore in Tobit, or the pseudosophisticated "wisdom" of Ecclesiasticus, and 2 Maccabees covers much of the same history as 1 Maccabees but "spices things up" considerably to make the events recorded seem more dramatic.

2. Interpolations by the hands of men. This language would seem to favor the view that the extra books, and particularly the additions to existing books, were added (or interpolated) to the Greek translation rather than deleted from the Hebrew.

3. It is not needful that the Apocrypha should be translated. Joseph's instructions that the Apocrypha did not comprise part of his translation obligation left the very clear implication that the Apocrypha is not to be considered part of the Latter-day Saint canon of scripture.[3] This verse essentially defines the Latter-day Saint biblical canon along Protestant lines: the Old Testament is rightly understood to consist of the books found in the Hebrew Old Testament rather than in the Greek Septuagint.

4. Whoso readeth it. Nevertheless, it should not be understood that the Saints are forbidden to read the Apocrypha or that these books are without merit. The Holy Spirit can bear witness to truth even on the stony ground of the Apocrypha.

5. Shall obtain benefit therefrom. Grammatically, the most plausible meaning here is that the benefit comes not from the Apocrypha as documents but from the process of reading them "by the Spirit" (v. 6). This principle would be just as true if one were reading any other type of literature, such as a newspaper or a good novel, but reading it "by the Spirit."

6. Cannot be benefited. Unlike the scriptures, the truths of the Apocrypha are not readily apparent even to the discerning reader and require personal revelation through the Spirit to be detectible. When compared with the scriptures, the Apocrypha is less fruitful soil for spiritual growth without greater than usual assistance from the Spirit. Therefore, these books will be of less value to the Saints than the Old and New Testament scriptures, and Joseph is not required to translate them. Again, the difficulty was not with the existing translation of the Apocrypha, but with the nature of the documents themselves (see v. 1 and Commentary). While historians and scholars can find much in these documents of importance to their research, average Church members will receive a greater spiritual return on their investment of time by reading the Bible and the other standard works than they will by reading the Apocrypha.

1. See LDS Bible Dictionary, s.v. "Apocrypha."
2. Smith, *History of the Church,* 1:331.
3. See Robinson, "Background to the Testaments," *Ensign,* Dec. 1982, 25–26.

92

BACKGROUND

On 8 March 1833, Joseph Smith received Doctrine and Covenants 90 at Kirtland, Ohio, which dealt with the organization and duties of the Presidency of the High Priesthood, or First Presidency. Section 90 confirmed the calling of Frederick G. Williams as a counselor in the First Presidency in place of Jesse Gause who had been excommunicated three months earlier. One week after section 90 was received, it was revealed to the Prophet that Frederick G. Williams should also become a member of the united order or united firm.[1] The minutes of the Kirtland High Council record for 15 March 1833 read as follows: "Thursday, received a revelation making known that F. G. W. should be received into the united order in full partnership agreeable to the specification of the bond."[2]

COMMENTARY

1. The commandment previously given. That is, Doctrine and Covenants 78:11; see also Doctrine and Covenants 82:11–20.

2. Lively member. In 1828 the term *lively* was an exact equivalent to our term *active*. It would not be enough for Brother Williams merely to be a member of the Church or of the united order. He was to be a "lively member," that is, one active and involved. Since this is the "only true and living Church" (D&C 1:30) on the earth, its members (or component parts) must also be "true" and "living."

1. See Background to D&C 78 and Commentary on D&C 78:9, 11.
2. Collier and Harwell, eds., *Kirtland Council Minute Book,* 11; spelling, punctuation, and grammar standardized; see also D&C 78:11; 82:11, 15.

DOCTRINE AND COVENANTS

9 3

BACKGROUND

Doctrinally, Doctrine and Covenants 93 is one of the more informative and important revelations in the Doctrine and Covenants, yet the Prophet gives almost no historical information concerning its reception. He simply recorded, "May 6.—I received the following."[1] The Kirtland Revelation Book and many other early manuscripts agree with *History of the Church* that this revelation was received on 6 May 1833.[2] Doctrine and Covenants 94 was received later on that same day. At this time, Joseph and Emma and their two small children were still living in rooms above the Whitney store in Kirtland, and sections 93 and 94 were probably received in Joseph's translation room there.

Although the Prophet was not yet aware of it, mobs had begun combining against the Saints in Missouri in April 1833, a month before Doctrine and Covenants 93 was received. By July mobs would attack the Church printing office in Independence and destroy most copies of the Book of Commandments, which was then in the process of being printed. The defection of some leading members, both in Kirtland and in Missouri, would soon bring a threat of apostasy in both places and even the threat of a possible division between the Church in Kirtland and the Church in Missouri.[3] This was a time when the Church would need additional light and knowledge to comfort the members and to strengthen their testimonies.

Though there is little explanation of the purpose of Doctrine and Covenants 93 in the historical record, the revelation itself states (see v. 19) that its purpose is to teach the Saints what they worship and how they are to accomplish that worship, in order that they may come to the Father through the Son and receive of the Father's fulness. Building on information given in Doctrine and Covenants 76 and 88, section 93 clarifies the nature of the relationship between the Father and the Son. It declares the eternal nature of all human beings, and it clarifies how human beings may become like the divine Father and Son (compare John 17:3). The doctrines of the premortal existence of spirits and the human potential eventually to become like God begin to be taught here in Doctrine and Covenants 93 (see D&C 132:20 and Commentary).

COMMENTARY

1. It shall come to pass. The promise given here is sure, but the timing of its fulfillment is not. According to Doctrine and Covenants 88:68, this promise will be fulfilled for those who qualify "in [the Lord's] own time, and in his own way, and according to his own will." It is possible, perhaps even likely, that many who qualify for this blessing will, in their own best interests, not receive its full benefits until after this mortal life.

1. Every soul . . . shall see my face. Note that the divine promise previously given to the leadership of the Church that they may be privileged to see the face of Jesus Christ and know for themselves that he lives (see D&C 50:45; 67:10, 14; 76:116–118; 88:68) is now extended here to every faithful member. Of course, there is a sense in which everyone, faithful or not, member or not, will eventually see Christ and know that he exists. This will take place on that great and last day, when Jesus returns to this earth in his glory. The sight of him on that occasion will lift up the righteous and incinerate the wicked (see D&C 5:19; 45:44–50).

In addition, it is true that those who are faithful but who do not see the face of Christ during their mortal lives will still, according to his promise, see him in the millennial kingdom (see, for example, 1 John 3:2). However, it seems likely here that the reference is not to the last day, or even primarily to seeing Jesus in the kingdom, but to that remarkable privilege extended to many faithful Saints of seeing the face of Christ and of receiving him in this life as the second Comforter (see D&C 88:3–4; 68:12 and Commentary).

The promise of Doctrine and Covenants 93:1 comes with five conditions, listed in logical order, for receiving the blessing referred to. These conditions together constitute a process of purification that will lead one eventually to see the face of the Savior. They are that a person must (1) forsake his or her sins (see D&C 58:43 and Commentary), (2) come unto the Savior (see Matthew 11:28–30; Moroni 10:32), (3) call upon his name, (4) obey his voice, and (5) keep his commandments. Having done all this, a person will, in the Lord's own time and in his own way (see D&C 88:68) have the right to see the face of the Savior and know that he lives.

1. Cometh unto me. To come unto Christ is to enter into the covenant of the gospel and thereby become one with Christ as his son or daughter in his kingdom (see D&C 25:1 and Commentary; John 17:21–23). Coming to Christ implies movement, yet one can come to Christ without moving physically, apart from receiving the ordinances of the gospel. When we come unto Christ through faith, repentance, and baptism (which is, according to Ammon, "all we *could* do"; Alma 24:11; emphasis added; compare 2 Nephi 25:23), we put all other concerns into his hands and trust him to save us from all other hazards (see 2 Nephi 4:19–21; 31:19; Moroni 6:4). Through coming to Christ and becoming one with him in this way, we cease to belong to this fallen world and become "fellowcitizens with the saints" (Ephesians 2:19). By coming to Christ we move spiritually from one world to the other, from this telestial Babylon to the kingdom of God. As long as we remain faithful to our covenants with Christ—even with our mortal imperfections—we also remain one with him and are linked to him and to his kingdom, wherever he, or we, may be.

1. Calleth on my name. To call upon the name of Christ is to seek his power and authority in our lives, in our prayers, and in our ordinances by doing all that we do "in the name of Jesus Christ." By calling upon his name, we accept Jesus Christ as Lord and Savior. We accept his role as mediator between ourselves and the Father; we accept him as the Atoning One who makes us worthy of his Father's kingdom; and we accept his power and authority, or in other words, his Spirit and his holy priesthood, in improving and governing our lives (see Moses 5:8).

1. Obeyeth my voice. This can be understood to mean obedience to Christ's voice either through the personal promptings of the Spirit or through the voice of his legitimate servants (see D&C 1:38 and Commentary). The Spirit of God may prompt one person in a different way or a different direction than another person in matters of individual importance or choice, whereas commandments to the whole Church and directives through its leaders are the same for everyone.

1. See my face and know that I am. See Doctrine and Covenants 76:117–18 and Commentary. In connection with Doctrine and Covenants 76:6–18, note the same wordplay here on the term "I am" that is also found in the Gospel of John (for example, see John 8:58; 18:6), where the underlying allusion is to the great "I Am," the name of God as revealed to Moses in Exodus 3:14.

President Kimball said: "I have learned that where there is a prayerful heart, a hungering after righteousness, a forsaking of sins, and obedience to the commandments of God, the Lord pours out more and more light until there is finally power to pierce the heavenly veil and to know more than man knows. A person of such righteousness has the priceless promise that one day he shall see the Lord's face and know that he is."[4]

2. I am the true light. See John 1:9; Doctrine and Covenants 84:45–46; 88:11–13.

3. The Father and I are one. Latter-day Saints accept both the "oneness" or unity of God and also the "threeness" or separateness of God (Father, Son, and Holy Ghost) as these are taught in the scriptures. However, we reject the attempt to explain this simultaneous oneness and threeness of God by the traditional doctrine of the trinity as it was developed in postbiblical times. We do not believe that God consists of one being in three co-equal and co-eternal persons. Neither this formula nor even the word *trinity* can be found in the Bible itself, and the experience of the Prophet Joseph Smith in the grove and the teaching of latter-day revelation on this topic make this an impossible concept for the Saints (see, for example, D&C 130:22).

However, sometimes in our desire to emphasize that the Godhead consists of three separate and distinct individuals (the "threeness" of God as Father, Son, and Holy Ghost), we fail to give proper attention to the unity and oneness of God as expressed in this and other passages of scripture. Our disagreement with the nonbiblical doctrine of the Trinity should not lead us into denying the scriptural teaching that God, or the Godhead, is somehow perfectly one. Latter-day Saints do believe, must believe, that the Father, Son, and Holy Ghost are one God (see, for example, D&C 20:28 and Commentary; Testimony of Three Witnesses; 2 Nephi 31:21; Mosiah 15:1–4; Alma 11:44; Mormon 7:7; John 10:30). These three divine persons, though separate beings, are perfectly one in purpose, one in mind, one in intent, and so on. Therefore, to know the mind, heart, and personality of one member of the Godhead is to know the mind, heart, and personality of all three (see John 14:7–9), for they are alike. In the beginning, the Father shared his power and will—his personality—so perfectly with the Son, and the Son voluntarily accepted it, conformed to it, and obeyed it so perfectly that the Son can now be said in one sense to be *both* of them (see Ether 3:14; Mosiah 15:2–4, 7; Alma 11:39–40; Mormon 9:12; Isaiah 9:6; JST Luke 10:23). The Father's personality and mind are in the Son, and vice versa. Nevertheless, they remain separate and distinct physical beings.

Moreover, just as the three separate persons of the Godhead are one in this manner without compromising their individual existence, so also may faithful disciples truly become one with the Father and with the Son in the same manner without losing their separate or individual existence. As John teaches, the oneness that exists between the members of the Godhead is the same quality or type of oneness that should exist between faithful disciples, or between God and his disciples (see John 17:21–23). This is not a physical oneness, but a oneness of mind and purpose. As we voluntarily conform to the character and obey the will of God as the Son has done before us, God is able to share with us also his divine energy, light, truth, intelligence, and spirit, so that we become more than we once were and more like he is. This is also one reason why Zion cannot be established until the Saints are "of one heart and one mind" (Moses 7:18), that is, at one with the heart, mind, and character of God.

Normally, human minds prefer straight lines and clear distinctions and delineations. We prefer blacks and whites to shades of gray. We identify things by their borders, and so we tend to focus on the distinctions between the Father, Son, and Holy Ghost in order to understand them as individuals. But the message of verse 3 is that such a neat division between their respective roles is sometimes difficult to make—for their complete unity of thought, personality, and purpose usually makes them better understood by their oneness, by their "alikeness," than by their differences. This unity of the Godhead is so perfect that it sometimes confuses us, as when Christ speaks as the Father, or when the Holy Ghost speaks as the Son (see Moses 1:6; 5:9; D&C 29:1, 42). As we teach the truth concerning the separate physical natures of the Father and the Son, we must be careful not to separate them in any other sense, for the Father and the Son are "in" each other

(John 14:10) and are one in a way difficult for mortals to fully appreciate, though in a way that does not compromise their separate and individual being.

4. The Father because. Jesus may be said to be the Father, or to be "in" the Father (v. 3), because the Father has given everything, that is, "his fulness," to the Son. From the beginning, Jesus has had access to all the Father has and is. He is a partner in all the Father does, and he is the agent through whom the Father does it. Whatever Christ may do, it is the Father's will being expressed (see John 5:19; 6:38; 7:16; 12:49–50; etc.). By being so perfectly the agent of the Father, and by so perfectly representing the Father's mind and character to us, Jesus becomes the Father for us in function by doing exactly as the Father himself would do (see Mosiah 15:7; see also D&C 20:28 and Commentary).

4. The Son because. On the other hand, Jesus is the Son, and the Father may be said to be "in" the Son (v. 3), because of Jesus' divine paternity in the flesh. The Father is part of the physical, biological nature of the Son in a way not true of any other human being. Then, as Jesus grew in knowledge "in the world," he learned and obeyed the will of the Father to perfection. Thus, the mind and will of the Father were manifest "in" the works and words of Jesus.

The Father is also in the Son because of Jesus' divine spiritual parentage in the premortal life. In the beginning, God chose Christ to be his Firstborn and to put into Christ his own fulness, that Christ might function as God, Jehovah, even before his personal incarnation and resurrection.

6. John saw and bore record. Many Latter-day Saint writers on Doctrine and Covenants 93, including President John Taylor, Elder Orson Pratt, and Brother Sidney B. Sperry, have concluded that the "John" mentioned here is John the Baptist.[5] According to Elder Bruce R. McConkie: "From latter-day revelation we learn that the material in the forepart of the gospel of John (the Apostle, Revelator, and Beloved Disciple) was written originally by John the Baptist. By revelation the Lord restored to Joseph Smith part of what John the Baptist had written and promised to reveal the balance when men became sufficiently faithful to warrant receiving it. Verse 15 of this passage is the key to the identity of the particular John spoken of. This verse should be compared with Matt. 3:16–17 to learn the identity of the writer."[6]

So, it would appear that John the Beloved Apostle has incorporated into his account of the Savior's ministry an account of events surrounding the baptism of Jesus which was somehow transmitted to him from the earlier John the Baptist. However, this makes it all the more mysterious as to why the actual baptism itself is not described in John's Gospel.

7. And he bore record, saying. Note that Doctrine and Covenants 93:7–17 constitutes an alternate version of John 1:1–16. Verses 6–7 seem to indicate that Doctrine and Covenants 93:7–17 are quoted from the "record of John" (v. 18) as it read before plain and precious things were taken out of it (see 1 Nephi 13:26–28; 14:18–27). Scholars have long recognized that of the four New Testament Gospels, John's bears the most evidence of editing by a later hand (see, for example, John 21:24, where the pronoun "we" identifies John's editors). Doctrine and Covenants 93:6, 18 and 1 Nephi 14:25–27 indicate that "the record of John" is yet to be revealed to the Church in its original condition with its original clarity. Doctrine and Covenants 93:7–17 is very similar to John 1:1–16, but the Doctrine and Covenants contains important clarifications not found in the New Testament text.

8. The Word, even the messenger. In human interaction, one brain does not interface directly with another. Rather, we communicate through the medium of language, that is, by words. The brain of one individual formulates words and speaks them; another individual hears the words spoken and transmits them to his or her own brain in order to understand. Thus, language, or the word, is a third entity that acts as a mediator or messenger between two minds. In just the same manner, we human beings do not encounter the Father directly. His mind is represented to us through his mediator, the Word, Jesus Christ. By hearing and receiving Christ, the perfect expression of his Father's will, we know the mind and will of the Father. Thus, the title "the Word" is an excellent way of referring to Christ, who is the representative of the Father to us, just as language, or the word, represents one mind to another.

9. The Spirit of truth. Before his mortal incarnation, Jesus was, indeed, a spirit—the Spirit of truth. Thus, Ammon's description of Christ to King Lamoni as the "Great Spirit" was at that time technically correct (Alma 18:26–29; ca. 90 B.C.). Scriptural distinctions between "the Spirit of the Lord," "the Holy Spirit," and several other designations of the persons and power of members of the Godhead are sometimes very tenuous—another example of the complete oneness of the Godhead (compare, for example, 1 Nephi 11:11 with 1 Nephi 11:27). The scriptural title "Spirit of truth" sometimes describes Christ (as here in v. 9), and sometimes describes the Holy Ghost (as, for example, D&C 50:17–19), and may correctly be applied to either of them.

10. See parallels in John 1:3, 10; Doctrine and Covenants 76:24; 88:41.

11. See parallels in John 1:14. The author of the record of John had seen in vision the glory of the premortal Christ and testifies here of his divine premortal existence (v. 7; John 1:1–3). Then, in Doctrine and Covenants 93:12–15, he describes "the condescension of God" (1 Nephi 11:26; see also Philippians 2:5–8), in which Jesus Christ (God the Son) submitted to the limitations and the testing of mortality until he was again glorified and received the fulness of the Father (see vv. 16–17). Thus, the fulness of the record of John contains an account of the role and ministry of the Savior, Jesus Christ, from the beginning of time to the end of the world (see "all things" in 1 Nephi 14:26).

11. The Spirit of truth. See Commentary on verse 9. In these verses, the term "Spirit of truth" refers not to the Holy Ghost, but to Jesus Christ. Before the incarnation, Christ was a spirit, and it was his influence and power, the light of Christ or the Spirit of truth, that made and gave life to all things (see D&C 88:6–7).

With the incarnation and resurrection of Christ into a glorified physical body, his spiritual power and influence have not become limited or been diminished, but rather have increased. Thus, he is still now, as he was then, the Spirit (or power, influence, light, etc.) of truth (see v. 26).

The process of exaltation does not make Jesus, or us, cease to be spirits. Rather we are "added upon," that is, we become spirits with increased powers and attributes, including physical natures and the ability to create using physical matter.

12–14. These three verses constitute part of what was taken from the fulness of John's original record. They are restored here to clarify the nature of the relationship between the Father and the Son and to clarify the process through which the mortal Jesus eventually received the fulness of his Father—a process which the Saints may emulate. Thus, these verses are the first detailed indication in the Restoration scriptures of what has come to be called the principle of progression or of becoming like God. Just as Jesus went through a progression from the beginning until he received the fulness of the Father at his resurrection, so his Saints may experience a similar progression "from grace to grace" (v. 13) until we, through Christ, also receive the fulness of the Father (see v. 19).

12. He received not of the fulness at first. Jesus Christ was God the Son and possessed the fulness of the Father and of the Father's divine glory from the beginning of time (see John 1:1–3; 1 Nephi 19:10, 12). He was, by the will and permission of the Father, fully and completely God. However, when he condescended to lay his divine status aside and become incarnated as a human being, he experienced life as all other humans do. The phrase "at first" refers here not to the beginning of time in the premortal state but rather to the beginning of Jesus' mortal life. Thus, President Lorenzo Snow taught that "when Jesus lay in the manger, a helpless infant, He knew not that He was the Son of God and that formerly He had created the earth. When the edict of Herod was issued, He knew nothing of it; He had not power to save Himself; and His [guardian and step-father Joseph] and mother had to take Him and [flee] into Egypt to preserve Him from the effects of that edict. . . . He grew up to manhood, and during His progress it was revealed unto Him who He was, and for what purpose He was in the world. The glory and power He possessed before He came into the world was made known unto Him."[7]

Before his mortal birth, Jesus Christ possessed the glory of the Father through the will of the Father. But everyone, even the Son of God, must be tested and tried in mortality, and so Christ laid aside his divine status and became a human being (see 1 Nephi 11:26–33; Philippians 2:5–8). By his perfect obedience in mortality, Jesus then regained the glory which had once been his by the will of the Father (see John 17:5). However, after Jesus' resurrection, having personally done all and having overcome all, that glory had now become his also by right, through his own experience and victory, by his own merits and obedience as well as by the will of his Father.

12. Grace for grace. In mortality, as Jesus responded to the grace (or gifts) of God with grace of his own (that is, with voluntary obedience, service, and sacrifice), he received yet further grace, or gifts, from God. As the mortal Jesus obeyed, served, and emulated his Father, the Father bestowed additional gifts, understanding, and powers upon him. It is critically important to remember that the reciprocal nature of "grace for grace" begins with the grace of God (see Mosiah 2:23–24) and *not* with the merit of the individual (see Alma 22:14), and it continues only as long as we respond graciously. The process is not one of merit and reward so much as one of gift and grateful response. As long as we respond to the gifts of God with graciousness of our own, with devoted obedience to God and loving service to others, he will continue to stay ahead of us, to give us additional gracious gifts, until we eventually receive all things (v. 20; see also Mosiah 2:21–25). This should not be understood as "earning" grace (an impossibility), for in every case God's blessings are greater than our performance actually deserves, and we remain indebted to him for his gracious gifts to us (see Mosiah 2:24). There is a quid pro quo of sorts, but it is one in which God always leaves us in *his* debt.

13. Grace to grace. The key to this verse is the word *to,* indicating that there are levels of grace, or degrees to which one may enjoy the grace of God and act graciously toward others. Thus, from birth on, we move forward in a process of learning and responding to God's grace, which process can, if we continue in it, lead us to receive a fulness of God's grace, or gifts. The Savior has shown us how this process works and how one may grow from one level of grace to another higher level, and he invites us to emulate him in doing so.

15–17. See parallels in John 1:32–34. Verse 17 marks the end in Doctrine and Covenants 93 of the quotation from the "fulness of the record of John."

18. See verse 6 and Commentary.

19–20. That you may understand and know how to worship. The Lord here states the primary purpose of Doctrine and Covenants 93. The actual formula for correct worship comes in verse 20: "For if you keep my commandments you shall receive of his fulness, and be glorified in me as I am in the Father." We worship God by emulating him and following his course. As Jesus kept the Father's will and was glorified, so we can imitate Jesus' course of action, keep his will, and be glorified in him. Just as imitation is the sincerest form of flattery, so also it is the truest form of worship. True worship is to imitate the Son of God and conform to his example in seeking God and in moving from grace to grace. Ultimately, the highest and truest form of worship is to become like the One we worship.

23. You shall receive grace for grace. The eternal principles by which Jesus Christ passed through mortality to enter into a glorious exaltation (see v. 13) are the same principles by which we, as his brothers and sisters in the spirit, may follow his example and become what he is (see v. 23). This was a revolutionary idea in the time of Joseph Smith. As we respond positively to the grace and gifts of God in acts of voluntary obedience, service, and sacrifice, God will grant us additional gifts. Among these gifts are the provision of a Savior and atonement for our sins and mistakes. These are gifts which Jesus Christ himself did not need. The principle of progress from grace to grace remains the same both in his case and in ours, but for us, if our desires are right (see Ether 3:2), the gifts of God also include mercy, forgiveness, and ultimately even salvation itself (see D&C 6:13; 14:7 and Commentary).

21. I . . . am the Firstborn. Jesus Christ was the very first of our Heavenly Father's spirit children in the premortal life (Colossians 1:15: "the firstborn of every creature"). Christ was chosen from the very beginning for his role as the Creator, as the Word, and as the Savior of humanity.[8]

22. Those who are begotten through me. Compare John 1:12–13. One must remember that while Jesus Christ was our Elder Brother in the premortal state, in this life he must also become our Father (see D&C 25:1 and Commentary; Mosiah 5:7; Ether 3:14). He is the Father of the "born again," the Father of our eternal, resurrected selves. If we are born again as Christ's sons and his daughters through the gospel plan, we shall share in his glory. Since one of Jesus' titles is "the Firstborn" (v. 21), those who are born again and are sealed by the holy spirit of promise are part of the church of the Firstborn and receive with Christ, the Firstborn, the fulness of the Father (see D&C 76:54, 67, 71).

23. Ye were also in the beginning with the Father. This is the first real indication in the Doctrine and Covenants of the doctrine of the premortal existence of souls. God did not create human beings *ex nihilo* (Latin, "out of nothing"). Rather, some part of us has always existed, first as mind or intelligence (see v. 29) and then as begotten spirit children of heavenly parents. Our eternal course has already followed that of our Elder Brother, Jesus Christ, in many respects. That eternal existence, which most people ascribe only to God, applies also to us, his children.[9] The great truth taught here is that we are the same species of being as the Father, Son, and Holy Ghost. We have not yet reached their full glory, but through the grace of God and obedience to his principles, we may in time do so. Our heavenly parents have begotten us as spirits, loved us, improved us, and seek to make each of us glorified and exalted beings as they are. The "parental" and "family" language of scripture is not just allegorical. We are the literal spirit offspring of heavenly parents and were the younger brothers and sisters of Jesus Christ in a premortal life. We also become the children of Christ when we enter into his covenant by baptism and are born again through his blood and his atonement into eternal life (see D&C 25:1; 50:41–43).

23–30. The Spirit of truth. Compare verses 9, 11 and Commentary. "The Spirit of truth" here seems to refer to the Father, with whom we dwelt in the beginning (see v. 26). However, some measure of intelligence, truth, mind, or light seems to be inherent in each individual from all eternity, "otherwise there is no existence" (v. 30). According to verse 29, "Intelligence, or the light of truth, was not created or made, neither indeed can be." Thus, as the Prophet Joseph taught, each of us has from all eternity had some native intelligence or light that was and is uncreated by God.[10] However, we know virtually nothing about conditions before our spirit birth except that such intelligence plus a spirit body make a spirit individual.[11]

As spirit children of our heavenly parents in a premortal life, we also had agency. Certainly, as spirits we were able to choose between Christ and Satan when there was rebellion in heaven (see Revelation 12:7; Moses 4:1–3; Abraham 3:27–28; Alma 13:3–5).

It seems, then, that the term *intelligence* is used in two ways in these verses. There is our own native intelligence that has been part of us forever and which cannot be made or destroyed. In addition, at least since our birth as spirit children of God, we have had the capacity of *increasing* in intelligence, truth, light, and glory from an outside source—from God himself, but only as we use our agency to keep his commandments and therefore to receive that truth and light (see v. 28).

God gives us the power, if we so choose, to receive further intelligence, to be added upon, unto a *fulness* of light and knowledge, through the light of Christ, through the gift of the Holy Ghost, through keeping his commandments (see v. 27), through the ordinances of the gospel, through resurrection, salvation, and exaltation in his kingdom. This capacity for light, truth, and glory—this gracious endowment from God—is what we gain or lose, depending on our response to God's gifts to us, depending as we grow or fail to grow "from grace to grace" (v. 13; see also v. 20).

24. Truth is knowledge of things as they are. See Jacob 4:13. In philosophical terms, this passage is a declaration that there is an objective reality in the universe. Things are not merely whatever they are perceived to be, or believed to be, or interpreted to be. They are as they *really* are. Reality is objective rather than subjective. To grow in light, knowledge, intelligence, and glory is to learn the reality of things as they are, rather than as they seem or as they appear to be. This is accomplished through the guidance of the Spirit of truth, which is the power of God and which leads us to true understanding. The light and knowledge conveyed through the Spirit of truth will give us understanding, not only of how things really are now but of what they were in the past and of what they will be in the future. Of necessity, these things would include a testimony of the truths of the gospel of Christ and also the spirit of prophecy (that is, things "as they are to come"). However, since the Spirit of truth will lead us into "all truth" (v. 26), this progress in knowledge would also include the truths of science, history, mathematics, and so forth.

While it is true that from a human perspective truth often seems relative, it is only our understanding that is relative, incomplete, or that suffers from limited perspective or information. With God, all things are certain (see 2 Nephi 9:20). They are as they are and no other way. Through the Spirit of God, those who trust his word can receive intelligence and certainty beyond their own abilities, as the light and intelligence of God is added to their own native intelligence (see 2 Nephi 9:13).

25. More or less than this is the spirit of that wicked one. See Doctrine and Covenants 10:68 and Commentary; see also D&C 98:7; 124:120; 3 Nephi 11:40; 18:13. While the Spirit of truth seeks to teach us the objective reality of things in the universe as they *really* are (see Jacob 4:13), the spirit of that wicked one, Satan, seeks to teach us that truth is subjective or relative, that it is different things to different people, or that truth is whatever it seems or appears to be. Satan was "a liar from the beginning" because he taught what was not true. He was able to convince many of our Heavenly Father's children that his lies were true, but obedience or conformity to the facts of existence, to the objective realities of the universe, was never part of his makeup.

26. John bore record of me. Compare verses 6–17 and Commentary. Here the Savior identifies himself as the Spirit of truth.

27. Unless he keepeth his commandments. While it would be impossible to receive the fulness of the Father before we can keep all the commandments of the Father, we must remember that in this life we cannot expect to achieve such perfection. This is why from Adam to the present humans have been in need of a Savior (see Moses 7:59). In mortality the requirement is that we *desire to keep his commandments* (see D&C 6:8–9; 11:21), that we are "willing to . . . keep his commandments" (D&C 20:77), and that we "list to obey" his commandments (D&C 29:45; see also Alma 3:27). After the resurrection, there will be time to perfect our performance, receive the desires of our hearts, and eventually to keep all the commandments, therefore ultimately receiving the fulness of the Father.

29. Man was also in the beginning with God. Like our Savior, Jesus Christ, in the premortal life each of us also existed with God before the creation of this world. Joseph Smith taught that "the intelligence of spirits had no beginning, neither will it have an end. That is good logic. That which has a beginning may have an end. There never was a time when there were not spirits; for they are co-equal [that is, co-eternal] with our Father in heaven."[12] It should be noted that the Prophet used the terms "intelligence," "spirit," "mind," and "mind of man" in this statement apparently interchangeably to refer to that native intelligence which existed in us before our spirit birth.[13]

It should perhaps also be noted that modern Church custom often uses the term *intelligences* for our state *before* spirit birth, and *spirits* for our state *after* spirit birth. However, the scriptures and the statements of the Prophet Joseph *do not support this distinction.* From Abraham 3:22–23, which contains the only occurrence of the word *intelligences* as a plural noun in scripture, it is clear that spirit children ("souls" or "spirits") are meant.[14] Similarly, Joseph Smith sometimes used the term *spirit* to refer to the native state in which we existed before our spirit birth.[15] Modern Saints should avoid becoming too technical in their use of these terms that are only broadly defined by the prophets or the scriptures, though to be understood by one another, we should be able to define the terms we use within the bounds of scripture.

29. Intelligence . . . was not created. A certain intelligence is native to each individual; it was not created by God but has existed independently from all eternity.[16] God's work and glory are to improve us; first to make us his very own children, and eventually to save and exalt us to become as he is (see Moses 1:39). But he can only work with what we were when he gave us spirit birth. Ultimately, we and not God are responsible for our own natures, although God gives us ample opportunity to change our natures through the atonement of Christ *if we so desire.* A part of us has existed from all eternity, and we have also been given the special gift of agency, which together make it impossible to hold God accountable for what we choose to become. God enables us to become whatever we *want* to become, but only we can choose what that is. We choose; God enables.

It is also important not to confuse the spiritual quality of intelligence with what humans call I.Q. Some persons with the highest I.Q.s have the least intelligence in the spiritual sense, and vice versa. Satan, as a "son of the morning" (D&C 76:26), was no doubt very bright. In psychological terms, he surely has a very high I.Q., high enough to deceive the smartest and most sophisticated of human beings, yet he lacks absolutely that intelligence that comes from God as we "receive grace for grace" (v. 20). Since intelligence, or light and truth, "forsake that evil one" (v. 37), those who embrace Satan and his plans may have quick wits, but they lack true intelligence.

Intelligence comes in two ways. There is that intelligence which is native to each individual, which is eternal, and which cannot be created or destroyed (for example, see vv. 29–30). However, this native element is capable of being added to or enlarged from that fulness of intelligence possessed by the Father when we use our agency to obey him (see v. 37; D&C 130:18–19). This latter intelligence is not native to ourselves but comes to us through the gift and grace of God (see v. 28; note the frequency of the verb "receive" in vv. 26–34). This latter intelligence, that which comes from God through obedience to law, can also be diminished or lost entirely through disobedience to God (see v. 39).

30. All truth is independent. Eternal truths cannot be contravened; things are as they are. Not even God can make what is eternally so into what is not. Truth will operate in its determined course whether human beings accept it or not, whether they believe it or not, or whether they even know of it or not. Similarly, beings possessing truth must also be allowed to operate according to their own choices. Water must be allowed to find its own level. Like must be allowed to seek out like. This is the grand doctrine of agency (see v. 31). Just as eternal laws must be allowed to operate as they really are and cannot be contravened, so also we must be allowed to express our true nature without divine coercion. Under any other circumstances, existence itself would not be possible.

31. Here is the agency of man. See Commentary on verse 30.

31–32. Here is the condemnation of man. Compare John 3:18–19. The common condemnation of human beings is that God has revealed himself to some degree to all humans and that all humans have in some degree ignored, disbelieved, or disobeyed him. Even the best among us have at times chosen darkness rather than light. Such choices might not be habitual, but at some time or other each of us has fallen under the condemnation of choosing sin. It is not even necessary for one to know Christ or his gospel to sin against the light which God has given everyone who has come into this world (see D&C 84:44–53; 88:7–13 and Commentary; see also John 1:9). Therefore, in some degree, all who reach a sufficient age and mental capacity may be held accountable for choosing darkness rather than light on some occasion. And because of this free and wilful choice of darkness instead of light, it is necessary for God to provide a Savior and a plan of salvation for the redemption of those who will repent of such sins and mistakes, the wrong choices that have brought them guilt and condemnation.

33. For man is spirit. Here we must point out, in relation to the Commentary on verses 7–17, that the parallels to the Gospel of John in Doctrine and Covenants 93 extend well beyond the first few verses of John 1. For example, while the King James Version of John 4:24 states that "God is a Spirit," the cross-reference refers to Doctrine and Covenants 93:33 (as well as to D&C 130:22, which further indicates that God also has "a body of flesh and bones as tangible as man's"). Doctrine and Covenants 93, in conjunction with John 4:24, elaborates on the theme of becoming like God (see vv. 19–23, 27–30) by teaching that part of man's eternal nature, like God, is spirit. We are the same type of being.

The term *man,* of course, is being used in its nineteenth century sense of all human beings, both male and female. Moreover, *spirit* in this sense is not something in a different category from matter but is itself a type of matter that is more refined (see D&C

131:7). Deprived of our basic and eternal element, our spirit, our present bodies die.

33. The elements are eternal. In agreement with the physical laws of the conservation of matter and energy, Joseph Smith declared through revelation that the elements, the building blocks of all physical matter, are themselves eternal. Such elements may be organized or disorganized, and as a result they may obey law to one degree or another (see D&C 88:7–13). The elements may even change their form and can apparently be transformed from element to energy or back again, but they can neither be created nor destroyed. The elements are co-eternal with God.

Since spirit is one type of pure and refined matter, it is important to know that matter is eternal, whether in the form of "spirit" or in the form of element, or "matter" (D&C 131:7). Of course, this directly contradicts the traditions of the historical Christian churches, which have adopted the theological view that God created all things out of nothing (Latin, *ex nihilo*) and that spirit and matter are totally and eternally different categories of existence. Most Christian theologians would claim that God made everything out of nothing and that he also created the space to put it in. However, according to modern revelation, space, matter, intelligence, light, and truth are all eternal. God is the organizer, or the builder, of the universe, but the raw materials out of which he creates his worlds and universes, unorganized matter and elements, are as eternal as he is. Just as our physical parents beget our physical bodies, so our heavenly parents begot our spiritual bodies. God's work and glory are to bring to his children—other beings like himself but less mature—the same kind of life and glory that he now enjoys (see Moses 1:39).

33. Spirit and element, inseparably connected, receive a fulness of joy. A common view in traditional Christianity, following Hellenistic Greek ideas, has been that God and things eternal are spiritual in nature and that nothing physical or material in nature could be eternal. Thus, while material elements exist, they are transitory and detract from the spiritual bliss to be enjoyed by nonphysical entities in the eternities to come. In one Greek view, the material world was created by mistake by a lesser god known as the demiurge, who, while playing in the mud, so to speak, created physical matter and accidentally trapped spirits within it. For many Greek thinkers, the physical universe was a prison-house in which pure spirits had sadly become entrapped. Many Greeks, therefore, believed that the goal of eternity was to free ourselves from all things physical and to become, like God, totally nonphysical in our being.[17] While Jews and early Christians believed in the literal resurrection of the dead, many in the Greek world preferred to believe only in the immortality of the soul (spirit). In time, denial of the importance or the eternality of the physical body led Christianity to the denigration of family relations and familial love, or the "continuation of the lives" or "continuation of the seeds" (D&C 132:22, 19; see also v. 30). The restoration of the gospel through Joseph Smith taught once again that both matter and spirit were eternal (see D&C 93:33) and that true and lasting eternal felicity can occur only when these two eternal entities are permanently joined together by the light and power of God.

34. When separated, cannot receive a fulness of joy. Since both spirit and matter are eternal, it follows that a fulness of eternal joy can only be had by those who can control and comprehend both of these materials. Were our natures limited to either spirit or element, we could not experience the full spectrum of reality. To truly comprehend and control the eternal worlds, we must be able to deal with what exists in all its forms. Physical bodies without spirits know nothing. Spirits without physical bodies have intelligence but cannot experience physical reality. To become like our Father in heaven, we must know and control all things, whether of the spirit or of the physical elements; otherwise, we cannot create as he creates in both spirit and element. Even with a memory of the pains of mortality, those spirits now inhabiting the postmortal spirit world view the absence of their spirits from their physical bodies as bondage (see D&C 138:50).

Without both aspects of eternity, both the spiritual and the physical, they cannot experience a fulness of joy.

It is common to describe resurrected beings as consisting of two component parts, of a spirit and a body, and this is certainly correct. Yet, there is also a third ingredient which we will receive in the resurrection, what Paul called "our house which is from heaven" (2 Corinthians 5:2). This other characteristic is the glory of God (see v. 28). Thus, ultimately, we will possess spirit bodies and physical bodies as they were in mortality plus that additional degree of glory, or intelligence, or light and truth, which is bestowed upon us by God as we progress from grace to grace (see vv. 13, 20, 28).

35. The elements are the tabernacle of God. Since the light or spirit of Christ permeates all organized matter, all matter may be said to be the tabernacle or dwelling place of God. The creative power of God dwells within every atom and molecule—every particle—of creation and holds the universe together from moment to moment (see D&C 88:7–13 and Commentary; Colossians 1:17).

35. Man is the tabernacle of God. Since the light of Christ permeates every part of matter that makes up our physical being, and since the influence of our Heavenly Father is part of our spiritual being, so to a certain extent every human being, both in body and in spirit, is a tabernacle of the divine, and the influence of God is felt by all of us in some degree in both our spirits and our bodies. And since the light of Christ and divine parentage are present within us, our mortal bodies are to a certain extent temples or dwelling places of the divine. In this life, as we receive the gift of the Holy Ghost and grow from grace to grace, we receive further light and truth and become holier and holier temples, that is, we become more and more sanctified vessels of divine power and influence. But even the lowest of humanity possess divine parentage in their spirits and the light of Christ in their physical bodies (see D&C 88:7–13); and, so, we receive so much the greater condemnation for defiling our spirits or our bodies—dwelling places of the divine (see also 1 Corinthians 3:16–17).

35. God shall destroy that temple. Since the elements are eternal (see v. 33), "destroy" as used in this verse does not mean that a person will cease to exist. But those who defile their bodies will be cast out of the presence of God.

36. The glory of God is intelligence . . . light and truth. See Commentary on verse 29. The Prophet Joseph Smith and the Restoration scriptures often use such terms as light, truth, spirit, glory, and intelligence interchangeably. When we use our agency to obey God, we are enriched by additional glory or intelligence as a gift from God (see v. 20). This latter kind of intelligence is neither a formal education, nor a quick mind, nor a high I.Q.; rather, it is that light and truth of the spirit that is available to shepherds, fishermen, and farm boys alike.

37. Forsake that evil one. To forsake means to abandon. Because of the Fall, all of us have at one time or another been associated to some degree with the evil one. As we grow in light and truth, we learn to leave him alone. One definition of true intelligence might be "agency freely choosing truth." When we demonstrate this kind of intelligence, choosing God and abandoning Satan, we are enlarged by further glory or intelligence from God. As we become one with God, first in the gospel covenant and then further by imitating his thoughts and actions (see v. 19 and Commentary), we move further and further from the devil, ultimately forsaking him altogether. Moreover, as we receive light and truth from God, our power to resist evil and the evil one increases.

38. Every spirit of man was innocent in the beginning. "In the beginning" refers here to our lives in the premortal spirit world. When we were first born as spirit children of heavenly parents in that premortal life, we were innocent of any sin. Through the atonement of Christ, any "original" sin associated with mortality and the Fall has been removed from us (see also Moses 6:54). Thus, as infants in mortality we are once again, just as when we were infant spirits, "innocent before God." Because of the Atonement, the fall of Adam and Eve and the sins of our mortal forbears convey no hereditary sin upon us, and we can be held accountable only for sins committed after we reach the age of accountability (see Articles of Faith 1:2; D&C 68:25–27 and Commentary).

39. And that wicked one. That is, Satan.

39. Taketh away light and truth. Just as true intelligence might be defined as "agency freely choosing truth," so loss of intelligence comes from agency choosing falsehood. This loss of truth and light can come about from wilful disobedience to God or through deception by human philosophies, the traditions of our fathers. We lose light and truth by our own personal rebellion or by accepting human wisdom in place of the revealed word of God.

40. I have commanded you. See, for example, Doctrine and Covenants 20:70; 55:4; 68:25–28, 31–32. There may also have been private revelation to these Church leaders on the subject of their families in which such commandments were issued.

41. My servant Frederick G. Williams. Notice that the Lord does not hesitate to rebuke publicly even his leaders when they neglect the proper instruction of their children. If children are taught the truth and then stray, the condemnation is upon their own heads. However, if the Saints, even Church leaders, are too busy doing Church work (or anything else) to instruct their own children, then the condemnation is upon the parents' heads.

At this time, all of the First Presidency (Joseph Smith, see vv. 47–48; Sidney Rigdon, see v. 44; and Frederick G. Williams, see vv. 41–43) and the bishop of the Church in Kirtland (Newel K. Whitney, see v. 50) were rebuked by the Lord for problems with their families. The exact nature of these brethren's family difficulties are left unspoken here, for they are private matters. It is a credit to the humility and integrity of the Prophet that these verses were not taken out of the revelation but were left in for all to read.

42. That wicked one hath power. Though individuals might hold high office, be personally worthy, and do much good in the world, should they neglect the proper instruction of their children, this alone will give Satan some power over them and will serve as a cause of affliction in their lives (see v. 42).

45. Servant . . . friends. Personally, the Prophet and his associates have the right to be called the friends of Christ, for their relationship goes beyond that of merely servants and master. However, from the perspective of the world, these brethren and their successors can still be called the servants of Christ, for they are at the very least his servants—and more besides. Moreover, because of their close relationship with Jesus Christ, they are also willing to be the servants of all other persons for Christ's sake (see Mark 9:35; 10:44; 1 Corinthians 9:19).

47. Joseph Smith . . . rebuked. This rebuke comes only two months after Joseph was absolved of all his sins (see D&C 90:1). One need not conclude that Joseph was guilty of some great, hidden sins, or that he had been rejected here by the Lord. Rather, like all of us, Joseph and the other leaders of the Church were human and continued to struggle with the limitations of mortality. They, like all of us, were under the necessity of continually praying and continually repenting in order to avoid the power of that wicked one (see vv. 48–49).

48. Your family. It is important to note that the Prophet's children were still very young, all under the age of accountability, and therefore not capable of repentance. Therefore, this warning can only have been meant for the Prophet's wife, Emma, for his parents, or for his brothers and sisters.

49. Pray always. See Doctrine and Covenants 10:5 and Commentary. Note the use of the prepositions *in* and *out* in this verse. If Satan gains power "in" us, he will move us "out" of our place in the kingdom.

51. Sidney Rigdon go on his journey. Perhaps Sidney was called on a preaching mission at this time. However, either he did not go or his mission was fairly short in duration, for he was back in Kirtland at least by 21 June and probably by 3 June.[18]

53. Hasten to translate my scriptures. Again, this passsage refers to Joseph Smith's translation of the Bible. The New

Testament of the Joseph Smith Translation had been completed on 2 February 1833. Work on portions of the Old Testament continued until 2 July of that year (see D&C 35:20; 73:3–4; 90:13; 91:3 and Commentary).

53. All this for the salvation of Zion. In this verse, note the importance of secular education ("history," "countries," "kingdoms," "laws of . . . man," etc.) as well as of divine revelation ("laws of God") in the salvation of Zion.

1. Smith, *History of the Church,* 1:343.
2. See Woodford, "Historical Development," 2:1209–10.
3. See *Doctrine and Covenants Student Manual,* 217.
4. Kimball, *Ensign,* Mar. 1980, 4.
5. See Taylor, *Mediation and Atonement,* 55; Pratt, *Journal of Discourses,* 16:58; Sperry, *Doctrine and Covenants Compendium,* 472–73.
6. McConkie, *Doctrinal New Testament Commentary,* 1:70–71.
7. Snow, in Conference Report, Apr. 1901, 3.
8. See also Commentary on D&C 76:54.
9. See Smith, *Teachings of the Prophet Joseph Smith,* 352–53.
10. See Smith, *Teachings of the Prophet Joseph Smith,* 354.
11. See Smith, *Answers to Gospel Questions,* 4:127.
12. Smith, *History of the Church,* 6:311.
13. See also Smith, *Teachings of the Prophet Joseph Smith,* 353–54.
14. See the First Presidency statement, 1916, in Talmage, *Articles of Faith,* 466.
15. See Smith, *History of the Church,* 6:311, in which "soul," "mind of man," and "immortal spirit" equate with what contemporary Latter-day Saints usually mean by "intelligences."
16. See Smith, *Teachings of the Prophet Joseph Smith,* 354; Smith, *Answers to Gospel Questions,* 4:127.
17. For example, see the discussion in Dodds, *Greeks and the Irrational,* 149.
18. See Smith, *History of the Church,* 1:354, 352.

BACKGROUND

In December 1832 (see D&C 88:119) and again in March 1833 (see D&C 90:7–9), the Saints in Ohio were commanded to build a temple at Kirtland. On 23 March 1833, a conference of Church leaders met in the schoolroom above the Whitney store to arrange for the purchase of land for future Church buildings, and on 4 May 1833, another conference appointed Hyrum Smith, Jared Carter, and Reynolds Cahoon as a building committee for the Church in Ohio.[1] These brethren were to raise money and supervise construction of Church properties in Kirtland. Sometime after May 4, probably on May 6, but possibly as late as 2 August, Joseph Smith received the revelation now known as Doctrine and Covenants 94, in which the Lord revealed that Kirtland was to be "the city of the stake of Zion" (v. 1).[2] Doctrine and Covenants 94 is not actually concerned with the Kirtland Temple. Rather, it gives instructions for two *additional* Church buildings, a Church administration building (see v. 3) and a printing office (see v. 10), to be located south of the proposed temple site. A letter from the First Presidency to Edward Partridge and the Saints in Zion clarifies the scope of the Lord's intended building projects. "Having here given you two revelations [D&C 97 and 98], we accompany them with the following explanations: the revelation [D&C 94] respecting the two houses to be built in

Kirtland in addition to the one we are now building [the Kirtland Temple]—one for the presidency and the other for the printing—is also binding upon you. That is, you at Zion have to build two houses as well as the one of which we have sent the pattern [the temple in Independence] and mentioned in the first revelation above written [D&C 97]. You are also, in addition to this one [that is, the temple], to build two others—one for the presidency and one for the printing."[3] Nevertheless, work on these additional two Church buildings, the administration building and the printing office, both in Kirtland and in Missouri, was not to begin until the Lord gave further specific commandments concerning them (see v. 16). There is currently no evidence that such further commandments were ever given, and these two supporting structures were never built. In response to the practical needs of the Church in Kirtland, the following year a smaller structure was built west of the temple which eventually housed both the School of the Elders and the printing office and also provided offices for Church leaders.[4]

Doctrine and Covenants 94 further reveals that as "the city of the stake of Zion," Kirtland would be a planned community of Saints, with the temple serving as the center point. The rest of the city would be laid out by lots north, south, east, and west of the temple. The two lots immediately south of the temple would be for the proposed Church administration building and printing office. Three other lots were to be reserved for the members of the building committee in return for their faithful service.

Doctrine and Covenants 94 cannot be dated with complete certainty. Joseph Smith's account states that he received this revelation on 6 May 1833; on the same day, he also received Doctrine and Covenants 93.[5] However, the oldest copy of section 94 appears in the letter which the First Presidency sent to the Saints in Zion on 6 August 1833. The language of this letter can be understood to imply that section 94 was received along with section 97 on 2 August 1833. In addition, the Kirtland Revelation Book specifically dates Doctrine and Covenants 94 to 2 August.[6]

Nevertheless, it is likely that 6 May 1833 is the correct date. In addition to the Prophet's statement in *History of the Church,* it should be noted that the 6 August letter to Zion does not specifically assign a date to section 94, only to section 97. From the full text of this letter, it is likely that section 97, the commandment to build a temple in Missouri, was received on 2 August. Section 94, left undated in the letter, was added to section 97 to make it clear that two structures in addition to the temple were to be built and that the dimensions of these structures would be revealed later. Doctrine and Covenants 98, received 6 August, the same day the Prophet's letter was sent, was then added to address rumors of trouble brewing in Missouri.[7]

COMMENTARY

1. A commandment. The commandment given in Doctrine and Covenants 94 was not for the Saints to build a city as a stake in Zion. Rather it was to "commence . . . preparing a beginning and foundation" for such a city. It is likely that the tentative nature of the language here reflects the knowledge that the settlement at Kirtland would not be permanent (see also D&C 64:21). The foundations obediently laid by the Saints in Kirtland are still there in eastern Ohio to this day, and someday the completed "city of the stake of Zion" will be there also, but it was only necessary for Joseph and the Saints of his day to make a beginning. At the time section 94 was received, only one hundred to one hundred fifty active Saints were living in the Kirtland area.[8] Thus, the obligation for building the temple and the two auxiliary structures described here fell on a Church population smaller than an average ward today.

1. The city of the stake of Zion. See Commentary on Doctrine and Covenants 82:13.

1. My house. That is, the Kirtland Temple.

2. The pattern which I have given you. This likely refers to a pattern for the city itself, rather than a pattern for the various houses of God to be built there. Specific, detailed instructions concerning the architecture of the three buildings had not yet been received (see vv. 5–6, 12). Since these plans were received by revelation in early June, this is another argument for dating Doctrine and Covenants 94 to May 1833.[9]

3. A house for the presidency. The first lot south of the temple was to be a two-story administration building measuring, like the Kirtland Temple itself (see D&C 95:15), fifty-five by sixty-five feet in its inside dimensions.

5. The pattern which shall be given unto you hereafter. See Commentary on verse 2. Specific details for the construction of these buildings had not yet been given by the Lord at the time Doctrine and Covenants 94 was received. Neither are they contained in this revelation, but they would come a month later, in the first week of June.

6–9. It shall be dedicated unto the Lord. Church buildings, even office buildings and printing offices, are dedicated to the Lord for the performance of his work upon the earth. What is said here of the proposed structures at Kirtland applies equally to Church properties of every sort today. While most of these may not be temples, they still belong to the Lord; they are intended for his service; and so they are his houses and are set apart and dedicated to him. Thus, there is an obligation on the part of the Saints today to keep Church properties clean and undefiled both physically and spiritually, just as there was such an obligation on the Saints in Kirtland.

10. A house . . . for the work of the printing. The proposed printing office was to publish Joseph Smith's translation of the Bible, which was essentially finished on 2 July, two months after Doctrine and Covenants 94 was received, although Joseph continued working on it until his death.[10] In addition, the printing office in Kirtland was also to reprint *The Evening and the Morning Star* which had originally been published in Independence, Missouri, by W. W. Phelps. This reprint of the *Star* was eventually published in the temporary printing office west of the temple, but the Saints left Ohio before the Joseph Smith Translation could be published there. However, in 1835, the first edition of the Doctrine and Covenants was published at the printing office in Kirtland, Ohio. The *Messenger and Advocate* was also printed there. This building was burned to the ground in January 1838.[11]

14–15. Hyrum Smith . . . Reynolds Cahoon and Jared Carter. These three brethren had been appointed as the building committee for the Church in Ohio by a conference of high priests held on 4 May 1833, two days before the probable date of Doctrine and Covenants 94. While the Lord directed that these three should receive city lots, the responsibility and burden of constructing homes on these lots was to rest upon the individuals themselves. However, the following year, in April 1834, the united order at Kirtland was temporarily dissolved and reorganized.[12] As a result, the lands mentioned in Doctrine and Covenants 94 were distributed differently than was directed here. As a result of "covetousness" in the Church (D&C 104:4), the instructions of section 104 superseded all previous revelations concerning the disposition of properties and funds in Kirtland (see D&C 104:4, 11–16).

16. These two houses are not to be built. The administration building and the printing office were not to be built either in Kirtland or in Missouri until the Lord gave further instructions concerning them. Since building the Kirtland Temple exhausted both the Saints and their resources in Ohio and mob action drove the Saints from Jackson County in Missouri, these two auxiliary "houses" were never constructed in either location, although a smaller structure was built for Church offices, the printing office, and the Elders' School in Kirtland.

1. See Background to D&C 95.
2. See Smith, *History of the Church,* 1:343–46.
3. Joseph Smith to "Beloved Brethren," 6 Aug. 1833, Church
   Archives; spelling, punctuation, and grammar standardized; see the

full text in Woodford, "Historical Development," 2:1226; Cook, *Revelations of the Prophet Joseph Smith,* 196.

4. See Cook, *Revelations of the Prophet Joseph Smith,* 196–97.
5. See Smith, *History of the Church,* 1:346.
6. Kirtland Revelation Book, 64.
7. See Background to D&C 97–98.
8. See Backman and Cowan, *Joseph Smith and the Doctrine and Covenants,* 85; Robison, *First Mormon Temple,* 28.
9. See Background to D&C 95; Robison, *First Mormon Temple,* 8; Backman and Cowan, *Joseph Smith and the Doctrine and Covenants,* 85–87.
10. Smith, *History of the Church,* 1:368–69.
11. Cook, *Revelations of the Prophet Joseph Smith,* 197.
12. See Background to D&C 104.

95

BACKGROUND

During his first mission to Missouri in the summer of 1831, barely a year after organizing the Church, Joseph Smith had received revelation from the Lord concerning a temple to be built in the town of Independence in Jackson County, Missouri (see D&C 57:3). A site for this temple was dedicated 3 August 1831, during that journey.[1] However, more than a year later no progress had been made toward construction of this temple in Zion. Then, on 27 December 1832, in the revelation known as the Olive Leaf, the Lord further instructed Joseph and the Saints in Ohio that they were also to build a "house of God" at Kirtland (D&C 88:119). Thus, there were to be two temples—one in Independence, Missouri, and one in Kirtland, Ohio. But again, during the winter of 1833, little progress was made toward building either of these two sacred structures.

In March 1833, Levi Hancock wrote in his journal that the Saints in Kirtland "had no place to worship in. Jared Carter went around with a subscription paper [that is, a pledge sheet for promised donations] to get signers. I signed for two dollars. He made up a little over thirty [dollars] and presented it to Joseph. The Lord would not accept it and gave a command to build a Temple."[2]

On 23 March 1833, a conference of high priests and elders

met in the schoolroom above the Whitney store in Kirtland to discuss purchasing land for the proposed temple and other Church buildings. It was decided that Ezra Thayre and Joseph Coe should be appointed agents for the Church in purchasing the farms of Peter French, Elijah Smith, and Isaac Morley.[3] These purchases, together with property belonging to F. G. Williams, eventually provided land for the Kirtland Temple and associated Church holdings. Then, on 4 May 1833, another conference of high priests met at Kirtland to take "into consideration the necessity of building a school house," as the Saints had been commanded the previous December (see D&C 88:119) and again in March (see D&C 90:7–9).[4] At this conference Hyrum Smith, Jared Carter, and Reynolds Cahoon were appointed to act as a building committee for the Church. They were to raise funds and also to supervise construction of the temple and other Church buildings. It should be remembered that in all these proceedings and in the associated revelations, the term *schoolhouse* or *school* actually referred to the temple, or at least to that part of the temple that would be used for the School of the Prophets.

Still, the Saints did not seem to catch the vision of the Kirtland Temple. At a conference held in early June 1833 to consider constructing the temple, Lucy Mack Smith reported: "Some thought that it would be better to build a frame house. Others said that a frame house was too costly, and the majority concluded upon putting up a log house and made their calculations about what they could do towards building it." To these suggestions Joseph responded, "And shall we, brethren, build a house for our God of logs? No, I have a better plan than that. I have the plan of the house of the Lord, given by himself. You will see by this the difference between our calculations and his idea of things." Joseph's mother then wrote that Joseph "then gave them the full plan of the house of the Lord at Kirtland."[5]

According to contemporary accounts, the First Presidency had already been shown the plan of the Kirtland Temple in a remarkable vision received on 3 or 4 June 1833.[6] Frederick G. Williams later described this vision to those who were building the temple: "Carpenter Rolph said, 'Doctor [Williams], what do you think of the house?' [Williams] answered, 'It looks to me like the pattern precisely.' He then related the following: 'Joseph [Smith] received the word of the Lord for him to take his two counselors, Williams and Rigdon, and come before the Lord, and He would show them the plan or model of the house to be built. We went upon our knees, called on the Lord, and the building appeared within viewing distance, I being the first to discover it. Then we all viewed it together. After we had taken a good look at the exterior, the building seemed to come right over us, and the makeup of the Hall seemed to coincide with that I there saw to a minutiae.'"[7]

With only one hundred to one hundred fifty Saints in Kirtland to fund construction of the temple and the other Church properties commanded in Doctrine and Covenants 94, it is understandable that they would originally make rather modest plans for the house of God. However, once the plans of the Lord had been revealed to the First Presidency, and with the divine rebuke contained in section 95 (see vv. 1–6, 12) ringing in their ears, the Saints commenced work in earnest. On 23 July 1833, the cornerstones of the Kirtland Temple were finally laid.

Even though the Saints knew that their stay in Kirtland was only temporary (see D&C 64:21 and Commentary), there were several reasons why a temple would be needed there. Among other things, the Prophet, the First Presidency, and the headquarters of the Church would remain in Kirtland for several years to come. A sacred temple would be necessary in order for additional priesthood keys and instruction to be transmitted to the Prophet Joseph and his associates. Once those keys had been received, a temple would also be necessary for performing some of the ordinances associated with them. Without these further keys, instructions, and ordinances, it would not be possible to organize and train a quorum of Twelve Apostles (see D&C 95:4), and the Church would be hindered or eventually even stopped in its progress. Moreover, without the benefit of a holy temple, individual members could not receive the fulfillment of certain promises made to them in earlier revelations (for example, D&C 76:116–18; 88:68; 93:19–20; see also 97:16).

According to Joseph Smith, Doctrine and Covenants 95 was received on 1 June 1833.[8] On that date, the building committee of Hyrum Smith, Reynolds Cahoon, and Jared Carter issued another subscription, or pledge sheet, exhorting the Saints to sacrifice for construction of the temple in order that the elders "may gather themselves together, and prepare all things, and call a solemn assembly [see D&C 88:70, 117 and Commentary], and treasure up words of wisdom."[9]

COMMENTARY

1. Whom I love I also chasten. "Chasten" should be understood here to mean primarily "to correct by punishment" but also "to purify from errors or faults."[10] The emphasis here is not on the punishment the Saints are to receive, but on their intended correction and their purification from error. There are times when the path to being more like God leads us of necessity through suffering for our mistakes, yet God's primary concern is not that we be punished, but that we be corrected. Still, the primary goal of bringing about repentance is often assisted by punishment which God administers in love to those he loves.

3. The great commandment. In their difficult financial circumstances, the Saints had collectively ignored the commandment to build a temple in Kirtland (see D&C 88:119; 90:7–9). At the very least, they had also underestimated, as some Saints still do today, the importance of the temple for their future well-being and their eternal progress.

4. For the preparation wherewith I design to prepare mine apostles. There was a real need for the Kirtland Temple to be built. "The Kirtland Temple was necessary before the apostles (who had not yet been called), and other elders of the Church could receive the endowment which the Lord had in store for them. The elders had been out preaching the Gospel and crying repentance ever since the Church was organized and many great men had heard and embraced the truth, nevertheless the elders could not go forth in the power and authority which the Lord intended them to possess until this Temple was built where he could restore keys and powers essential to the more complete preaching of the Gospel and the administering of its ordinances."[11]

4. Prune my vineyard. See Doctrine and Covenants 21:9 and Commentary on Doctrine and Covenants 24:19.

4. My strange act. The work of the Lord often seems strange, puzzling, or even foolish when judged from the perspective of human wisdom and worldly leadership (see D&C 101:92–95; 1 Corinthians 2:5–8, 14). In Isaiah 28:21 the Lord refers to both his immediate and his long-term intentions as "strange" as judged by the worldly leaders of Judah in that day (see Isaiah 28:15–21). From our modern perspective, both the Restoration and the Second Coming would be examples of the strange works of the Lord.

4. Pour out my Spirit upon all flesh. See Joel 2:28; Acts 2:17. The events described in verse 4 are associated with the coming of Christ to the earth and in this case to his imminent second coming. Perhaps it is only when the wicked have been pruned out of his vineyard that the Holy Ghost can truly be poured out upon *all* (remaining) human beings.

5. Many . . . called but few of them are chosen. To be "called" is to be invited or summoned out of the world into the Church and kingdom of God, to be called upon to perform certain duties there (our Church callings), and be called to keep the Lord's commandments. To be "chosen" is to have answered God's call positively and to have performed one's duties so faithfully with the proper attitude that God selects, elects, chooses, or judges an individual to be in fact an heir of the celestial kingdom. Most of the Saints will be chosen, or will be selected by God as heirs of the kingdom, at the judgment. These are called but are not yet chosen. However, to be chosen or elected in this manner while still in the flesh is to be evaluated or judged by God, to be found worthy, and in some sense of the term to be sealed up to eternal life (see D&C 68:12 and Commentary). Ultimately many of the Saints will be found worthy of the celestial kingdom, but not all who will be so blessed receive both their calling and their election (being chosen) while still in mortality (see D&C 121:34–40 and Commentary). Thus, "many are called but few of them are chosen" while still in the flesh.

6. Walking in darkness at noon-day. One purpose of the gospel is to bring light to those who are in darkness (see D&C 45:28; Isaiah 42:6; 49:6; 60:3). To sin in ignorance, or in darkness, is remedied by accepting the light of the gospel and by repenting in the gospel covenant. However, to sin wilfully against God's light after we already know the truth is not an act of ignorance but an act of rebellion. Those who rebel against what they already know *choose* to walk in darkness, even though there may be light all around them, and sinning in rebellion against the light is more "grievous" than sinning in ignorance.

7. Solemn assembly. That is, as commanded in Doctrine and Covenants 88:70, 117.

7. The Lord of Sabaoth. Normally, *sabaoth* in the Old Testament comes from the Hebrew *sabaot,* meaning "hosts" or "armies" (see D&C 87:7 and Commentary). Here, however (if *sabaoth* is Hebrew, as it appears), it would come from the very similar root *sh-b-t,* the plural of which could be understood in New Testament times as "the first day of the week."[12] Thus, the significance of the term here would be that Jehovah, as Jesus Christ, is Lord and creator of both Sabbaths, the Jewish Sabbath on the last day of the week and the Christian Sabbath on the first day of the week.

8. I gave you a commandment that you should build a house. See Doctrine and Covenants 88:119; 90:7–9.

8. I design to endow those whom I have chosen. See Commentary on Doctrine and Covenants 38:32 for "endow."

Many of the brethren had been ordained to the priesthood but not all of them were at that time worthy to receive the ordinances that would be made available in the Kirtland Temple. In Doctrine and Covenants 105:33–35, the Lord would instruct the Prophet that the time had come for those who had been ordained, and who were also judged worthy, to receive an endowment of power in the Kirtland Temple. The *Far West Record* for 23 June 1834 lists those high priests chosen to receive the blessings of the Kirtland Temple. It is important to remember that the complete endowment as we know it today was not revealed to the Saints in the Kirtland Temple. Those who were chosen at that time received only preparatory ordinances. The full endowment would eventually be revealed to the Saints in the Nauvoo Temple a decade later.

9. Tarry, even as my apostles at Jerusalem. See Luke 24:49; Acts 1:4.

10. A very grievous sin. The tardiness of the Saints in building the temple and the contentions which arose in the School of the Prophets are characterized as sins grievous enough to require the chastening of the Lord.

12. The love of the Father shall not continue. When we reject the gospel and its covenant obligations, we also reject the relationship with the Father that we might have enjoyed had we remained faithful (see Alma 13:4).

14. Let the house be built. The best readily available discussion of the Kirtland Temple can presently be found in Robison, *First Mormon Temple.*

16. Lower part . . . for your sacrament offering. The ground floor of the Kirtland Temple was to serve as a common meetinghouse for the Kirtland Saints much like a ward or branch meetinghouse of today.

17. Higher part . . . for the school of mine apostles. The upper floors of the building were to be specifically dedicated for the more sacred purposes associated with training and preparation of the apostles and other Church leaders for other purposes associated today with temple work.

17. Son Ahman. See Commentary on Doctrine and Covenants 78:20.

17. Alphus . . . Omegus. Alpha and omega are the first and last letters of the Greek alphabet. Their use as titles for Jesus Christ emphasize his role as the first and the last (see D&C 19:1 and Commentary; see also Revelation 1:11). In this verse, the names of the Greek letters have been given the Latin masculine ending -us.

1. See Background to D&C 57 and Commentary on D&C 57:2–5.
2. Levi Hancock Journal, as cited in Woodford, "Historical Development," 2:1222; spelling, punctuation, and grammar standardized; compare D&C 90:7–9, given 8 Mar. 1833.
3. See Smith, *History of the Church,* 1:335.
4. Smith, *History of the Church,* 1:342–43; Collier and Harwell, eds., *Kirtland Council Minute Book,* 14.
5. Proctor and Proctor, eds., *Revised and Enhanced History of Joseph Smith by His Mother,* 321, 322.
6. See Robison, *First Mormon Temple,* 8.
7. Truman O. Angell Journal, as cited in Robison, *First Mormon Temple,* 8.
8. See Smith, *History of the Church,* 1:350–52.
9. Smith, *History of the Church,* 1:349.
10. Webster, 1828 *Dictionary.*
11. Smith, *Church History and Modern Revelation,* 1:406; compare D&C 110.
12. See references in Bauer, Arndt, and Gingrich, *Greek-English Lexicon,* 739.

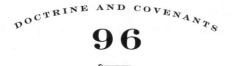

96

BACKGROUND

O n 23 March 1833, a conference of high priests was held at Kirtland in the School of the Prophets, which met above Newel K. Whitney's store. This conference decided that the Church should purchase several pieces of property in Kirtland upon which a temple and Church administration buildings could be constructed. The largest of the desired parcels of land was known as the Peter French farm, and Mr. French agreed to sell his 103 acres to the Church for five thousand dollars.[1] However, it was then necessary to send the brethren of the school out into the world to preach and to raise money for the proposed purchases.[2] Negotiations were soon concluded for acquisition of all the necessary properties, though all the funds needed to meet this obligation would not be raised for some time to come. On 4 May 1833, another council of high priests appointed Hyrum Smith, Jared Carter, and Reynolds Cahoon to serve as a committee to oversee construction of the proposed Church buildings on the newly acquired property.

After this 4 May meeting, some disagreement remained among the brethren over exactly who should ultimately be in charge of Church-owned properties (see D&C 95:10). For this reason, yet another meeting of high priests was held on 4 June 1833, this time in Joseph's translating room adjacent to the schoolroom above Newel K. Whitney's store. This council, failing to agree among themselves, inquired as to how the Lord wanted matters handled, and the Lord's answer was given at that time in the revelation now designated as Doctrine and Covenants 96.[3] This revelation also provided the Church with an example for future similar questions by explaining the principles involved in the matter and by reemphasizing that the bishop was the Lord's steward in the administration of temporal things, particularly in the disposition and use of Church property (see D&C 72:9–23). Although there was not yet an office of Presiding Bishop over the whole Church,[4] Newel K. Whitney was the Lord's bishop in Kirtland, and he was therefore to have charge of the Lord's properties there (see vv. 2–3).

The oldest known copy of Doctrine and Covenants 96 is found in the Kirtland Revelation Book and was recorded there in the handwriting of Orson Hyde. It was copied sometime before August 1834.[5]

COMMENTARY

1. This stake. See Doctrine and Covenants 82:13–14 and Commentary.

2. Newel K. Whitney. In answer to their prayer of inquiry, the Lord informed the brethren that the person with responsibility for the Lord's properties in Kirtland was the bishop in Kirtland, Newel K. Whitney. The building committee was to oversee construction, but control of Church-owned properties and the structures built upon them would remain with the bishop.

3. Let it be divided into lots. Part of the recently acquired properties were to be divided into lots for those who had consecrated all their possessions according to the system of stewardship revealed in Doctrine and Covenants 70:7–16 and elsewhere. Assignment of these stewardships, or inheritances, was also to be Bishop Whitney's responsibility.

4. Mine order. Some of the newly acquired land was also designated for the literary firm, which consisted of those Church leaders responsible for publication of the revelations.[6] Receiving such stewardships, or inheritances, would make it possible for these brethren to devote their full time to the work of the Lord.

5. This is the most expedient. The most important duty of the Church leadership at this time was to publish the Lord's modern revelations to the world.

5. Subduing the hearts. Making the Lord's revelations to the Church publicly available to all interested parties not only educates the members, but also informs nonmembers about the actual beliefs of the Church—usually with positive results.

6–9. John Johnson. Brother Johnson was a member of the Church living in Hiram, Ohio.[7] The Smith and Rigdon families had lived at the Johnson farm while Joseph, with Sidney as scribe, translated much of the Joseph Smith Translation. Joseph and Emma occupied part of the Johnson home, and Joseph received several revelations there, including Doctrine and Covenants 76. The Johnson home was also the location of several Church conferences. Here also Joseph and Sidney were tarred and feathered by a mob.[8] Unavoidably, all of these things had put additional burdens upon the Johnson family. For bearing these patiently, the Lord here blesses Brother Johnson and directs that he be made a part of "the order" (v. 8), or united order.[9] Members of this order consecrated their possessions to the Church, agreeing to conduct their affairs according to the law of consecration for the benefit of the Church, and Brother Johnson was to put up the security to pay off the Peter French property for the firm (see v. 9).[10]

7. He is a descendant of Joseph. John Johnson, like many in the Church today, was informed that he was a descendant of Joseph, the son of Jacob (Israel) who was sold into Egypt. His lineage would be through either Ephraim or Manasseh, and he would therefore be heir to the blessings of the Abrahamic covenant and the promises made to the Patriarchs, or "his fathers" (see also Abraham 2:6–12).

9. Incumbrances that are upon the house. This refers to the Peter French property upon which the Kirtland Temple would eventually be built. The property, upon which an inn was located, was still under a mortgage when the Church acquired the property.[11]

1. See Background to D&C 95.
2. See Zebedee Coltrin Journal, as cited in Cook, *Revelations of the Prophet Joseph Smith*, 198–99; see also D&C 95:10.
3. See Smith, *History of the Church*, 1:352–53.
4. See Commentary on D&C 72:23.
5. Kirtland Revelation Book, 60–61; Woodford, "Historical Development," 2:1244.
6. See Background to D&C 70 and Commentary on D&C 70:3; Background to D&C 78.
7. See Background to D&C 64.
8. See Background to D&C 82.
9. See Background to D&C 78; 104 and Commentary on D&C 78:9, 11.
10. See Backman, *Heavens Resound*, 144.
11. See Cook, *Revelations of the Prophet Joseph Smith*, 198–99.

97

BACKGROUND

Almost no information concerning the reception of Doctrine and Covenants 97 is found in Joseph Smith's *History of the Church*.[1] However, in a letter dated 6 August 1833, Joseph wrote to "Beloved Brethren" in Missouri and included with that letter copies of Doctrine and Covenants 94, 97, and 98.[2] In Joseph's letter to Missouri, the date of Doctrine and Covenants 97 is given as 2 August 1833. Exactly one month earlier, on 2 July 1833, Joseph had noted in another letter to Missouri that he had finished his translation of the Bible (Joseph Smith Translation, or JST), although he continued to make adjustments to the manuscript after that time.[3] In Kirtland, Joseph was greatly relieved that the Joseph Smith Translation had been completed and took some time to rejoice and relax. Nevertheless, a little more than two weeks after completion of that manuscript, and less than two weeks before Doctrine and Covenants 97 was received, the ax of disaster was to fall on the Church in Missouri (see v. 7).

By the time Doctrine and Covenants 97 was received, the Church had had a presence in Independence, Missouri, for about two years. While little more than one hundred Saints remained behind in Kirtland, the number of Latter-day Saints in Independence and the surrounding country rose from zero to around one thousand members, or about 25 percent of the total population, in that same period of time.[4] These rapidly rising numbers and the public designation of Independence as "the city of Zion" (D&C 57:2) and a gathering place for an ever-increasing number of Saints (see D&C 57:1) caused great alarm among the non–Latter-day Saint population there. Fearing to become eventually a religious, political, or economic minority in a Latter-day Saint majority, the original settlers of Jackson County banded together in a "secret combination" with the stated intention of driving the Mormons from their society "peaceably if we can, forcibly if we must." Hundreds of these earlier settlers of Jackson County, including judges, constables, and justices of the peace, signed a document stating the mob's illegal agenda for the expulsion of the Saints and setting 20 July 1833 as the day for the mob to gather to achieve that end.[5]

On 20 July, leaders of the mob delivered their demands to Church leaders in Independence, who were caught somewhat off guard. When the Saints understandably refused to leave the county immediately, the mob, variously estimated at three hundred to five hundred men, descended upon the Latter-day Saint printing office and destroyed the press, together with most copies of the 1833 Book of Commandments, which was then being printed.[6] Some copies of the printed text were bravely rescued by two teenaged sisters.[7] The mob also demolished the brick home of W. W. Phelps, in which the press was located. They then ransacked the Gilbert and Whitney store and tarred and feathered Bishop Edward Partridge and Charles Allen. Temporary peace was restored on 23 July when several leading Church members, under threat of violence from the mob, signed an agreement to leave Jackson County by 1 January 1834. In the meantime, the Saints in Missouri sent word to Joseph Smith in Kirtland requesting his aid and instructions. Oliver Cowdery, the special messenger, left Missouri on 25 or 26 July 1833.[8] (Oliver signed the agreement with the mob on 23 July and left Missouri two or three days thereafter).

It is possible that Joseph Smith learned of anti-Mormon

feelings in Missouri from a now-lost letter from Oliver Cowdery dated 9 July 1833. Receipt of such a letter is mentioned by Joseph in his 6 August letter to Missouri. Yet Joseph makes no allusion in that letter to persecutions in Missouri. While there had been anti-Mormon feelings in Jackson County for some time, the immediate catalyst for mob action there had been an article in the July issue of *The Evening and the Morning Star* entitled "Free People of Color," which was distorted by non-Mormons who claimed falsely that the Saints were "tampering with [their] slaves."[9] When the Saints in Missouri realized what the reaction to the article had been, they immediately published an "extra" edition of the *Star*, dated 16 July, to set the record straight. But this is a full week after Oliver's 9 July letter to Joseph, so Oliver may not have known the true mood of his non-LDS neighbors on 9 July. Even if Oliver had written about trouble brewing in Missouri, it was humanly impossible for Joseph Smith to have known about the mob activities of 20–23 July by 2 August when Doctrine and Covenants 97 was received, or even by 6 August, when Doctrine and Covenants 98 was received and sections 94, 97, and 98 were sent to Missouri. Joseph first learned of these events when Oliver arrived in Kirtland from Missouri sometime in mid-August (the *Painesville Telegraph* stated in its 16 August edition that Oliver had just arrived in Kirtland). Nevertheless, Doctrine and Covenants 97 and 98 already contained exactly the divine counsel and instructions the Missouri Saints were seeking in their perilous circumstances. In other words, the answers were sent to Missouri before the questions were received in Kirtland. If the body of the Saints were to remain in Missouri, it was critical that they should receive, hear, and obey these revelations.

COMMENTARY

1. I say unto you my friends. The salutation here is directed to Joseph Smith and the Church leaders in Kirtland. Even though there were serious problems among the members in Missouri, Church leaders in Kirtland were still the Lord's "friends."

1. My will concerning . . . Zion. Doctrine and Covenants 97 contains instructions for the Saints in Jackson County, Missouri, in their distress, but also important information on the nature and the future of Zion generally.

1. Many of whom are truly humble. It is possible to overestimate the internal problems of the Missouri Saints. Since Zion is ultimately a people "of one heart and one mind" (Moses 7:18), many of the Saints in Missouri could be properly obedient and yet still be unable to establish Zion collectively because of the behavior or attitude of a relative few among them. In trying to establish Zion collectively, the behavior of the few does affect the success of the many, for Zion can only have *one* heart and *one* mind. Thus, while the unfaithfulness of one individual may not affect another in establishing Zion in himself or in his family, such unfaithfulness does have a negative impact on the ward, the stake, and the Church collectively. However, the attitude of members toward the less faithful should not be one of force or militance, but of love and patience. The Lord will prune his own vineyard in due time by bringing chastening trials upon it (see D&C 95:2). Individuals can then self-select for or against the kingdom as they endure these trials or leave the Church because of them.

3. The school in Zion. Joseph's letter to Missouri dated 6 August 1833 contained the following introduction to Doctrine and Covenants 97: "Having received Brother Oliver's letter of July 9th as well as one from the brethren composing the school, we now answer them both in one letter as relates to the school in Zion. According to your request, we inquired of the Lord and send this letter—the communication which we received from the Lord concerning the school in Zion. It was obtained August 2nd and reads thus [D&C 97 follows]."[10]

The school in Missouri was patterned after the School of the Prophets in Kirtland and was referred to as the School of the Elders, with Elder Parley P. Pratt called as teacher. It was intended to train the Missouri leadership in the principles of the gospel and also to provide them with an elementary secular education. Elder Pratt recorded his experiences with this school as follows: "A school of Elders was also organized, over which I was called to preside. This class, to the number of about sixty, met for instruction once a week. The place of meeting was in the open air, under some tall trees, in a retired place in the wilderness, where we prayed, preached and prophesied, and exercised ourselves in the gifts of the Holy Spirit. Here great blessings were poured out, and many great and marvelous things were manifested and taught. The Lord gave me great wisdom, and enabled me to teach and edify the Elders, and comfort and encourage them in their preparations for the great work which lay before us. I was also much edified and strengthened. To attend this school I had to travel on foot, and sometimes with bare feet at that, about six miles. This I did once a week, besides visiting and preaching in five or six branches a week."[11]

6. The residue of the school. According to the 1828 edition of Webster's *American Dictionary of the English Language,* the word *residue* meant "that which remains after a part is taken, separated, removed or designated." The word did not have the negative connotation that it often does in contemporary English. The Lord has stated his approval of Parley P. Pratt, and he is willing to show mercy to the other members of the School of the Elders in Missouri. However, it appears from the language here that some members of the school required punishment from the Lord for secret sins which he would also make public.

7. The ax is laid at the root of the trees. The quotation here corresponds most closely with the language of Alma from the Book of Mormon (see Alma 5:52) but also closely parallels Matthew 3:10 and Luke 3:9. In the Book of Mormon, this warning is given to the people of Alma who were about to experience the great Lamanite wars. In the New Testament, it was delivered to the Jews who would soon be devastated by their failed First Revolt against Rome. The same warning is now addressed here specifically to the faltering Saints in Missouri, for whom persecutions had already begun but for whom deliverance was still possible if they would only repent.

Trees can't move; they can't run away or hide from the woodsman's ax. Their *only* defense against being cut down for firewood lies in producing valuable fruit. Many of the Missouri Saints had moved there contrary to the instructions of the Prophet.[12] Some were arrogant or otherwise foolish in their dealings with the original settlers of Jackson County, and too few were committed to living the law of consecration as they had been commanded. Now the fire was upon them. Those who produced no fruit would be cut down and burned, but Zion might still be established if the Saints would as a body repent and keep the Lord's commandments.

8. Their hearts are broken . . . spirits contrite. See Commentary on Doctrine and Covenants 20:37; compare Psalm 51:17. It might be noted that the Hebrew word for "contrite" in the Bible is *dakka,* meaning "bruised," or "crushed." The primary definition given for "contrite" in Webster's 1828 *American Dictionary* is "worn or bruised."

8. Willing to observe their covenants by sacrifice. In ancient times, covenants were entered into by offering sacrifices. Even contracts or other agreements between individuals were sealed with a sacrifice. In fact, the Hebrew idiom for "make a covenant" is *karat berit,* literally "to *cut* a covenant," referring to the animal that was customarily sacrificed and eaten in token of the covenant being made (see, for example, Genesis 31:44–55). According to the law of sacrifice, Abraham offered sacrifices when he covenanted with the Lord (see Genesis 15:9–18). According to the same law, Moses slaughtered oxen to seal the covenant at Sinai (see Exodus 24:3–8). The covenant of the gospel was sealed with the blood of Jesus Christ, the Lamb of God, whose flesh and blood we are symbolically reminded of when partaking of the sacrament. Other covenants are also accompanied by sacrifices—of one kind or another, such as the Lord may require—and without sacrifice of some kind, there is no covenant. Both in ancient and modern times, covenants are kept by making sacrifices. Only then may one enjoy the blessings that follow sacrifice.

8. They are accepted of me. In this case, the fruits to be enjoyed as a result of sacrifice would be the acceptance of the Missouri Saints by the Lord—something they did not at this time collectively enjoy.

9. Planted in a goodly land. In the short term, the "goodly land" is Independence, Missouri. However, the Lord's promise here to the faithful Saints would be fulfilled in the intermediate future by settlement in the valleys of the mountains in the West and in the long term will be fulfilled ultimately by the establishment of an extended Zion in the millennial age (see v. 18).

10. A house should be built unto me in the land of Zion. The chief sacrifice that the Lord required of the Missouri Saints was that they should build a temple in Independence, just as the Kirtland Saints were being required to build one in Ohio. This commandment cannot have been a complete surprise for the Missouri Saints, for a temple site had been selected and consecrated two years earlier, yet no further action had been taken. They had received an explicit commandment to proceed, together with rough plans for their temple, of which the Kirtland Temple was a duplicate, in a letter dated 25 June 1833, well before Doctrine and Covenants 97 was sent to them.[13] However, they took no action to begin construction. Doctrine and Covenants 97 makes it clear that the commandment to build this temple was as binding upon the Missouri Saints as building the Kirtland Temple was on the Ohio Saints (see D&C 95:3), and still they took no action.

According to verses 18 and 25–26, had the Missouri Saints kept the commandment to build a temple, Zion would have been established, never to be removed. Had the Missouri Saints collectively been as committed to building a temple as the Ohio Saints were, the Lord would have opened up the way for them to succeed. However, as Elder Parley P. Pratt, who taught the elders in Missouri, observed: "This revelation was not complied with by the leaders and Church in Missouri, as a whole; notwithstanding many were humble and faithful. Therefore, the threatened judgment was poured out to the uttermost, as the history of the five following years will show."[14] The obligation of this commandment was formally removed from the Saints as a practical impossibility in 1841 (see D&C 124:49–51), though it would have been possible in 1833 had they collectively proved more faithful.

And yet, again, it is possible to overemphasize the failings of the Missouri Saints, as compared to the body of Church members today. These were good people, but they expected a paradise of milk and honey, and the sacrifice of one's personal expectations in order to build the house of God was as difficult, or even more difficult, then as it is now. According to Brother Pratt: "They lived in peace and quiet; no lawsuits with each other or with the world; few or no debts were contracted; few promises broken; there were no thieves, robbers, or murderers; few or no idlers; all seemed to worship God with a ready heart."[15]

11. Let it be built . . . by the tithing of my people. Usually, the term *tithing* is used in the scriptures to indicate a tenth part of one's interest, or increase, annually (see D&C 119:4). However, in this verse, the word is used as it is in Doctrine and Covenants 64:23 and 85:3 to mean freewill offerings generally. Certainly, more than a tenth part of the Saints' resources would have been necessary to construct a temple in Independence, even as more than a tenth was required in Kirtland. Besides the cost of land and materials, offerings of time and labor would also have been required under the financial aspects of the law of consecration which remained in effect in Missouri and the rest of the Church until 1840.[16]

12. For the salvation of Zion. A temple might be likened to a doorway through which the full blessings of heaven are poured out upon the Saints. If the Saints want those special blessings, they must begin by constructing that portal—a temple. Salvation in the highest degree of the celestial kingdom can only come by receiving the ordinances performed in temples (see D&C

131:1–4). Temporally, the very safety and protection sought by the Missouri Saints would have been theirs if only they could have built a temple, for the Lord promised if they would do this, they would escape the coming chastening (vv. 18, 25). Both temporal and spiritual powers come from the presence of a temple. As President Ezra Taft Benson observed at the dedication of the Jordan River Temple: "The saints have been commanded to stand in holy places, such as this temple, in order to avoid the tribulations which are to come in the latter days. . . .

"The saints in this temple district will be better able to meet any temporal tribulation because of this temple. Faith will increase as a result of the divine power associated with the ordinances of heaven and the assurance of eternal associations.

"I repeat what I said at the groundbreaking of this temple two years ago: This valley will be preserved, our families will be protected, and our children will be safeguarded as we live the gospel, visit the temple, and live close to the Lord."[17]

13. For a place of thanksgiving. The temple is a place the Saints can go and, if they are humble and repentant, put themselves and their loved ones ultimately beyond the powers of Satan. Through the atonement of Christ, whole families can be sealed together in the kingdom of God, and surely any place where we may receive such blessings is "a place of thanksgiving."

14. A place of instruction. A full understanding of the Lord's plan comes only with that panoramic view of history from the beginning, to the present, and until the end, that is communicated in the ordinances of the temple. The temple provides us with our own guide to time and space that teaches us who and where we are, what went before, and what comes hereafter. Those who are lost cannot be saved by others who are also lost, but only by those who have their spiritual bearings, who know where they are and how to get home. It is entirely understandable, then, that missionaries and others who are called to the ministry in the kingdom of God should first be instructed in the temple of God before they are sent out to show others the way to God.

14. In theory, in principle, and in doctrine. The English word *theory* is derived from the Greek, *theoreo,* meaning "to see or perceive." Taken in this sense, it does not refer to anything speculative or hypothetical, but to a knowledge of the relationships between individual principles, the sum total of which is doctrine. As Webster's 1828 *American Dictionary* phrases it, theory is "an exposition of the general principles of any science," or "the science distinguished from the art." Note the parallel between this verse and Doctrine and Covenants 88:78.

15. Do not suffer any unclean thing to come into it. The responsibility for maintaining the sanctity of the temple lies not upon the Lord, but upon the Saints themselves. For this reason, it is necessary for the Church, through appointed leaders, to inquire into the life and habits of those wishing to attend the temple. By complying with this requirement, both those who seek recommends and those who grant them participate in a process designed to keep the temple holy, which is the obligation laid upon the Saints. The personal desires of those who might want to attend the temple but who will not keep the covenants set forth in the temple cannot be allowed to prevail over the strict command of the Lord. Otherwise, "my glory shall [not] rest upon it," and the very purposes of temple attendance will be lost to all. The equality of this system is that any member may repent and receive a recommend, but the decision not to repent is also a decision not to attend the temple.

16. The pure in heart . . . shall see God. This is the same promise made by the Savior in the sixth Beatitude (see Matthew 5:8; 3 Nephi 12:8). Note that the promise here does not guarantee that the pure in heart will see God *in the temple,* though they may, but only that they *shall* see God (compare Moses 5:4, 10).

17. I will not come into unholy temples. When the Savior came onto the grounds of the Jerusalem Temple, he drove out those who "made it a den of thieves" (Matthew 21:13), who defiled a place that should have been holy. Whether it is applied to our modern temples, or to that temple which is made up of all the members collectively (see Ephesians 2:19–21; 1 Peter 2:5), or that temple which is each member individually (see 1 Corinthians 6:19), the principle is the same. When the Savior comes in, that which is unholy must be cast out, for he will not inhabit the same tabernacle with uncleanness.

18. Zion . . . shall prosper, and become . . . very great. See Commentary on Doctrine and Covenants 84:4. The contemporary Church may sometimes underestimate the glorious future of Zion. During the Nauvoo period, the Prophet revealed to the Church in a general conference that "the whole of America is Zion itself from north to south, and is described by the Prophets, who declare that it is the Zion where the mountain of the Lord should be, and that it should be in the center of the land."[18] Brigham Young added later, "This American continent will be Zion; for it is so spoken of by the prophets. Jerusalem will be rebuilt and will be the place of gathering, and the tribe of Judah will gather there; but this continent of America is the land of Zion"[19] (see Ether 13:2–12). On another occasion, Joseph taught the Saints that "the whole of North and South America is Zion," and in the twentieth century, modern prophets have revealed that "every nation is the gathering place for its own people."[20] Thus, while the Doctrine and Covenants might have directed the nineteenth century Church to Missouri as the *center* place of Zion (see D&C 57:3), when that holy place is finally established physically, neither the state nor the continent will any longer suffice to contain the whole of it.

18. And very terrible. In contemporary English, *terrible* has a certain negative connotation. However, Webster's 1828 *American Dictionary* offers as an alternate meaning for "terrible" what is likely intended here: "adapted to impress dread, terror or solemn awe and reverence." The power and glory of the physical Zion, when it is established, will impress dread and terror upon the wicked and solemn awe and reverence upon the righteous.

20. Her high tower. In ancient times, a high tower was a defensive structure and was the most secure place in a city wall or in the city itself. For Zion the power of God will be her defense.

21. This is Zion—THE PURE IN HEART. Zion is both a people and a place. The Church has now among its members many Zion people and many Zion families. There are doubtless even Zion wards and Zion stakes, for spiritual Zion is the pure in heart. Nevertheless, the physical Zion, which the Church will establish at some time in the future, is not simply "wherever the pure in heart may dwell," for the formula *Zion is the pure in heart* describes the people themselves and not necessarily the place they live. Physical Zion will be established only when a Zion people inhabit a Zion place, when the pure in heart live in a place that has been consecrated to the purposes of the Lord. Ultimately, that physical place will take in all of the American continent and beyond (see Articles of Faith 1:10; Commentary on v. 18). Eventually, Asia will be Zion for the Asian Saints, Africa for the African Saints, and so on, for every nation will be Zion for the Saints who inhabit it. Surely, there will be administrative centers at all levels, but the time is long past when all the Saints can be gathered into one country, let alone into one state or one tiny county.

23. The Lord's scourge shall pass over by night. The language here is reminiscent of Isaiah 28:15, 18–19. That passage prophesied the invasion of Israel by the Assyrian army together with the destruction and chaos it would cause. Here it refers to the judgments that will come at the end of this dispensation as they are described in Doctrine and Covenants 29:14–17; 45:26–33, 40–50; 87:5–8. Whether the Church suffers from such calamities with the rest of the world or is protected from them by the Lord, their high tower, depends upon whether or not they can establish Zion. When the Jackson County Saints failed in their attempt to establish Zion, an "overflowing scourge" (D&C 45:31) fell upon them.

23. It shall not be stayed until the Lord come. The "overflowing scourge" (D&C 45:31) of the last days will reduce the world, with the exception of Zion, to a state of anarchy and chaos that will continue until the second coming of Christ (see D&C 87:6–8). As the end approaches, all the peoples of the earth will have to choose one kingdom or the other: the risks and plagues of Babylon, or the joys and the safety of Zion.

25–26. Zion shall escape if. Zion is a pure people (see v. 21) dwelling in a consecrated land (see D&C 57:2–3), who are of one heart and one mind with one another and with their God, dwelling in righteousness with no rich or poor among them (see Moses 7:18). The promise of the Lord is that a truly Zion people will dwell in safety forever (see Moses 7:20) but only *if* they are truly Zion and thus keep his commandments. In the present text, the immediate commandment requiring the obedience of the Independence Saints if they are going to establish Zion is that they build a temple (see vv. 10–12).

On Saturday, 3 June, Joseph Smith indicated the proposed dimensions of the Kirtland Temple, and Hyrum Smith went out that very evening and began digging the foundation trench himself. Hyrum resumed his digging the following Monday.[21] Unfortunately, there is no indication that any steps were taken in Missouri to begin construction of a temple in the two years following the dedication of the temple site or even in the months that followed the reception of Doctrine and Covenants 97. Failing collectively to keep the Lord's commandment, those Saints were driven out of Jackson County the following November, and over the next five years all the woes listed in verse 26 also fell upon them.

---

1. See Smith, *History of the Church*, 1:400.
2. See Background to D&C 94; 98.
3. See Smith, *History of the Church*, 1:368–69; Matthews, *Plainer Translation*, 41–48.
4. See Backman, *Heavens Resound*, 140, 163.
5. Smith, *History of the Church*, 1:372–76.
6. See *Times and Seasons* 1 (18 Dec. 1839): 18; John Whitmer described the mob as consisting of "the whole County," *Early Latter-day Saint History*, 93.
7. See Backman and Cowan, *Joseph Smith and the Doctrine and Covenants*, 3.
8. See Smith, *History of the Church*, 1:395.

9. Smith, *History of the Church,* 1:375; for the article "Free People of Color," see Smith, *History of the Church,* 1:378.

10. Woodford, "Historical Development," 2:1226; Cook, *Revelations of the Prophet Joseph Smith,* 200; spelling, punctuation, and grammar standardized.

11. Pratt, *Autobiography,* 93–94.

12. See Commentary on D&C 58:44.

13. See Smith, *History of the Church,* 1:362–63; Robison, *First Mormon Temple,* 9–16.

14. Pratt, *Autobiography,* 96.

15. Pratt, *Autobiography,* 93.

16. See Smith, *History of the Church,* 4:93; Ludlow, ed., *Encyclopedia of Mormonism,* 4:1481.

17. *Church News,* 22 Aug. 1981, 8.

18. Smith, *History of the Church,* 6:318–19.

19. Young, *Journal of Discourses,* 5:4.

20. Ehat and Cook, *Words of Joseph Smith,* 363; Harold B. Lee, *Ensign,* July 1973, 5; Graham W. Doxey, *Ensign,* Apr. 1979, 65.

21. See L. M. Smith, *Biographical Sketches of Joseph Smith and His Progenitors for Many Generations,* 203; Smith, *History of the Church,* 1:353.

98

BACKGROUND

Although Joseph Smith wrote almost nothing about the reception of Doctrine and Covenants 98 in his *History of the Church,* that revelation was one of three Joseph included in a letter dated 6 August 1833 and addressed to "Beloved Brethren" in Zion.[1] The other two revelations contained in the 6 August letter were Doctrine and Covenants 94 and 97.[2] In Joseph's letter to the Missouri Saints, he mentions having received an earlier letter dated 9 July 1833 (now lost) from Oliver Cowdery who was in Missouri at that time. It is possible that Oliver's letter to Joseph contained some information about anti-Mormon feeling on the rise in Jackson County or that Joseph had learned of such feelings by other means. However, no mob activity had taken place by the time of Oliver's letter on 9 July, and the first indication of any organized opposition against the Saints in Jackson County is reflected in an "extra" edition of *The Evening and the Morning Star* dated 16 July, or one week after Oliver's letter had already been sent to Kirtland. Prior to that date, editions of the *Star* make no mention of anti-Mormon feelings in Jackson County. It is improbable that any details of the mob activity of 20–23 July could have reached the Prophet in Kirtland by 6 August, the date on which he sent Doctrine and Covenants 94, 97, and 98 to Missouri, and he may have had no knowledge of the troubles there at all. The first detailed information concerning mob activity in Missouri did not reach Joseph in Kirtland until mid-August with the arrival of Oliver Cowdery as a special messenger from the Missouri Saints.[3]

In fact, it runs somewhat counter to the evidence to assume that Doctrine and Covenants 98 was intended *primarily* for the Missouri Saints. Neither Zion nor Missouri is specifically mentioned in this revelation, but the church at Kirtland is so mentioned (see v. 19). The use of the second person plural throughout this revelation, with the exception of verses 19–21, which mention the Kirtland church in third person, indicates that it was directed through Joseph and his associates to the whole Church with a specific warning to Kirtland, in much the same way as Doctrine and Covenants 97 was directed through Joseph to the whole Church with specific instructions and a specific warning to Missouri. While it is true that the mention of "afflictions" and "enemies" would fit the situation in Missouri in the summer and fall of 1833, it would also fit the situation in Kirtland since at least the fall of 1831.[4] The principles, promises, and wisdom of Doctrine and Covenants 97 and 98 would prove invaluable to the entire Church in all the days to follow 6 August 1833.

COMMENTARY

1. I say unto you my friends. Although Doctrine and Covenants 98 begins with the same salutation as Doctrine and Covenants 97, the revelation is not directed primarily to or about the Saints in Missouri, as is Doctrine and Covenants 97, but to the whole Church generally and to the "church at Kirtland" specifically (v. 19). Having in the earlier revelation warned Zion to repent, in this one the Lord now warns Kirtland to repent. Moreover, Doctrine and Covenants 98 would serve as a guide to the Church in all its persecutions over the next several decades and is still pertinent for members today, especially in areas where the Church is faced with opposition or discrimination.

1. Rejoice evermore and in everything give thanks. This is possibly one of the less well-kept commandments in the Church today, but in the context of the early persecutions in Missouri and Ohio, it is all the more surprising. No matter what the opposition or how desperate their physical circumstances, the Lord's Saints may rejoice and offer thanks for the spiritual blessings of the gospel of Christ and for the assurance that if they remain faithful, the kingdom is theirs (see D&C 25:1; 37:27; 38:9; 50:35; 62:9; 78:18; 82:24, etc.; note the present tense in all these passages).

2. Waiting patiently on the Lord. To "wait on" the Lord has two possible meanings, according to Webster's 1828 *American Dictionary*. On the one hand, it means "to attend, as a servant" or "to be ready to serve; to obey" the Lord (compare 2 Chronicles 17:19; Psalm 25:3, 5). On the other hand, it means "to look watchfully," or to wait *for* the Lord to appear (see Mark 15:43) or to answer the prayers of his Saints. The language here strongly favors this last meaning.

2. The Lord of Sabaoth. See Commentary on Doctrine and Covenants 87:7.

2. And are recorded with this seal and testament. The righteous prayers of the Saints have all been recorded in the heavens and will all be granted in the due time of the Lord. This is also the Savior's promise in the Sermon on the Mount (see Matthew 7:7; Luke 11:9–13). The seal and testament that guarantee this ultimate fulfillment are God's. God has sealed those prayers, and no power but our own unfaithfulness can break that seal. He who cannot lie here testifies and swears that our righteous prayers will not be lost, or forgotten, or overlooked, but will all be granted. However, this promise does not guarantee that the righteous prayers of the Saints will be granted right now, or even in the short-term or in the intermediate future. Nevertheless, all these things will be granted and fulfilled by the time the exalted Saints receive "all that my Father hath" (D&C 84:38; see Romans 8:17, 32).

3. An immutable covenant. *Immutable* means "unchangeable" or "unalterable." The agreement between the Saints and their God cannot be changed, altered, or repealed. If they will just be faithful, every single one of their righteous prayers will eventually be granted. God swears to us that this is so (see v. 2). The scope and inclusiveness of the divine promise and the strength of the divine guarantee are seldom fully appreciated by the Saints of any generation. What, after all, is not included in "all things"?

3. All things wherewith you have been afflicted. This is a rather dark verse, for the Saints are shown that accepting the gospel carries with it no immunity from affliction. In fact, the Saints are here warned once again (see D&C 54:10; 58:4; 95:1) that they should *expect* trials and afflictions.

3. Shall work together for your good. No suffering is meaningless or wasted. All suffering is ultimately redemptive. The inclusiveness here is the Lord's own wording: "All things wherewith you have been afflicted shall work together for your good." While we might not see or understand how this trial or that pain can ever result in good, the Lord assures us that it is so. A fine distinction must be made here. The Lord does not say that affliction is good, that suffering is good, that trials or abuse are good, or anything of the kind. In the Gethsemane experience of the Savior, we are not asked to believe that his pain was not hideous, that his suffering was not monstrous, that his penalty was not grotesquely undeserved. We are asked only to believe that it all worked together for our good. Neither are the Saints asked to believe in the face of their own trials or in the trials of those around them that they should be happy because evil is just good in disguise or because trials are just blessings in disguise. We are not asked to accept naively or without a second thought that whatever happens is God's will, or that because what happens is God's will, then pain isn't really hideous and evil isn't really ugly. We are only asked to believe that in the end all our pains and trials will not have been for nothing. Rather, they will work for our good, they will give us redemptive power, and in eternity, as in mathematics, negative values can strangely but truly add up to a positive total.

4. Concerning the laws of the land. The major theme tying Doctrine and Covenants 98 together might be the answer to the question, "As a member of the Church and kingdom of God upon the earth, what are my obligations as a member of society living under civil authority?" In the context of the United States in 1833, the short answer would be to obey God (see v. 4), to keep the law of the land (see vv. 5–8), to vote for good leaders (see vv. 9–10), to keep the covenant and keep the peace (see vv. 11–22), to observe the higher law of retaliation for families (see vv. 23–32) and for nations (see vv. 33–38), and to observe the law of forgiveness for individuals (see vv. 39–48).

4. All things whatsoever I command them. The Saints' first and highest obligation is always obedience to the Lord and faithfulness to their covenants with him. Nevertheless, once this has been made clear, it is usually wise to remind ourselves of how the will of the Lord is revealed to the Church. Pertinent passages would include Doctrine and Covenants 1:38; 26:2; 29:2; and 43:3–6.

5. That law of the land which is constitutional. In the historical context in which this revelation was given, that of the United States in 1833, the United States Constitution would have consisted of the Constitution itself and the first twelve amendments, including the Bill of Rights. Undoubtedly, as additional amendments were made to the Constitution, Church members in the United States would also be justified in observing laws based upon them, until or unless such laws might conflict with their highest obligation—to obey the command of the Lord (see v. 4). Absent such a conflict, if a law is constitutional and if it supports the Constitution in maintaining rights and privileges, then it is the common law for all of us, Latter-day Saints and non–Latter-day Saints alike, and we are all justified in living by it.[5]

5. Supporting that principle of freedom. Grammatically, *that* is a demonstrative pronoun, and so it must point something out to us. In this case, it points back to the noun *Constitution,* implicit in the adjective *constitutional,* as being "that principle of freedom." It is the Constitution itself, rather than any or all of the myriad of laws built upon it, that is the framework and scaffolding of freedom in the United States. Individual laws are justifiable only to the extent that they conform to that principle of freedom inherent in the Constitution. According to the Prophet Joseph: "The Constitution of the United States is a glorious standard; it is founded in the wisdom of God. It is a heavenly banner; it is to all those who are privileged with the sweets of its liberty, like the cooling shades and refreshing waters of a great rock in a thirsty and weary land."[6]

5. Belongs to all mankind. Although early Saints sometimes assumed a strictly American context for this revelation, there is no reason why contemporary members cannot assume an international context and seek to govern themselves by the principles of freedom as they are found in the Constitution of the United States to the degree that this is politically possible in their individual situations. Moreover, many nations that have emerged since 1776 have adopted legal systems styled upon that Constitution. In any case, however, Latter-day Saints "believe in being subject to kings, presidents, rulers, and magistrates, in obeying, honoring, and sustaining the law" wherever they might live (Articles of Faith 1:12).

5. Is justifiable before me. Although it is true that individual members will be justified in obeying the constitutional law of the land, it is not necessarily the case that the constitutional law of the land always defines what the Lord would otherwise ask, prohibit, or allow in a Zion society. Lack of blame, or being justified, is not the same thing as praise or commendation. Being justified by observing the present civil code is our refuge from blame before the Lord in matters of civil law, but one day being commended or praised by the Lord for establishing a Zion society ought to remain our collective hope and aspiration.

6. In befriending that law. What a noble word is *befriending!* It says just enough and yet not too much. In fact, to say more or less than this in regard to the civil law "cometh of evil" (v. 7). The law is our friend, and we may, therefore, embrace it. We respect the law, but we do not worship it. Civil law is good, but it is not divine. It may be our partner, but it is not our deity.

7. Whatsoever is more or less than this. Law which is less than constitutional, which bypasses the constitutional balance of powers (for example, legislation by executive or judicial decree, and so forth) comes of evil and leads to further evil. Moreover, individuals sometimes want to exalt the Constitution too highly by refusing to accept amendments to the Constitution or Supreme Court decisions interpreting the Constitution, consequently despising the civil law too much. Sometimes the opposite tendency is seen. Either point of view "cometh of evil." Usually when people say that something is unconstitutional, what they really mean is that in a more perfect world something wouldn't be allowed. They may even be correct, but that is beside the point. Our present civil law can be less than perfect, less than a Zion law, and yet still be in fact the constitutional law of the land, and we are still bound to obey it.[7]

8. I, the Lord God, make you free. The freedom referred to here is our individual God-given moral agency. According to Moses 7:32, "In the Garden of Eden, gave I unto man his agency." Because our moral agency to choose to sin or not to sin is God-given, it cannot be taken away from us, and we are, as this verse states, "free indeed." It is *impossible* for anyone else to make us guilty without our permission and cooperation.[8]

8. The law also maketh you free. In addition to the God-given moral agency that cannot be taken from us, there is a broad range of political liberties that are the function of human law. These may be more or less permissive or prohibitive depending upon where we live and the laws in force under which we live. For example, may I own a cow and keep it in my yard? What kind of papers do I need to travel within my country or between countries? Under what conditions may I drive a car? In some cases, these might be freedom *to,* like the freedom to own cows or to drive a car, and in some cases these might be freedom *from,* like being free from next-door neighbors with cows in their yard or from ten-year-olds driving cars.

9. When the wicked rule the people mourn. Despite the finest philosophical principles of government embodied in the Constitution and despite the best-intended body of constitutional laws based upon those principles, if the men and women who hold elective and appointed offices in any country are wicked, then the rest of the people will live in misery. No system of government, no matter how inspired, can long survive being managed by the wicked.

10. Honest . . . good . . . and wise men. In contrast to some religious viewpoints, active participation in government is a religious obligation for faithful Latter-day Saints. Not only are we commanded to vote, we are commanded to seek out honest, good, and wise candidates for whom to vote. We may not throw up our hands in despair and retreat from politics any more than we may retreat from our wards or from the Church. We do not necessarily need to run for office ourselves, but we do need to vote intelligently for men and women of wisdom and of good character.

10. Whatsoever is less than these cometh of evil. Note that this is not simply a repeat of the refrain in verse 7. There it was "more or less" and it was singular, "this." Here it is just "less" and it is plural, "these." The language is clearly adapted to fit specifically verse 10. Thus, to vote for anything less than honest, good, and wise candidates "cometh of evil."

11. Forsake all evil. Literally, this phrase means "to quit it," "to abandon it," or "to leave it alone." In the present context, this would also include evil political philosophies and evil office seekers (see vv. 7, 10).

11. Cleave. See Commentary on Doctrine and Covenants 11:19.

12. He will give unto the faithful line upon line, precept upon precept. These phrases may be understood in two opposing senses, both of which are true. They are most often understood to mean that God will continue to reveal things to the faithful in an unceasing stream of revelations until finally they know the truth of all things. We know that this is true by such revelations as Doctrine and Covenants 42:61 or 76:7.

The other sense of "line upon line, precept upon precept" is that the Lord will give the faithful only a *little* bit of revelation at a time. Then he will wait and test the reaction of the Saints to what has been given. If they prove faithful, he will then add another little bit, another line or precept, then wait and test or try them again, and so on.

In verse 12, two things argue strongly for the second meaning in its original context. First, "line upon line, precept upon precept" would appear to be an allusion to Isaiah 28:9–13, where it is used for speech given bit by bit to stubborn children who are being drilled and tested. Second, the Lord explicitly states in the end of this verse his intention of testing and trying the Saints with the very lines and precepts he is revealing to them. So, in this instance, "line upon line, precept upon precept" means that the Lord will give his Saints a little bit of revelation and then test them. If they prove faithful, he will then give them a little bit more and test them again, and so on.

13. Whoso layeth down his life . . . shall find it again. This had also been the Savior's assurance to his Saints in former days (see Matthew 10:39; Mark 8:35; Luke 9:24). Now, for some of the Latter-day Saints, their own time of dying was about to begin.

14. Be not afraid of your enemies . . . even unto death. No one gets through life uninjured, and no one gets out alive. Unfortunately, the faithful have little advantage over the wicked in avoiding the common pains and trials of mortality. And everyone makes enemies. Usually one's only choice is whether one's enemies will be the wicked or the righteous. It is certain that the faithful will make enemies and suffer persecution (see Matthew 10:34–39). In fact, the most faithful will often make the most bitter and vicious enemies, and often they suffer the most persecution, but such persecution, though difficult at the time, is a sure indicator of future joy (see Matthew 5:10–12).

14. I will prove you in all things. All our life is a test and a trial, not just in the big and difficult things, but in the little everyday things as well. We don't normally think of an afternoon at the library, an hour on the Internet, or a moment daydreaming as tests, but they are. You can only read one book or magazine at a time; you can only view one screen on the computer at a time; you can only think one thought at a time. And so, with all the books in the library, with all the screens on the Internet, with all the thoughts in the universe to read, view, or think, to choose this or that single one—to the exclusion of all others—says something about what our heart desires and, therefore, about what we are.

15. Abide in my covenant. Can you remain faithful to your covenants even when life turns on you? Can you remain faithful to your covenants when life turns on you so viciously that it seems God himself has turned on you? At some point in life, most people will face a test like Abraham's (see Genesis 22:1–14); they will reach a point where it seems that God is not living up to his promises or to their expectations. It may seem that he is not keeping his side of the covenant and that when this is pointed out, his only response is, "So what?" At such a time, it would be wise to consider that this may not be a betrayal by God so much as it may be an important question on the final exam of life. The only right answer in this situation is to say with Job, "Though he slay me, yet will I trust in him" (Job 13:15).

16. Therefore, renounce war and proclaim peace. The word "therefore" is important here, because it ties this verse to the last as a conclusion that may be drawn from it. Since you are not worthy of Christ if you do not abide his covenant, then keep his covenant by renouncing war and proclaiming peace. In times to come, this commandment would prevent the Saints from making preemptive strikes or first strikes against their enemies. In addition, it also forbade them from adopting the Old Testament *lex talionis,* or law of retribution—"eye for eye, tooth for tooth"

(Deuteronomy 19:21)—and which pertained to the lesser law of Moses.[9] Instead, the Saints will be given at this time a higher law of retaliation congruent with the principles of the gospel (see vv. 23–48). The ancient Nephites also lived the higher law of retaliation (see Alma 48:14–16), since they also had kept the Melchizedek Priesthood and the fulness of the gospel.

16. Turn the hearts of the children to their fathers. This is one of those scriptures that has more than one correct application. While we normally associate these words from Malachi 4:6 with family history and temple work, it is unlikely that very many in the 1833 Church could have so understood it, since none of the revelations, keys, or temples needed were yet in place. Family history and temple work were unknown doctrines for most of the Saints at this time.

Given the context of the passage in verse 16 of renouncing war and proclaiming peace, it is likely that most of the Saints would have understood the allusion to Malachi quite literally as making peace between and among families (see also v. 23). Only later would they see the deeper meaning that could be read beneath the surface of extended human families being sealed together through temple ordinances.

17. The hearts of the Jews unto the prophets. Our initial instinct is to understand this passage in terms of the final restoration of Judah in the last days. This may well be so. But, again, since there were very few Jews in the environment of the 1833 Church, it may also be that the term *Jew* was meant to be understood here as it was in Doctrine and Covenants 57:4, to refer to Native Americans, with whom the Church had then and continues to have now considerable interest and experience.[10]

18. In my Father's house are many mansions. Most people think of a mansion as being larger than a house. The intent of the passage is simply to convey the maximum sense of personal reward to the faithful while at the same time conveying the maximum sense of personal closeness with our heavenly family.

19. I, the Lord, am not well pleased with many . . . at

Kirtland. Just as Doctrine and Covenants 97 delivered a specific warning and commandments to the Church in Missouri, so Doctrine and Covenants 98 delivers a specific warning to the Church in Kirtland. Remember that at this time there were only about 150 members of the Church in the Kirtland area.

20. They do not forsake their sins. Of course, the Lord is speaking of the Kirtland Saints collectively and not individually.

20. Observe the words of wisdom. The use of the plural here indicates that the intended meaning is not confined to Doctrine and Covenants 89, what we know as the Word of Wisdom, but refers to all the revelations of the Lord to the Saints.

20–22. These verses contain the same kind of promises and warnings that were given to the Saints in Missouri (compare D&C 97:24–27).

23. I speak to you concerning your families. The topic of verses 23–37 does not actually concern family interrelationships but, rather, discusses family defense. Since these verses are similar to verses 39–48, it should be noted that the English pronoun *ye,* used here frequently, is plural and is not found at all in verses 39–48. This would seem to indicate that the instructions in verses 23–37 are to be understood as directed *primarily,* though not exclusively, to families collectively or to heads of families collectively, while the instructions in verses 39–48 are directed specifically to individuals. Also this section deals with principles of retaliation, while the latter verses, though similar in structure, deal with principles of forgiveness.

Since the Saints are going to be afflicted by their enemies and persecuted contrary to the law, at what point are they justified in taking the law into their own hands and resorting to violence in retaliation against their enemies? The law of Moses in the Old Testament seemed to allow appropriate retaliation after being injured the first time (see Leviticus 24:19–20; Deuteronomy 19:20–21). Because the law of retaliation, the *lex talionis,* or "an eye for an eye" (Matthew 5:38), is both fair and biblical, it could be argued that it was a good standard for the Latter-day Saints.

The Old Testament law of retribution, although strictly just, was part of the preparatory gospel given to ancient Israel, fulfilled with the resurrection of Christ, and was an inadequate law for living the gospel or establishing Zion in the latter days.[11]

23. If men will smite you, or your families, once. In effect this verse has the same force as Matthew 5:38–39 in the Sermon on the Mount. There the Savior explicitly states that the law of retaliation in the law of Moses, "an eye for an eye," is no longer sufficient for a Christian. Now the law must be, "Whosoever shall smite thee on thy right cheek, turn to him the other also" (Matthew 5:39).

23. Revile not against them, neither seek revenge. To be rewarded, it is not enough simply to forgo revenge. We must bear the insult patiently and revile not. That is, we must not lose our temper and lash out physically or verbally. Like Christ our Savior, we must absorb evil and reflect back good.

23. Ye shall be rewarded. In the Sermon on the Mount, the reward for those who make peace is to be called the children of God (see Matthew 5:9); the reward for those who are persecuted for righteousness' sake is the kingdom of heaven (see Matthew 5:10); and loving our enemies is the way in which we become truly our Heavenly Father's children (see Matthew 5:45).

24. If ye bear it not patiently . . . a just measure unto you. If we retaliate in kind when offended, then it doesn't really matter who hit whom first. Both sides end up victims to the same extent, and both sides end up aggressors to the same extent, and so justice has no further interest in the matter. We got even; so we're even. By our own hand, the scales of justice have been balanced, and *everything* is now fair. The actions of both sides are justified by reason of the penalties they have mutually suffered and exacted. However, had we not retaliated, then the law of justice would have remained outraged, and God would have been obliged to reward us and to demand satisfaction of our enemies.

26. Doubled unto you four-fold. Since the second offense has already paid off a hundred fold (see v. 25), this would seem to make the third offense pay off a total of eight hundred times more than the first offense if we bear it patiently, though the number is likely meant to be symbolic of overflowing blessings rather than to be taken literally.

27. These three testimonies. The three attacks, or afflictions, of one's enemies stand as three witnesses under the law of witnesses that "in the mouth of two or three witnesses every word may be established" (Matthew 18:16; see Deuteronomy 19:15). On the third occurrence, the evil intent of our adversary may be deemed a matter of record. The third time we are injured, his or her behavior cannot be misunderstood as a mistake, or a coincidence, or a misinterpretation. There is a clear pattern of aggression, and we are justified in assuming that this is so and in taking appropriate *defensive* measures. In such a case, even an ambush might be self-defense.

28. If that enemy shall escape my vengeance. Sometimes the Lord himself punishes the wicked by bringing upon them the very plagues and destructions they sought to bring upon the Saints. Just as Pharaoh planned to slay the firstborn of Israel only to lose his own firstborn, sometimes the Lord takes his own vengeance upon the enemies of the Saints.

28. Ye shall see to it that ye warn him in my name. After the third offense the righteous are still under obligation to put an offender on notice that they are liable to retaliation if they should attack or offend again. The Lord is interested not in maximizing the scope of retaliation but in minimizing prospects for revenge. Nevertheless, such a warning is sufficient "unto the third and fourth generation" and ought to be taken seriously.

29. I have delivered thine enemy into thine hands. The testimony of three separate offenses (see v. 27) clearly establishes the continuing evil intent of our enemies. If we issue a fair warning of retaliation against further attacks (see v. 28), then any action we must take to secure justice following a fourth attack will be acceptable to the Lord. Once our enemy's malice is a matter of record, as well as the repeated nature of his attacks, then any measures we are forced to take may be understood as justifiable self-defense. Note that we are not justified in taking vengeance in such a case, for "vengeance is mine; I will repay, saith the Lord" (Romans 12:19; see also D&C 98:45). Rather, we are justified by the principle of self-defense.

30. If thou wilt spare him. It should be pointed out that even after a fourth attack, we are not instructed or required to smite our enemies. We may be justified in doing so, but if we choose not to, we will be further rewarded for our mercy and restraint and will bring blessings upon our heads and upon the heads of our children for generations.

33–38. This is the law that I gave unto mine ancients. It is likely that the term "mine ancients" is meant to refer to those peoples who had the fulness of the gospel. Three things argue in favor of this. First, the Patriarchs and the Nephites mentioned in verse 32 all had the Melchizedek Priesthood and the fulness of the gospel; none of those mentioned comes from the Bible between Moses and Malachi, the period of the law of Moses. Second, the evidence of the Old Testament clearly shows that the practice of ancient Israel between Moses and Christ, the period of the lesser law with its *lex talionis,* was markedly different from what is described in verses 23–38. Deuteronomy 20:10, for example, states that "when thou comest nigh unto a city to fight against it, then proclaim peace unto it." But this is not an offer of peace in the modern sense, and certainly not an offer of peace to foreign invaders, but is merely an offer to allow a city that Israel has attacked to surrender peacefully or be destroyed (see Deuteronomy 20:12–13). The native Canaanite peoples were not given even that choice, however (see Deuteronomy 20:16–17; 1 Nephi 17:32–35, 41). Similar examples are common between Exodus and Malachi. By comparison, the practice of the Nephites was vastly different and in accord with verses 23–38 (see Alma 48:14–16; 3 Nephi 3:20–21; Mormon 3:10–16). Third, the Savior himself says in the Sermon on the Mount regarding the lesser law of retaliation in the law of Moses and the higher requirement of the gospel: "Ye have heard that it hath been said, An eye for an eye, and a tooth for a tooth: But I say unto you, That ye resist not [the] evil[doer]: but whosoever shall smite thee on thy right cheek, turn to him the other also" (Matthew 5:38–39). So it would seem that when the Lord took the fulness of the gospel and the holy priesthood away from Israel and gave them the preparatory gospel in its place, he also allowed them to operate under a lesser law of retaliation from Moses until Christ.[12]

38. This is an ensample unto all people. *Ensample* is an old spelling of *example.* Thus, even when a nation is not led by prophets or does not worship the Lord, the principles of retaliation taught in verses 23–37 would serve as a useful and beneficial example for them to follow.

39. After thine enemy has come upon thee. Verses 39–48 deal with matters of individual forgiveness. Many people are confused by what they consider to be conflicting instructions in scripture on the topic of forgiveness. On the one hand, the Savior says to forgive "seventy times seven" (Matthew 18:22) and "of you it is required to forgive all men" (D&C 64:10). On the other hand, verses 39–48 seem to limit forgiveness to "three strikes and you're out."

The crucial distinction that allows us to resolve the apparent conflict is whether the offender in a given instance is repentant or not. If he or she is repentant and asks for our forgiveness, then we, as true children of a merciful Father in Heaven, must grant mercy and forgiveness even as we hope to be forgiven (see Matthew 6:12, 14–15; Commentary on D&C 64:9–10). Even when an offender is not repentant, we are required to forgive him or her at least three times without harboring any grudge. By extension, then, if we are commanded to forgive the *intentional* insults of our enemies without harboring a grudge, how much more, then, should we be expected to forgive the *unintentional* slights or mistakes of our friends! How can there ever be grudges between brothers and sisters or between members or families in the wards and stakes of the Church?

46. And upon his children. Since the Latter-day Saints do not believe in inherited guilt, it should be pointed out that this formula is descriptive rather than prescriptive. That is, it describes what is going to happen and not what the Lord is going to make happen. In this case, someone of such an evil character as this repeated offender is, by the natural laws of the universe, probably going to raise an equally unpleasant family. Violence and other abusive behaviors are usually learned at home. Should any off-spring of such a person turn to the Lord, they would be forgiven, and the chain of evil would be broken (see v. 47). But otherwise it will likely take generations for the sins of the fathers to become sufficiently diluted by time to cease influencing their posterity.

46. Unto the third and fourth generation. Note the parallel between the four offenses of the enemy and the four generations of his posterity against which the judgments of the Lord are poured out, one generation for each offense.

---

1. See Smith, *History of the Church,* 1:403–6.
2. See Background to D&C 94 and 97.
3. See *Painesville Telegraph,* 16 Aug. 1833; see also Background to D&C 97.
4. See Background to D&C 71; 82.
5. See the excellent articles by Rex E. Lee, "Constitutional Law," and Ralph Hancock, "Constitution of the United States," in Ludlow, ed., *Encyclopedia of Mormonism,* 1:315–19.
6. Smith, *History of the Church,* 3:304.
7. See also Commentary on D&C 10:68; 93:25.
8. See Commentary on D&C 29:36; 93:30.
9. See Commentary on D&C 84:24–27.
10. See also Commentary on D&C 2:1–3; 28:8; Background to D&C 32.
11. See Commentary on D&C 84:24–27.
12. See Commentary on D&C 84:23–27.

DOCTRINE AND COVENANTS

99

BACKGROUND

The Prophet Joseph does not mention Doctrine and Covenants 99 in his *History of the Church*. It is recorded, however, in the Kirtland Revelation Book as having been received on 24 August 1832 "by Joseph the Seer and written by F. G. Williams, Scribe."[1] It is further recorded that Doctrine and Covenants 99 was received in Hiram, Ohio, and this would make the most likely setting for its reception the John Johnson home in Hiram because Joseph did not move his family from there back to Kirtland until mid-September 1832. John Murdock's diary and journal also record the date of this revelation as August 1832.[2] All editions of the Doctrine and Covenants until 1876 dated Doctrine and Covenants 99 to August 1832. Beginning with the 1876 edition, the date was changed to August 1833, which means that Doctrine and Covenants 99 is now out of its natural chronological order in present editions of the Doctrine and Covenants where it would naturally fall between section 83 and section 84.

Doctrine and Covenants 99 is a mission call given to one of the great men of the early Church, Elder John Murdock. Brother Murdock, like Lehi of old, was "a visionary man" (1 Nephi 2:11), joining the Church just seven months after its organization as the missionaries to the Lamanites preached in Kirtland on their way to Missouri.[3] Between November 1830 and March 1831, Brother

Murdock preached the gospel of the Restoration and baptized between sixty and seventy persons.[4] A month later, on 30 April 1831, John's beloved wife, Julia, died just six hours after giving birth to twins. On that same terrible night, Emma Smith also gave birth to twins. Emma lived, but her twins died. Being widowed and with five children to care for, John Murdock agreed to having Joseph and Emma adopt the two babies. This they gladly did, naming the girl Julia after her mother and the boy Joseph after his adoptive father. Julia lived to adulthood, but little Joseph died ten months later as a result of exposure during a mob attack directed at the Prophet on the John Johnson farm.[5]

John Murdock was first mentioned in Doctrine and Covenants 52:8 when he received his first mission call to Missouri, just five weeks after the death of his wife. On his return to Kirtland from Missouri, he learned of the death of his young son, Joseph. Nevertheless, he accepted this additional mission call, recorded as Doctrine and Covenants 99, leaving a month later with Zebedee Coltrin on 27 September 1832, after providing for his children as advised in verse 6. In view of his steadfast obedience and faithfulness, it is not surprising that Elder Murdock's private journal contains the following notation of a vision he received after a promise made to him by the Prophet Joseph Smith in the School of the Prophets the next spring: "I saw the form of a man [the Savior], most lovely, the visage of his face was sound and fair as the sun. His hair a bright silver grey, curled in most majestic form, His eyes a keen penetrating blue, and the skin of his neck a most beautiful white and he was covered from the neck to the feet with a loose garment, pure white, whiter than any garment I have ever before seen. His countenance was most penetrating, and yet most lovely."[6] Brother Murdock remarried and moved to Missouri in the summer of 1836. After serving faithfully on the mission mentioned in this revelation and on many others, including Zion's Camp, Brother Murdock moved with the Church to the valleys of the West. Eventually, he was ordained a patriarch and died in Beaver, Utah, in 1871, at the age of seventy-nine.

COMMENTARY

1. Eastern countries. Based on Brother Murdock's itinerary, he seems to have understood this to refer primarily to the areas immediately east of Kirtland and in New York state but also to the other eastern states.

2. And who receiveth you receiveth me. The Savior taught this principle of representation to his disciples in the time of the New Testament Church (see Matthew 10:40–42; 25:30–35). It is in part an extension of the divine investiture of authority that is inherent in the priesthood. Just as the Son may speak in the person of the Father (for example, see Moses 1), or the Holy Ghost may speak in the person of the Son (see Moses 5:9), so a properly ordained apostle or prophet may say, "Thus saith the Lord," and then deliver the rest of his message in the first person as though it were the Lord himself speaking (for example, see Isaiah 50:1; D&C 1). Beyond this, however, anyone—male or female—under the guidance of the Holy Spirit may represent the Lord in many situations, e.g., missionaries, Sunday School teachers, or Relief Society presidents.

2. In the demonstration of my Holy Spirit. The language here was not without special significance for John Murdock, for as a child he had had a vision which had caused him to seek for the true church of Christ until he found it in November 1830. One thing that had particularly caused him to lose patience with one church after another was their lack of, or even denial of, the gifts and power of the Holy Spirit. Now in his second mission call, this visionary man was promised that he would preach the gospel in power and in the demonstration of the very Holy Spirit he had sought all his life and had only recently received as a gift after his baptism.[7]

3. Blessed are they, for they shall obtain mercy. According to the fifth Beatitude (see Matthew 5:7), it is the merciful who shall obtain mercy, but in the days of missionaries traveling without purse or scrip, to receive penniless strangers—to feed and house and clothe them, to nurse them when they were sick, to hide them from their enemies, as well as to listen to them preach—all of this was merciful indeed.

4. Cleanse your feet. See Commentary on Doctrine and Covenants 24:15.

5. I come quickly. See Commentary on Doctrine and Covenants 33:18.

5. As it is written of me in the volume of the book. "The book" referred to here could be the book of Enoch, which is the source of the quotation cited, the New Testament book of Jude, in which the quotation appears (1:14–15), or the Bible itself, which contains the book of Jude.

6. It is not expedient that you should go until your children are provided for. John and Julia Clapp Murdock had five children together, including the twins she died giving birth to. With the twins safely in the care of Joseph and Emma, Brother Murdock arranged for his three older children to be taken to Missouri by Caleb Baldwin and arranged for their support there by Bishop Partridge until he could join them. "Previous to this I had provided for my children and sent them up to the Bishop in Zion according to the revelation by Br. Caleb Baldwin and paid him thirty dollars for carrying them and [other] things. And after making proper preparations according to the revelation I journeyed forth. Sept. 27, 1832. Br. Zebedee Coltrin and myself started on a mission."[8]

6. Sent up kindly. That is, they are to be sent with affection and in such a manner that, having just lost their mother, they will not come to doubt the continuing love of their father. The Lord specifically instructs that they must not feel rejected or abandoned.

7. After a few years . . . thou mayest go up also unto the goodly land. Although Brother Murdock was soon reunited with his children in Missouri, he was also called upon to serve several missions and later become a bishop and partriarch. His daughter Phebe became ill and died in Missouri in 1834, but the two remaining sons lived to adulthood, went west, and served faithfully in the Church. In 1836, Brother Murdock married Amoranda Turner and settled with his children in Missouri, only to be driven from that state with the rest of the Church in February 1839.[9]

1. Kirtland Revelation Book, 20, though its table of contents lists the date as 29 Aug.
2. See Cook, *Revelations of the Prophet Joseph Smith,* 201–2; Woodford, "Historical Development," 2:1276–78.
3. See Background to D&C 32.
4. See Murdock, Journal, Church Archives, 1–2; *Deseret News,* 10 Feb. 1858, 384.
5. See the Background to D&C 82.
6. John Murdock Journal, as cited in Black, *Who's Who in the Doctrine and Covenants,* 202.
7. See Black, *Who's Who in the Doctrine and Covenants,* 201–2.
8. Murdock, Journal, Church Archives, 25; spelling, punctuation, and grammar standardized.
9. See Black, *Who's Who in the Doctrine and Covenants,* 201–4.

100

BACKGROUND

Joseph Smith had first learned details concerning the mob activities in Missouri in mid-August 1833 and had almost immediately dispatched Brothers Orson Hyde and John Gould to Independence with advice and support for the Saints in Zion.[1] Then, about six weeks later, on 5 October 1833, Joseph and Sidney Rigdon, in company with Freeman Nickerson, who provided a team and transportation, began a month-long mission to upstate New York and Canada. By 12 October the missionaries had reached the home of Brother Nickerson in Perrysburg, New York, which had been an intermediate destination.

It cannot have been easy for the Prophet to have undertaken a mission at this particular time. He was concerned about the persecutions in Missouri and the fate of Zion. He was concerned for Elders Hyde and Gould whom he had sent there, and he was concerned for the safety of his own family in Kirtland, where there were many enemies. Joseph kept a private journal during much of his adult life, and on the day he arrived at the Nickerson home in Perrysburg, he wrote in it, "Saturday the 12[th] [October 1833 to] the house of father Nicke[r]son I feel very well in my mind the Lord is with us but have much anxiety about my family &c."[2] Perhaps in response to these many anxieties weighing upon the heart of the Prophet, Joseph received that same day at the

Nickerson home the consoling and comforting revelation now recorded as Doctrine and Covenants 100. The Prophet later wrote in his *History of the Church,* "On the 12th, arrived at Father Nickerson's, at Perrysburg, New York, where I received the following revelation—Doctrine and Covenants 100."[3]

COMMENTARY

1. My friends Joseph and Sidney. It should not be supposed that Brother Nickerson, who accompanied Joseph and Sidney on much of this mission, is being excluded here. However, since he has just arrived home in Perrysburg at this time, he already knows that his family is well. Most of the remaining revelation concerns matters of Church leadership and is therefore properly directed to Joseph and Sidney.

1. Your families are well; they are in mine hands. In fulfillment of this assurance, the Prophet recorded in his private journal on his return to Kirtland: "Friday November 1 [1833]. Left Buffalo, N. Y. at 8 o'clock A.M. and arrived at home Monday, the 4th [November 1833] at 10, A.M. found my family all well according to the promise of the Lord, for which blessing I feel to thank his holy name; Amen."[4]

3. I have much people in this place . . . an effectual door shall be opened. Even though Joseph and Sidney spent only one month on this particular mission, they preached to many large and receptive congregations, they were impressed that the Holy Spirit was planting seeds in many honest hearts, and they baptized at least eighteen individuals.[5] However, the real fruits of their labors would come two years later when Parley P. Pratt would return to the same area in Canada through the "effectual door" that had been opened by Joseph and Sidney. What they had sowed, Brother Pratt harvested, preaching to thousands and baptizing hundreds. Among those converts were John Taylor, a future president of the Church, and Mary Fielding, the mother of

President Joseph F. Smith and grandmother of President Joseph Fielding Smith. The month-long mission of Joseph Smith and Sidney Rigdon to New York and Canada indeed opened an "effectual door" through which passed hundreds of Saints and three future Church presidents.

4. Suffered. That is, allowed.

4. It was expedient in me. This might be rephrased in more contemporary English: "It served my purpose," or "I found it useful."

5. Lift up your voices unto this people; . . . you shall not be confounded. It is not an easy thing to preach in public to strangers, to be thought deluded, malicious, or unbalanced. The world's view of proselyting is generally very negative, and so the Lord's promise here that they will not be confounded must have been comforting to the brethren.

6. For it shall be given you. The Lord then repeats to Joseph and Sidney the same promise he made when he sent out his New Testament disciples, that they would be inspired whenever they needed it with exactly what they were to say (see Matthew 10:19).

7. But a commandment I give unto you. "Unto whom much is given much is required" (D&C 82:3; see also the parable of the talents in Matthew 25:14–30). However, the blessings promised in verses 5 and 6 come with an obligation. Joseph and Sidney are commanded to keep in mind the seriousness of their work. Meekness, which is also mentioned here, is the ability to put the will of God before one's own will. Thus, to preach in meekness is to preach what *the Spirit* wants you to say and not what *you* might want to say, and always in the name of Jesus Christ.

8. I give unto you this promise. With the commandment in verse 7 comes an additional promise. If missionaries in meekness of spirit confine themselves to preaching only what the Lord inspires them to preach rather than what may please their own hearts and minds, then everything they say will be God's own truth, and the Holy Ghost will be able to bear powerful witness that it is so. When missionaries do not preach in meekness, that is, when they depart from what they have been sent out to teach and teach what pleases themselves instead, they cannot teach with the power of the Spirit, for the Spirit will not bear witness to the teachings of men—even if they *think* they are right.

9. Sidney should be a spokesman. Sidney Rigdon was a well-educated man with magnificent talents as a thinker and a writer but particularly as an orator. He had been a Reformed Baptist minister with several congregations in the Kirtland area before joining the Church in 1831. George Q. Cannon said of Elder Rigdon: "Those who knew Sidney Rigdon, know how wonderfully God inspired him, and with what wonderful eloquence he declared the word of God to the people. He was a mighty man in the hands of God, as a spokesman, as long as the prophet lived, or up to a short time before his death."[6] The Lord had earlier promised Sidney that he would "preach my gospel and call on the holy prophets [that is, the scriptures] to prove [Joseph's] words" (D&C 35:23).

The appointment of Sidney Rigdon as the spokesman for the Prophet Joseph fulfilled an ancient prophecy of that Joseph who was sold into Egypt: "And the Lord hath said: I will raise up a Moses . . . and I will make a spokesman for him" (2 Nephi 3:17). Thus, the relationship between Joseph and Sidney would be that of a modern Moses and Aaron, Joseph as Moses the prophet and Sidney as Aaron his spokesman (see Exodus 4:16). Elder Rigdon served in this capacity until sometime after his imprisonment in Liberty Jail. During the Nauvoo period, this role was gradually assumed by Hyrum Smith.

The fulfillment of 2 Nephi 3:17–18 and the role of the modern Aaron cannot be confined to Sidney Rigdon alone. In Doctrine and Covenants 8:6–7, the Lord had previously told Oliver Cowdery that he had the gift of Aaron, while Doctrine and Covenants 28:2–3 explicitly stated that Oliver was to be as Aaron to Joseph, who was to be to him as Moses. When Oliver Cowdery subsequently left the Church, Hyrum Smith received all the blessings, honors, gifts, and positions that Oliver had formerly held (see D&C 124:95). This would include Oliver's former position of an Aaron to Joseph's Moses. And just as Aaron really was Moses' elder brother, so Hyrum really was Joseph's elder brother and died with him at Carthage, a true Aaron and a true brother to the last, after Oliver and Sidney had lost that calling.

10. I will give unto him. That is, to the Prophet Joseph.

11. I will give unto thee. That is, to Sidney Rigdon.

11. To be mighty in expounding all scriptures. Sidney's calling is to use his knowledge of the scriptures and his gifts of explanation and oratory to preach the truths of the restored gospel as they are revealed through the Prophet Joseph Smith. However, Joseph—not Sidney—is the one who receives those revelations. No one on the earth, no matter how intelligent, gifted, or highly placed, has the authority to declare new doctrine to the Church except the prophet.[7]

13. Zion shall be redeemed, although she is chastened for a little season. Beginning just nineteen days after this revelation was received, the Saints were driven out of Jackson County, Missouri, altogether. This was the chastening foreseen by the Lord. Some might think that two hundred years or so from the time the promise of redemption was given until its fulfillment might be more than "a little season." It must be remembered, however, that John the Revelator uses "a little season" in a context that seems to describe the dispensation of the fifth seal, which some interpret to last as long as a thousand years (see Revelation 6:10–11). The primary meaning of *redeem* is to recover by purchase what has been lost or sold. The promise of the Lord is that Zion will in time be redeemed, but only when he has prepared "a pure people, that will serve me in righteousness" (v. 16).

14. Orson Hyde and John Gould. These two brethren had been sent at considerable risk to Jackson County with counsel for the Saints from the Prophet, and Joseph is concerned that they will run afoul of mobs on their journey. Elders Hyde and Gould did, in fact, return safely on 25 November, and Elder Hyde brought the first accounts of the expulsion of the Saints from

Jackson County and of their miserable conditions, dispossessed of practically everything they owned and facing the coming of winter in the unsettled country north of the Missouri River.

15. All things shall work together for good. See Commentary on Doctrine and Covenants 98:3.

15. And to the sanctification of the Church. The trials and tribulations of the Saints sanctify the Church, or make it holy, in at least two ways. First, the individual Saints who remain faithful through periods of trial are purified by the experience of overcoming adversity. They pass through the refiner's fire, which can be agonizing but which also burns away that part of them which is unholy. Second, those members who are not willing to keep their covenants and endure trials for the Savior's sake will be driven from the Church by their chastening, and the Church will be collectively purified by their departure.

17. All that call upon the name of the Lord . . . shall be saved. Note that the promise is not that they shall be *safe,* but that they shall be *saved.* Many worthy Saints died in Missouri, in Illinois, on the plains, and elsewhere. Righteousness brings no guarantee of physical health and safety in this life, but it is a guarantee of salvation in the kingdom of God in the life to come.

---

1. See Smith, *History of the Church,* 1:407.
2. Jessee, *Personal Writings,* 18.
3. Smith, *History of the Church,* 1:419–20.
4. Jessee, *Personal Writings,* 24.
5. See Smith, *History of the Church,* 1:421–23.
6. Cited in George Q. Cannon, *Journal of Discourses,* 25:126
7. See Commentary on D&C 28:2; 43:3–6.

101

BACKGROUND

In late August 1833, in response to the report of Oliver Cowdery who had just arrived in Kirtland from Missouri bearing news of the mob activities of 20–23 July, Joseph Smith dispatched Elders Orson Hyde and John Gould to Jackson County with advice for the Saints there. Among other things, he advised the Saints to exhaust every legal appeal, including a petition to the governor of Missouri, Daniel Dunklin. The Missouri Saints did petition the governor, reviewing for him the breakdown of law and order in Jackson County and requesting "a sufficient number of troops, who, with us, may be empowered to defend our rights, that we may sue for damages for the loss of property . . . that the law of the land may not be defiled . . . but peace be restored."[1] The governor's response was one of bureaucratic evasion. He refused to send any troops; rather, he encouraged the Saints to apply to their local officials, many of whom were members of the mob, for justice: "I would advise you to make a trial of the efficacy of the laws. The judge of your circuit is a conservator of the peace. . . . [O]btain a warrant, let it be placed in the hands of the proper officer. . . . [T]he law is open to redress; I cannot permit myself to doubt that the courts will be open to you, nor [believe] that you will find difficulty in procuring legal advocates to sue for damages therein."[2] Accordingly, on 30 October 1833, the Saints in

Independence retained the firm of Wood, Reese, Doniphan and Atchison to pursue their case in the local courts. Within hours the mob was aware of this action and interpreted it as a repudiation by the Saints of their illegally coerced promise to leave Jackson County by January 1 and as a decision to remain and pursue their civil rights instead. The very next day—fittingly enough, Halloween, 31 October 1833—the infuriated mobbers descended again upon the Missouri Saints.

For the next two weeks, mobs attacked the Saints' homes and farms between Independence and the Indian Territory and especially along the Big Blue River, west of Independence, virtually unhindered by any civil authority. On 5 November Lieutenant Governor Lilburn Boggs did call out a militia with the stated purpose of disarming both sides in the fighting, but since Colonel Thomas Pitcher and most of this militia favored the mob, the guns of only the Mormons were actually collected. This left the Saints defenseless and with no recourse but to flee for their lives from an armed enemy unopposed by any state or local authority. By mid-November twelve hundred Saints were scattered on the prairies or across the Missouri River in Clay, Van Buren, and other counties. More than two hundred homes were burned and an estimated $175,000 in damages inflicted upon the Missouri Saints. There were dead and wounded on both sides during the first days of the fighting, but more Saints died during the hard winter that followed when they huddled dispossessed in northern Missouri.[3]

Joseph Smith and the Kirtland Saints received several incomplete accounts of the expulsion of the Saints from Jackson County between 25 November, when Elders Hyde and Gould returned to Kirtland, and 10 December, when the full story reached them from Bishop Partridge and the brethren in Clay County, Missouri. Joseph grieved, "Oh my brethren! my brethren. . . . [W]ould that I had been with you, to have shared your fate. Oh my God, what shall I do in such a trial as this!"[4] During that time, many Kirtland Saints agonized over the unknown fates of friends and loved ones.

Oliver Cowdery, for example, did not know whether his wife, Elizabeth, whom he had left behind in Jackson County, was dead or alive or to where she might have fled. In addition, those Saints who had fled Jackson County south to Van Buren County in November were driven out by the residents of that county again in December.[5]

And yet, although he apparently had not expected so complete and so sudden a disaster, these things were not a total surprise to the Prophet Joseph because, collectively speaking, the Saints in Jackson County had not been obeying the commandments the Lord had given them. Many of the Saints in Missouri had gone there in violation of the strict commandments of God concerning consecration and stewardship.[6] Many of the Missouri Saints were not keeping the special covenant of sacredness entered into when the land of Zion was dedicated in 1831.[7] On 27 November 1832, a year before the expulsion, Joseph again warned the leaders in Zion that the principles of consecration were not being properly implemented there and that those Saints who had moved to Zion contrary to commandment and who were seeking an inheritance without consecration should not be enrolled on Church records there.[8] On 11 January 1833, ten months before the expulsion, Joseph wrote again to W. W. Phelps, "[I]f Zion will not purify herself, so as to be approved of in all things, in His sight, He will seek another people . . . and they who will not hear His voice, must expect to feel His wrath. Let me say to you, seek to purify yourselves, and also all the inhabitants of Zion, lest the Lord's anger be kindled to fierceness. Repent, repent, is the voice of God to Zion; . . . hear the warning voice of God, lest Zion fall, and the Lord sware in His wrath the inhabitants of Zion shall not enter into His rest. . . . This from your brother who trembles for Zion and for the wrath of heaven, which awaits her if she repent not."[9] In addition, many individuals in Zion, including Church leaders, had to be reproved for their hard feelings and disobedience in the years before the expulsion.[10]

Finally, in August 1833, the Lord had warned Zion directly

and specifically one more time: "But if she observe not to do whatsoever I have commanded her, I will visit her according to all her works, with sore affliction, with pestilence, with plague, with sword, with vengeance, and with devouring fire" (D&C 97:26). In a letter written on 10 December 1833, shortly after their expulsion from Zion, Joseph spoke to the Missouri Saints: "I have always expected that Zion would suffer some affliction, from what I could learn from the commandments which have been given. . . . [B]ut how many will be the days of her purification, tribulation, and affliction, the Lord has kept hid from my eyes. . . . Now, there are two things of which I am ignorant. . . . Why God has suffered so great a calamity to come upon Zion . . . and . . . by what means He will return her back to her inheritance."[11] Thus, while Joseph had been expecting some kind of affliction to befall Zion for its imperfections, the sudden and complete loss of all LDS holdings in Independence and Jackson County left Joseph and the Church desolated and with many unanswered questions about the future of Zion and the suffering of her people. On 16 December 1833, many of those questions were answered for the Prophet in a revelation received in Kirtland and now known as Doctrine and Covenants 101.[12] Additional information and answers to questions on the topic of Zion would come to the Prophet and the Saints in Doctrine and Covenants 103 and 105.

COMMENTARY

1. The land of their inheritance. Every faithful member of the Church, every faithful Latter-day Saint, as the physical or spiritual seed of Abraham, has a right by lineage and by covenant under the law of consecration to a physical inheritance in a physical Zion, which will be established upon the earth in the latter days (see Galatians 3:7–9; Abraham 2:6, 9–11; Genesis 49:22–26; D&C 38:18–20; 52:2, 42; 85:3).[13]

2. I, the Lord, have suffered the affliction to come upon

them. The Lord allows the wicked of the world to afflict his people when they sin (see Isaiah 7:17–20; 8:6–8). The Assyrians, the Babylonians, the Greeks, the Romans, the Lamanites, the Missourians—though usually wicked themselves and ripening for their own destruction—have all been permitted at times by God to scourge and afflict his people and purify them of their disobedience. However, this does not render the wicked any less guilty or accountable for their sins against disobedient Israel, for which, in time, they will pay the uttermost farthing.

2. In consequence of their transgressions. Responsibility for the loss of Zion rested collectively upon the Saints who inhabited that land. While there were many righteous exceptions among them, and while even the sins of the many were not all that terrible by the world's standards, Zion cannot be established by the righteousness of a few individuals within the Church but must be established by the righteousness of the Church collectively. The unfaithfulness of a few can prevent the establishment of Zion by the many. A Zion society is not one of *almost* one heart or with only a *few* rich or poor among them, but a society of *one* heart with *no* rich or poor among them (see Moses 7:18; D&C 97:21). If only a certain percentage of the Saints are faithful, then the remainder must either repent, or be tried and plagued until the unrepentant are purged out through afflictions—or else Zion cannot be established.

3. I will own them. That is, I will claim them as my own.

3. My jewels. See Commentary on Doctrine and Covenants 60:4.

4. Chastened and tried, even as Abraham. Abraham was not a wicked man; neither were the Saints in Missouri, by the standards of the world, a wicked people. However, they were not sufficiently pure collectively to establish the holy Zion of God. Over and over again, the Lord has stated his intent of testing and trying his people (see D&C 58:4; 95:1; 98:12; 136:31), so it should not come as a surprise to the Saints when those tests and trials arrive. When such trials are so difficult as to make God himself seem unjust, or even to have broken his promises and betrayed his covenant with the Saints, then the seriousness of the test approaches that of Abraham who was commanded—as a test of his faithfulness—to slay his son Isaac (see Genesis 22:1–19).

The Prophet Joseph further explained the principle of an "Abrahamic test" in these words: "For a man to lay down his all—his character and reputation, his honor and applause, his good name among men, his houses, his lands, his brothers and sisters, his wife and children, and even his own life also, counting all things but filth and dross for the excellency of the knowledge of Jesus Christ [compare Philippians 3:8–9]–requires more than mere belief or supposition that he is doing the will of God. . . .

"Let us here observe that a religion that does not require the sacrifice of all things never has power sufficient to produce the faith necessary unto life and salvation. For from the first existence of man, the faith necessary unto the enjoyment of life and salvation never could be obtained without the sacrifice of all earthly things. It is through this sacrifice, and this only, that God has ordained that men should enjoy eternal life.

"It is vain for persons to fancy to themselves that they are heirs with those, or can be heirs with them, who have offered their all in sacrifice, and by this means obtained faith in God and favor with him so as to obtain eternal life, unless they in like manner offer unto him the same sacrifice and through that offering obtain the knowledge that they are accepted of him."[14]

5. Endure chastening. To continue trusting in God even when he seems to have abandoned you is to "endure chastening" and pass the test of Abraham. The effect on *individuals* who do this is the same as it was on Abraham: it sanctifies them or makes them holy and pure. The effect on the Saints *collectively* who do this is to weed out from their number those who will only serve or trust God when he is good to them and who cannot, therefore, be sanctified—who cannot be counted on in all times, and in all places, and in all circumstances. After the trials are over, the remaining Saints may be fewer in number, but they will also have been sanctified collectively by their endurance of the Lord's chastening, whereas the less faithful will have departed. Thus, when the Lord chastens his Saints, and at some point he always will, the afflicted then self-select for or against his kingdom either by humbly enduring his chastening or by becoming offended at it and leaving.

6. **There were jarrings, and contentions, and envyings.** The list of failings here reveals once again that the Missouri Saints were not a wicked people. There are no murders, no robberies, no assaults listed here, none of those sins that might be considered "the big ones." In a modern ward, such things as "jarrings, and contentions, and envyings" might be written off as everyday personal differences between otherwise faithful members, or as simple personality conflicts. "Lustful and covetous desires" might seem to be minor difficulties in controlling one's personal thoughts, especially where such thoughts are kept internally and are never acted upon. However, while such personal and internal flaws might be tolerated while the Church is "in the wilderness," so to speak, establishing the physical Zion of God requires that we be of one heart and one mind—no backbiting, no bickering (see D&C 38:24–27). Those of us with "difficult personalities" must repent and smooth down our rough edges, and those with private mental sins must disown them and clean them out if ever we are to establish a Zion. But, beyond this, we must eliminate these same internal sins even to establish a spiritual Zion in ourselves or in our homes and wards, "for this is Zion—THE PURE IN HEART" (D&C 97:21). Such minor sins as jarring, contention, envy, and inappropriate desires are cardiac impurities of a degree sufficient to pollute the Saints, destroy their unity, and put Zion out of their reach.

7. **They were slow to hearken.** By November 1833, the Saints in Missouri had had more than two years since the dedication of the temple site in Independence to make progress toward the establishment of Zion. In that time, they had been relatively free from persecution and had grown to a viable community of

over twelve hundred persons who very likely had as many or more combined resources than the Kirtland Saints. And yet, the specific covenant made at the dedication of the land was not kept, the commandments to purify their internal thoughts and desires were not obeyed, the principles of consecration and stewardship were not universally observed, and as of November 1833 not a single step had been taken toward construction of the temple or even toward preparation of the proposed temple site. Specifically and directly commanded in August 1833 to begin construction of the Independence Temple, the Missouri Saints neglected to do so for fear of antagonizing the Jackson County mobs. Having collectively been "slow to hearken unto the voice of the Lord" for more than two years, the Saints find the Lord was in no hurry to answer their prayers when they desperately needed his help. They had taken their personal relationships with God for granted.

8. In the day of their peace . . . in the day of their trouble. It seems to be a natural human failing to credit ourselves for our blessings in good times and to blame God for our afflictions in bad times. But this is a form of spiritual hypocrisy. All covenants—contracts with conditions laid upon both parties—are reciprocal; to be valid, they must bind all parties in both good times and in bad. Covenant promises can only be claimed by those who keep their covenant obligations. Therefore, we have no more rightful claim upon God for help in our times of trouble than he has received obedience and faithfulness from us in our times of peace, although he is often more merciful in this regard than we have any right to expect (see v. 9).

9. My bowels are filled with compassion. Webster's 1828 *American Dictionary,* aside from being "entrails . . . of man," also defines "bowels" as "the heart," "the interior part of anything," or "the seat of pity or kindness; hence, tenderness, compassion" when used in a scriptural sense.

9. I will not utterly cast them off. Though Zion has been chastened and the immediate plans of the Saints have been frustrated, the Saints have not been rejected as God's people, and God has not canceled his long-term plans for the physical Zion (see Ether 13:2–6). In his own time, all his intentions and commandments for Zion will be fulfilled sometime in this dispensation by faithful Latter-day Saints.

9. In the day of wrath I will remember mercy. In the short term, this statement could refer to the plight of the Missouri Saints, who were suffering a day of wrath (although D&C 98:22 is directed more to the Kirtland Saints than to the Missouri Saints) but whom the Lord would bless in times to come. More likely, however, this is a reference to the Lord's day of wrath before his second coming (see D&C 87:5–8; 97:22–25), when the Saints as a body will be shown mercy and be spared the fate of the nations through their establishment of Zion.

10. The decree hath gone forth by a former commandment. The "former commandment" referred to is apparently Doctrine and Covenants 35:14, "I will let fall the sword in their behalf, and by the fire of mine indignation will I preserve them."

11. Mine indignation . . . upon all nations. Compare with Doctrine and Covenants 87:2–3, 6. The term *measured* implies an appropriately gauged portion or a quantity with distinct limits and thus only a partial judgment of the world. But "without measure" tells us that the punishment to come won't be partial or parceled out a little here and a little there; rather, it will come like Noah's flood with unlimited and overwhelming power to make a full and complete end of all nations.

11. When the cup of their iniquity is full. Many contemporary Saints like to decry how wicked the world is becoming, and surely it is becoming more wicked all the time. However, by the standards of those societies whom the Lord has destroyed "when the cup of their iniquity is full," many areas with large numbers of Saints are not quite there yet. Good examples of what a society whose cup of iniquity is full can be found in 3 Nephi in the generation before the Savior's visit to the New World, or in ancient Jerusalem just before Lehi left, or again in Jerusalem in the generation after the death of the Savior (see also Helaman 13:14, 24).

12. And in that day. That is, in the day when the Lord comes to take vengeance upon the nations of the world.

12. All who are found upon the watch-tower . . . all mine Israel. In an ancient city, the tower was the strongest and most impregnable fortress in times of attack. It also gave the inhabitants of a city a commanding view of the surrounding territory and of the approach and tactics of their enemies. When the Saints are righteous, the Lord himself is their high tower, that is, their defense and their early warning system of approaching enemies (see D&C 97:20). In Doctrine and Covenants 101, the tower also seems to be connected with the temple of the Lord, and the Lord's true Israel are those who have obeyed him in building a temple and are protected by having received its ordinances. Had the temple in Zion been built in a timely manner, the Missouri Saints would have seen in advance the designs of their enemies and could have taken preventive measures to avoid the loss of the land (see v. 54).

13. And they that have been scattered shall be gathered. In the immediate circumstances, this might refer to those Saints who have been scattered onto the plains and into other counties in Missouri, and surely modern Israel would be, and will be, gathered together again. But in the long term, this verse also refers to the great latter-day work of gathering together from among every nation, kindred, tongue, and people *all* the dispersed of Israel, *all* the children of Abraham, which we will be best equipped to do after the establishment of the physical Zion when the rest of the world is in chaos and turmoil.

14. And they who have mourned. A repetition of the promise made in the Sermon on the Mount (see Matthew 5:4). Accepting the gospel offers the individual no protection against grief and mourning, for these are the common lot of mortality.[15] The promise is that the inevitable comfort of the Lord will more than compensate the faithful for all the sufferings and mourning imposed upon them in mortality.

15. They who have given their lives . . . shall be crowned. The promise here appears to allude to Revelation 2:10, "Be thou faithful unto death, and I will give thee a crown of life."

16. Let your hearts be comforted concerning Zion. Unlike Joseph and the Saints, God was not surprised by the loss of Jackson County. Neither did the immediate loss of Zion cause God to change his plans. Though he continually gives his Saints opportunities to succeed or fail, according to their faithfulness, his own plans and designs are never disappointed, for he knows the end from the beginning, and he is never surprised or caught unprepared. The loss of Zion was not a failure on God's part, but the failure of his people to keep their covenants. The disappointed Saints must now take refuge in the knowledge that God is still in charge, that he has prepared all things from the beginning, and that his plans have not been thwarted—though the Saints have lost their opportunity for a season.

16. Be still and know that I am God. This is an allusion to verse 10 of Psalm 46, which begins, "God is our refuge and strength, a very present help in trouble." In the context of the loss of Zion, the entire psalm should be read, for it is a reassurance that God has power over all of nature and over all the enemies of Israel, and the whole psalm provides exactly the divine reassurance needed by the Saints who had been driven out of Zion by their enemies. The exact sense of "be still" in Psalm 46 could be translated as "let it go" or even "stand back" and leave things to God.

17. Zion shall not be moved. Regardless of the short-term or intermediate events of history, or to where the body of the Saints may eventually be driven, the center stake of Zion is, was, and ever shall be, Independence, Missouri. Though her stakes may spread abroad and even fill the entire American continent, there is no other center place (see v. 20).[16]

18. They that remain, and are pure in heart, shall return.

One way in which the Lord allows the Saints to exercise their faith in him is by not revealing his timetable for the fulfillment of his prophecies. In the Lord's own time, Saints of this dispensation who are pure in heart—for Zion is the pure in heart—will return to Jackson County and establish a physical Zion. However, it is possible that the phrase "they and their children" (v. 18) should cause us to think in terms of generations rather than in terms of months or years before this event takes place.

18. To build up the waste places of Zion. While it is true that the generation in Missouri that persecuted the Saints suffered some of the worst devastations of the Civil War, the wasting of Zion referred to here is likely that of the last days, when the scourge of the Lord will descend upon the Gentiles and make a full end of all nations (see vv. 9–13 and Commentary). Only then will the Saints return to reclaim the lands they once possessed and which were taken from them, and there will be no one left in those waste places to oppose them or to interfere. Referring to this very passage, Elder Orson Hyde commented: "The scripture says, that in the last days His people will go forth and build up the waste places of Zion. But they must first be made desolate, before they can be called 'the waste places of Zion.' Then the hands of the Saints will be required to build them up."[17]

20. There is none other place appointed. One of the immediate problems faced by the Prophet in December 1833 was a rumor spreading among some of the Saints that Zion extended as far east as Ohio, and that Zion could therefore be established just as well by settling in Ohio as by trying to carve it out of the frontier.[18] Although Joseph had already acted to correct this notion, here the Lord himself makes it absolutely clear. When, in the due time of the Lord, the physical and political latter-day Zion is finally established, the center place will be Independence, Missouri. Zion's stakes may spread abroad from there, but there will never be another center place.

21. When there is no more room for them. The commonly held notion that at some future time *all* faithful Latter-day Saints will be called to go to Jackson County, Missouri, is probably incorrect. Surely the time has already passed when all the faithful Saints could fit in such a small space. From the beginning of this dispensation, the Lord has allowed for stakes of Zion to be built in addition to the center place in Independence, Missouri. These are extensions of Zion inhabited by the pure in heart and connected to the center place just as a tent stake is connected to the center post of a tent and is, therefore, part of the tent. Just as a tent would become unstable if all its stakes were uprooted and placed around the center pole, so Zion would not thrive if all her stakes were moved into one confined, central place. When the center place of Zion is finally established and built up, it will be strengthened by strong cords attached to many stakes in many places that will already have been established and will contribute to her greatness and her glory.

21. For the curtains. Besides holding the center pole steady, tent stakes also keep the tent walls, or "curtains," firm against the wind or other agitations.

22. Should gather together and stand in holy places. The gathering of the Saints of God has been a theme of the gospel since the days of Adam and the Zion of Enoch (see Moses 7:18–21). The ultimate gathering of the Saints will take place at the second coming of the Savior when he will gather to himself from off of the earth both the righteous dead and the righteous living. While the righteous are gathered to the Savior at his coming, the earth will be cleansed by fire of all wickedness and receive its paradisiacal or terrestrial glory (see D&C 45:45–50; 88:96–99; Articles of Faith 1:10; 1 Thessalonians 4:15–17). Until that ultimate gathering, however, the Saints are commanded to gather themselves together and stand in holy places (see D&C 87:8 and Commentary). This gathering need not be in Jackson County, Missouri, or in Salt Lake City, Utah. It can be in one of the many wards and stakes of Zion that have been or will be established before his coming. The great key to understanding this verse is remembering that Zion is the pure in heart (see D&C 97:21).

Therefore, wherever the pure in heart have gathered together to call on the name of the Lord is Zion and is a holy place. It is the pure in heart who make a place Zion and holy, and not the other way around. Otherwise—if the *place* could sanctify the *people*—the Saints would never have lost Zion in 1833.

23. Prepare for the revelation which is to come. The coming revelation is the second coming of Christ when his presence will be revealed to all who live upon the earth at the beginning of his millennial reign. The brightness and glory of his countenance will glorify the righteous who have prepared for his coming by establishing and gathering to Zion, and it will incinerate the wicked who are caught unprepared in their sins. Preparations for the Savior's coming have already begun. According to President Ezra Taft Benson, "There is a real sifting going on in the Church, and it is going to become more pronounced with the passing of time. It will sift the wheat from the tares, because we face some difficult days, the like of which we have never experienced in our lives. And those days are going to require faith and testimony and family unity, the like of which we have never had."[19]

23. The veil of the covering of my temple, in my tabernacle. The language here is difficult but seems to mean the veil that shields the earth from the full glory of the resurrected body of Christ (his temple) within the universe he has created (his tabernacle) and which contains all things both human and divine—thus creating the need for a separating veil between them. As things now stand, there is a veil which separates and protects the realm of the human from the realm of the divine within the universe and presently shields the earth from the full glory of the resurrected Son of God. At his second coming that shield, or veil, shall be removed and all humanity, prepared or not, will be exposed to the full brightness of his glory (see D&C 88:95; Revelation 6:14; Acts 1:9–11). While God and his angels have often passed through the veil in their great redeeming work, on rare occasions and with great faith this protecting veil has also been approached and even pierced by faithful seers from the human side (see, for example, Ether 3:6, 19–20).

24. And every corruptible thing. "Corruptible" refers to anything that is eventually going to oxidize, spoil, rot, or decay. At the second coming of the Savior, when the earth is raised from a telestial to a terrestrial state (see Articles of Faith 1:10), all living things will fall into two categories, those that are capable of abiding at least a terrestrial glory, and hence will be preserved incorruptible in that paradisaical state, and those that cannot receive such glory and will be consumed by it as corruptible material. For human beings, the criterion for judgment will be personal righteousness. It has not been revealed what the criteria will be for other living creatures or even whether they will be judged individually or perhaps as classes or species, but *all* living things will be judged and will be brought into a new ecological balance and a new ecological order.

25. All things shall become new. Not only will there be a new biology for this earth during the Millennium (see v. 24), but there will also be a new chemistry and a new physics. Indeed, the earth will become again as it was in the time of Eden, without the intervening changes caused by the Fall or the Flood. The energy involved in raising this present telestial world back to a terrestrial sphere will cause the very elements to melt and to reform in ways that will sustain the terrestrial physical laws of Christ's millennial kingdom. As the earth was once baptized in water, it will then be baptized by fire and be "born again." This should not be confused with the further change that will take place at the end of the Millennium when the earth undergoes a process analogous to death and resurrection to become a celestial sphere (see Revelation 21:1; D&C 77:1; 88:18–20, 25–26).

26. The enmity of all flesh, shall cease. At the second coming of the Lord, not only will there be a new biology, chemistry, and physics, but there will be a drastically new world ecology as well. Cats will no longer kill mice just because they are mice; dogs will no longer chase cats just because they are cats. Nothing that remains upon the paradisaical earth will harm anything else—ever. The limited details we have regarding these changes are found in Isaiah, where we are told that the wolf will lie down with the lamb, and the lion will eat straw like the ox (see D&C 11:6–7). But, the physical laws of biology and ecology in a terrestrial world are clearly different than they are in this present telestial world. For human beings, verse 26 means that anyone who continues to hold a grudge or to hate another person for any reason—that is, whose enmity will *not* cease—is not worthy of the new terrestrial, millennial kingdom. The wicked will have been incinerated already, and there ought not to be "jarrings, and contentions" (v. 6) between the righteous Saints of God. And even among the terrestrial mortals who remain, who are the honorable men and women of the earth (see D&C 76:75), there ought not to be malice or evil intent in any degree.

27. Whatsoever a man shall ask, it shall be given him. Because all those who inhabit the millennial kingdom will be the terrestrial and celestial righteous, their desires will also be righteous and can be granted without fear of any hidden malicious or evil intent.

28. Satan shall not have power to tempt any man. Compare Doctrine and Covenants 88:110–15 and 84:100 and Commentary; also Revelation 20:2–3; 1 Nephi 22:26. Satan will be bound and divested of power in two ways: (1) The righteous who remain upon the earth after the second coming of the Savior will pay no heed to him. (2) Satan will actually be bound by the priesthood power of the Savior himself so that he cannot act in his accustomed ways

29–31. There is no death. There will continue to be mortals upon the earth throughout the Millennium. These mortals shall continue to have mortal children, grandchildren, and so forth. But no mortal child born during the Millennium will die prematurely or tragically. No parents will outlive their children. And during the Millennium when such mortals reach their full age and pass on, there will be no funerals in the present sense, for in the twinkling, or blink, of an eye, the covenant faithful will change from mortality to their resurrected glory and be caught up to rest in the Lord.

There will also be those upon the earth who are "honorable men" (D&C 76:75) but who will not accept the testimony of Jesus while in the flesh or who were not sufficiently valiant in that testimony to merit celestial glory (see D&C 76:74–79). These terrestrial beings are still worthy of the resurrection of the just (see D&C 45:54) when their one hundred years are up, but their curse (see Isaiah 65:20) lies in the fact that they will be changed from mortality to terrestrial resurrection rather than receiving the celestial resurrection that might have been theirs had they accepted the gospel and its covenant obligations. So those who live into the Millennium will pass from mortality to resurrection without experiencing death as we know it, burial, or separation of their spirits from their bodies.[20] In fact, from the time of the Second Coming onward, the spirit prison will be emptied of those who are worthy of the resurrection of the just (a terrestrial or a celestial resurrection), and during Christ's millennial reign that great prison will be inhabited only by the spirits of the wicked who are destined to come forth at the last resurrection, the resurrection of the unjust at the end of the Millennium, to inherit telestial glory or to become sons of perdition (see D&C 43:18; 76:84–85; 88:101; Revelation 20:5).

30. His life shall be as the age of a tree. According to the prophet Isaiah in a similar prophecy concerning millennial conditions (see Isaiah 65:20, 22), the age of a tree is to be understood as one hundred years.[21]

31. Changed in the twinkling of an eye. See Commentary on Doctrine and Covenants 43:32.

31. His rest shall be glorious. Ultimately, to enter into the rest of the Lord refers to reaching the end of our probationary state when the test of mortality is over and the struggles of life are done. For some, this would occur at death. For others, this would normally include both phases of our probation—both our mortal life and our time in the spirit world before our resurrection.[22]

32–34. He shall reveal all things. Oh what a marvelous

promise! No matter what the scientific specialty or historical interest, the Savior will answer all questions when he comes. What is the correct relationship of the entire human family from Adam and Eve to the present? How old is the earth? How was it created? How are stars made? Why were there dinosaurs? How did the Egyptians build the pyramids? During the Savior's millennial reign, knowledge of all kinds and of all things will flood the earth, and every question about the whole of this creation will be answered.

35. Called to lay down their lives for my sake. All those who die faithful to the gospel covenant before the Millennium will miss out on nothing. They will be resurrected at the second coming of the Lord and will receive the same blessings of knowledge and of celestial glory as those who are "changed in the twinkling of an eye" (v. 31) during the Millennium (see v. 22 and Commentary).

36. In this world your joy is not full, but in me your joy is full. Life is not fair, and there is as much misery in the world as there is joy. Many people experience as much or even more pain in this life than they do happiness. This is one of the unavoidable consequences of living in a fallen world. No one in this life is truly happy all of the time, and despite what the television may tell us, true bliss is a rare and fleeting commodity. Joy is rare and never entirely full for anyone in this life. It usually comes only after a long time and considerable effort or sacrifice. Nevertheless, it is comforting to know that if we think upon the single most exquisite and glorious moment of our lives, it represents only a fleeting fraction of that ever flowing fulness of joy that awaits the faithful in the arms of their Lord.

37. Care for the soul. This verse and others like it are usually understood to mean we ought to care for the life of the spirit rather than the life of the flesh. But since the last few verses have dealt with the resurrection, it is probable that "soul" in this case should be understood as the resurrected self composed of spirit and body, in the sense used in Doctrine and Covenants 88:15, rather than simply as spirit. In other words, we ought to consider our eternal resurrected self rather than our transitory mortal self in making moral choices (see D&C 46:7).

38. In patience ye may possess your souls. The statement likely alludes to Luke 21:19 where the word "patience" in Greek is *hupomone,* which can mean "patience" and is so translated in the King James Version, but probably would better be rendered "endurance" or "steadfastness." The familiar phrase "the patience of Job" (James 5:11) is another place in the King James translation where the Greek *hupomone* was clearly meant to refer to Job's powers of endurance rather than to his patiently waiting for anything.

39–40. They are accounted as the salt of the earth and the savor of men. Savor is flavor or seasoning. Entering the gospel covenant lays upon each member the obligation of making a positive change in the lives of those around them just as salt improves the flavor of most foods in cooking. A little bit of salt can greatly improve the quality and flavor of a lot of food, and just as a little salt goes a long way in seasoning and preserving food, so the influence of individual Saints for good is greater than they know if they will only keep their covenants, live the gospel, and serve as a light to the world. Another term for being the "savor of men" is serving as a witness for God at all times and in all things and in all places.

In ancient times, the principal purposes of salt were for seasoning and preserving food. If salt should somehow lose its ability to do those things, if it should lose its salt-ness, it would become worthless and be thrown out in the street with everything else discarded as worthless or unclean. Village streets and alleys were the collective dumps and sewers where all such refuse was trodden into the mud by pedestrian and other traffic.

41. The children of Zion . . . were found transgressors. The language here, following hard on verses 39–40, would seem to indicate that the Missouri Saints who had recently been driven out of Jackson County had collectively been judged as salt that had lost its savor. This apparently applied to a large number of the

Missouri Saints, perhaps even to a majority of them, though certainly not to all.

42. He that exalteth . . . he that abaseth. Exalting oneself means arrogantly placing oneself above others in value and importance. Abasing oneself is to be humble in considering others to be of equal value and importance as oneself.

43–64. A parable . . . concerning the redemption of Zion. Parables by their very nature can often be interpreted on more than one level, but it seems that on at least one level the parable here might be interpreted as follows.[23] The nobleman is the Lord Jesus Christ. The choice spot of land in the Lord's vineyard is Zion in Jackson County, Missouri. The twelve olive trees represent the settlements of the Saints in Zion, twelve being the number associated with Israel and with the Church. The watchmen are the leaders of the Saints in Missouri, and the tower is the temple they were commanded to build and whose site had been dedicated more than two years earlier. The watchman on the tower would be the leader of the Church in Missouri.

Beyond laying out stones and logs to mark the foundation site, however, the Saints in Zion made no effort to build the temple that would have protected them in times of trial. Instead, they attempted to establish Zion without building a temple, and they put their resources into other enterprises instead. This led first to arguing, then to laziness, and then to breaking the commandments (see v. 50). At that point, the Lord allowed the mobs to descend upon them, first in July and then again in November 1833, and the Missouri Saints, whose watchmen were seemingly asleep on duty (see v. 53), found themselves defenseless and unprepared.

55–62. Take all the strength of mine house . . . and redeem my vineyard. This part of the parable refers to Zion's Camp, which the Lord would explain to the Prophet Joseph more fully in Doctrine and Covenants 103 and 105. Zion's Camp was an attempt by Joseph Smith and about two hundred brethren from the eastern churches to redeem Zion by force of arms. For several reasons that will be discussed in the Commentary on

Doctrine and Covenants 105, that attempt did not achieve its stated goal of regaining possession of the Jackson County properties. However, it is crucial to note that even at this early date when the servant in this parable (Joseph Smith) asks the Lord, "When shall these things be?" (v. 59), he is only vaguely answered, "When I will" (v. 60). We are then told that "*after many days* all things were fulfilled" (v. 62; emphasis added). Thus, it appears that the parable already anticipated a long interval between Zion's Camp and the eventual redemption of Zion.

63–66. Wisdom in me concerning all the churches. The Lord now relates his will to the Prophet concerning the continuing latter-day gathering of the Saints as alluded to in the parable of the wheat and the tares (see Matthew 13:24–30, 36–43; Commentary on D&C 86).

67. Continue to gather together unto the places which I have appointed. While Jackson County in Missouri has always been the center stake of Zion, there were at this time, as there continue to be now, other designated gathering places for the Saints, such as Kirtland in the East and Clay County, Missouri, in the West.

68. Let not your gathering be in haste . . . but let all things be prepared. One reason for the loss of Zion in Jackson County was the disobedience of the Saints regarding this very commandment.[24] The numbers of the Saints in Jackson County rose so rapidly that the original settlers were greatly alarmed, and social and economic relations were strained beyond their limits.

70. Purchase all the lands. Once again, the Lord clearly commands that Zion *must* be purchased with money. Despite the foolish, loose talk of some, there would not at this time be any conquest in Missouri like that of Joshua taking the promised land from the Canaanites (see D&C 105:28–32). If there is bloodshed over Zion at *this* time, the Saints will lose the battle, will be driven from place to place, and few of them will stand to receive an inheritance in Zion (see D&C 63:27–31).

71–74. In Jackson county, and in the counties round

about. The Lord wants the Saints to continue buying land in Missouri as close to the center stake of Zion as possible. As for the properties controlled by the mobs, the Church is to let that issue be resolved by the Lord for the present. If this is done in a slow and controlled manner, the eastern churches can purchase lands near Zion that will lead toward the eventual redemption and establishment of Zion itself (see D&C 105:28–32).

75. There is even now . . . sufficient . . . to redeem Zion. The Church has perhaps never lacked the physical resources to establish Zion; it has only lacked the collective commitment and righteousness to establish Zion. In 1833, as now, if all the Saints in all the wards and branches of the Church were personally obedient to the will of the Lord and collectively dedicated to establishing Zion, there would be more than sufficient resources available to accomplish the task.

76–77. Importune for redress . . . according to the laws and constitution of the people. The dispossessed Jackson County Saints are instructed to exhaust every legal avenue, successful or not, in seeking to regain their lost properties, retain their rights, and be fairly compensated for their losses. The Saints obeyed these instructions and pursued their rights unsuccessfully under the laws of Missouri and of the United States for years to come.[25]

77. For the rights and protection of all flesh. See Commentary on Doctrine and Covenants 98:4–7.

78. That every man may act . . . [and] be accountable. The enjoyment of political freedom as guaranteed by the Constitution allows men the political freedom to express their moral agency to the fullest degree of any political system on earth and therefore to be accountable for their choices to the fullest degree, since their actions are freely chosen and not coerced by government. The greater the political freedom, the greater the moral accountability. In this case, the laws of Missouri and the Constitution of the United States to which the Saints applied, and which were ignored by their enemies, as God knew they would be, increased the guilt and accountability of those enemies before the coming judgments of God.

79. Bondage. The bondage described here may be of at least two types: either governmental tyranny over population groups or personal tyranny over individual slaves.

80. I established the Constitution of this land. See Commentary on Doctrine and Covenants 98:4–7. President Gordon B. Hinckley stated: "There were men whom the God of Heaven had raised up who saw with a greater vision and dreamed a better and more inspired dream. On May 14, 1787, fifty-five of them met in Philadelphia. . . . there were differences of opinion, sharp and deep, and bitter. But somehow, under the inspiration of the Almighty, there was forged the Constitution of the United States. . . . It is the keystone of our nation. It is my faith and my conviction that it came not alone of the brain and purpose of man, but of the inspiration of God."[26]

81–85. The parable of the woman and the unjust judge. This parable may also be found in Luke 18:1–8. It is encouragement for the Saints to continue seeking redress through legal authorities.

87–88. The governor . . . the president. At this time, the governor of the state of Missouri was Daniel Dunklin. The president of the United States was Andrew Jackson.

89. And in his fury vex the nation. If the Saints cannot receive justice from those appointed to administer justice under the Constitution, then judgment will be poured out upon the nation by the Lord himself. The reference here is, among other things, to the Civil War and is further commented upon in Doctrine and Covenants 105:15.[27]

91. Even in outer darkness. Contemporary usage of the term "outer darkness" in the Church usually reserves it for the fate of perdition after the final judgment. However, it is probably used here also for that awful but temporary state shared by the wicked, the unfaithful, unjust stewards, hypocrites, and unbelievers enumerated in verse 90. In other words, it means that awful hell prepared for the wicked between death and resurrection where they will suffer the inevitable consequences of their sinful behavior before being brought forth in the last resurrection to receive a glory according to their works.[28]

93. That all men may be without excuse. If the Lord knows that the search of the Saints for justice and all of their expensive legal quests and petitions in seeking their constitutional rights will come to nothing, then why does he command them to pursue them? The answer to this question lies in this one verse—that all those who have persecuted the Saints contrary to the laws of man and God may stand without excuse when his judgments are poured out upon them in this life and/or the next.

94. Know that which they have never considered. The reference appears to be an allusion to a messianic passage in Isaiah dealing with the gathering of Israel in the latter days (see Isaiah 52:15). Something no one wise or powerful had considered of any significance, the restored gospel, will prove to be the most significant work of all in the latter days.

95. My strange act. See Commentary on Doctrine and Covenants 95:4. To the world, that The Church of Jesus Christ of Latter-day Saints turns out to be significant—let alone true!—will be too bizarre for words. Yet the strange work of the Lord will make it clear to all where Zion is and where Babylon is, where the righteous are and where the wicked are.

96–99. Contrary to my commandment . . . [to] sell my storehouse. At first it might seem to be to the Saints' advantage to sell the Jackson County properties, and especially the Gilbert and Whitney Store and its resources, for what cash they could get, especially if there was little hope of retrieving those assets anyway. However, these properties and resources were consecrated to the Lord and were sacred. To sell sacred, consecrated, and holy things to the Lord's enemies would involve the Saints in some degree of complicity in their desecration as a matter of principle and would therefore be a grievous sin. It would be better to hold onto a rightful claim that would never be recognized by wicked men than to give up such a claim for money.

100–101. They shall dwell thereon. Even at this point, if the Saints were to be dedicated and faithful, Zion could possibly still be redeemed in their lifetime (see vv. 74–75). However, it is more likely that this promise is meant in a millennial context to be fulfilled in the due time of the Lord.

1. Smith, *History of the Church,* 1:415.
2. Smith, *History of the Church,* 1:424.
3. See Smith, *History of the Church,* 1:426–40; Backman, *Heavens Resound,* 162–74.
4. Smith, *History of Joseph Smith,* 225.
5. See Smith, *History of the Church,* 1:456–57; Backman, *Heavens Resound,* 167.
6. See Commentary on D&C 85:1–3; 58:36, 44; and the excellent summary in Jessee, *Personal Writings,* 284.
7. See Background to D&C 58.
8. See Jessee, *Personal Writings,* 285; Smith, *History of the Church,* 1:298.
9. Smith, *History of the Church,* 1:316, 317; compare Jessee, *Personal Writings,* 292–93.
10. See examples of such rebukes in Smith, *History of the Church,* 1:316–21.
11. Smith, *History of the Church,* 1:453, 454.
12. See Woodford, "Historical Development," 2:1292.
13. See Commentary on D&C 97:18, 31.
14. Cited in Dahl and Tate, eds., *Lectures on Faith in Historical Perspective,* 92–93.
15. See Commentary on D&C 101:4.
16. See Commentary on D&C 97:18.
17. Hyde, *Journal of Discourses,* 10:376.
18. See Smith, *History of the Church,* 1:419.
19. Benson, *Teachings of Ezra Taft Benson,* 107.
20. See Hinckley, *Teachings of Gordon B. Hinckley,* 576; Smith, *Doctrines of Salvation,* 2:300.
21. See Commentary on D&C 63:50–51.
22. See Smith, *History of the Church,* 1:252.
23. See Sperry, *Doctrine and Covenants Compendium,* 520–22.
24. See Commentary on D&C 58:44, 56; 63:24.
25. See, for example, Johnson, ed., *Mormon Redress Petitions.*
26. Hinckley, *Teachings of Gordon B. Hinckley,* 15.
27. See also Background and Commentary on D&C 87:1–3.
28. See Commentary on D&C 76:84–85, 88–89, 103–6.

102

BACKGROUND

During the winter of 1834, while the Saints in Missouri were still in distress at having been driven out of Jackson County and the Kirtland Saints were making preparations to come to their aid, Joseph Smith continued to receive revelation on a number of other topics as well. One of these dealt with the organization of the first high council of the Church in this dispensation. On 12 February 1834, Joseph met with a council of high priests and elders at his home in Kirtland. On the subject of councils, Joseph remarked that "in ancient days councils were conducted with such strict propriety, that no one was allowed to whisper, be weary, leave the room, or get uneasy in the least, until the voice of the Lord, by revelation, or the voice of the council by the Spirit, was obtained, which has not been observed in this Church to the present time. . . . Ask yourselves, brethren, how much you have exercised yourselves in prayer since you heard of this council; and if you are now prepared to sit in council upon the soul of your brother."[1]

Five days later, on 17 February 1834, another council, consisting of high priests, elders, priests, and members, met again at Joseph's home for the purpose of proposing and sustaining twelve high priests to serve as members of the first high council of the Church in the latter days. These twelve would be presided over by the First Presidency of the Church, who also served as the stake presidency in Kirtland. The minutes of that meeting, as recorded by Orson Hyde and Oliver Cowdery, provide the text of Doctrine and Covenants 102. The minutes of the 17 February meeting were corrected by the Prophet and accepted by the council two days later, on 19 February.

On 3 July 1834, the Prophet organized another high council in Clay County, Missouri, with the Presidency of the Church in Missouri as its presidency. "In 1834, these two councils were sufficient to take care of all matters that properly belonged to and should be considered by high councils in the Church. As the Church grew and spread abroad it became necessary for high councils to be organized in each stake of Zion, over which the presidency of stakes presides, and it was no longer necessary for a general high council to sit or be organized, over which the First Presidency of the Church should preside."[2]

It will be observed that in some ways the first high council of the Church prefigured the Quorum of the Twelve Apostles which was organized a year later in February 1835. Once the Quorum of the Twelve was organized, and there were functioning high councils in the stakes of the Church, there was no need for general Churchwide high councils. Nevertheless, Doctrine and Covenants 102 remained as a model of organization and procedure for all future stake high councils. Verses 30 through 32 were added to this revelation by Joseph Smith in the 1835 Doctrine and Covenants after the organization of the Quorum of the Twelve to distinguish the decisions of that quorum from those of the high councils in Kirtland and Missouri.

COMMENTARY

1. A general council. To avoid confusion, it must be remembered that a general council of high priests, priests, and members (see v. 5) had met on this occasion to nominate and sustain twelve high priests and a presidency as a high council. The two bodies should not be confused.

2. For the purpose of settling important difficulties. While a primary purpose of high councils has always been disciplinary hearings, these are not the only matters nor even the majority of the matters a high council may deal with. "Under the direction of the stake presidency, the high council has important executive, legislative, and judicial powers (see D&C 102). Members of the stake high council serve as advisers to the stake presidency on any matter about which the presidency might seek counsel, and they carry out specific assignments. For example, a high councilor may have an assignment to represent the stake presidency, to assist in the training of a new ward bishopric, to attend ward priesthood executive committee meetings and ward council meetings, or to train and advise ward Melchizedek Priesthood quorum leaders."[3]

2. Difficulties which could not be settled by the . . . bishop's council. Today, this function almost always refers to cases involving serious transgression on the part of members. Bishops are the common judges in Israel and will act on all cases of transgression in their wards, with the most difficult cases being referred to the stake presidency and high council for resolution. Only the stake president, presiding over a stake high council, may excommunicate a member holding the Melchizedek Priesthood.

3. To be a standing council for the church. That is, members of the high council.

6. Cannot have power to act without seven. The newly installed high council must have a quorum of seven of its twelve members present in order to conduct business.

8. Whenever any vacancy shall occur. Members of the high council are called by the stake president and sustained by the membership of the stake according to the law of common consent (D&C 26).

9. Appointed by revelation. The underlying truth of the entire Restoration is the divine calling of the Prophet Joseph Smith. It is this calling and that of Joseph's successors that is acknowledged by the voice of the entire Church twice yearly, at each semiannual general conference of the Church. Local authorities, officers, and teachers are similarly sustained at semiannual stake conferences and also at ward conferences.

10. Appointed after the same manner. The President's two counselors are also to be appointed by divine revelation and accepted by sustaining vote.

11. The other presidents have power to preside. While this was true in the original high council of the Church as presided over by the First Presidency, it is not the case today in local high councils presided over by stake presidents. Unless otherwise directed by the First Presidency, the stake president himself must preside over stake high council disciplinary hearings.

12. To cast lots by number. Drawing numbers randomly assures that no human agency can bias the proceedings for or against the accused in a disciplinary council, since no one knows in advance which council members will be appointed to speak or which ones will be appointed to represent the interests of the accused.

13–17. In a disciplinary council meeting, all of the council members are committed to seeing that truth and justice prevail. Toward this end, half of the councilors, those who have randomly drawn even numbers, are charged with defending the rights of the accused. The other half are charged with defending the rights of the Church, or with the aggrieved party or parties. The facts of the case are then presented by one, two, or three pairs of councilors— depending on the degree of difficulty. This is not an adversarial procedure, however. There is no prosecution and no defense. No one argues a case or tries to persuade the council. No one attempts to "win" a verdict. There is only one object, which is to arrive at the truth and to let fairness and justice prevail.

18. A privilege of speaking for themselves. A basic principle of justice in any dispute is that both sides of the case be allowed to speak for themselves freely and without prejudice.

19–22. The president shall give a decision. While the

councilors offer valuable preparation, advice, and deliberation, they do not make the decision of the council. The decision in a disciplinary council lies with the president alone. The councilors then vote to sustain his decision after the fact. Should the high council vote not to sustain the president's decision, the proceedings can be reviewed for possible errors. If errors are found, then a rehearing of the case may be take place. But if there are no substantial errors, the original decision stands, and there is no rehearing provided a simple majority of the council sustains the president in his decision.

23. The president may inquire . . . of the Lord. It should be remembered that in its original context, the president in verse 23 was the Prophet Joseph Smith who was entitled to receive new doctrine for the Church by revelation. In the modern Church, stake presidents are still entitled to receive revelation and inspiration from the Lord concerning matters before the high council, and it is customary for them to retire briefly and seek the Lord's confirmation in prayer before reaching their decision. However, no one but the prophet receives new *doctrine* in the Church today (see D&C 28:2; 43:3–6).

24–29. The high priests, when abroad. The following verses allow for the creation of local high councils in the stakes of the Church as the numbers of high priests and other members shall warrant. These councils will not be general Church councils like that in Kirtland presided over by the President of the Church, nor like the Quorum of the Twelve which will be described in verses 30–32. They are termed "traveling" high councils because they are not central to Kirtland but are "located abroad" (v. 29), not because they move from place to place.

26. A copy of their proceedings. Note in this requirement the continuing growth of central record keeping for the Church. From the beginning, all decisions of disciplinary councils affecting membership were to be forwarded to Church headquarters.

27. They may appeal. The decision of any disciplinary council may be appealed to a higher Church council. The decision of a bishop's council may be appealed to a stake high council, and a stake high council decision may be appealed to the First Presidency. However, the Council of the First Presidency may choose to hear such an appeal or not and is not obligated to hear it (see v. 33).

28. The most difficult cases. While the bishop is the common judge in Israel (see D&C 107:72–74), a stake president can decide to bring any case before the high council, and cases involving Melchizedek Priesthood holders must be heard by the high council.

30–32. The high council . . . and . . . the twelve apostles. These three verses were added by the Prophet Joseph to Doctrine and Covenants 102 for the 1835 edition of the Doctrine and Covenants in order to distinguish the roles of the general high council of the Church from that of the newly formed Quorum of the Twelve Apostles.

---

1. Smith, *History of the Church*, 2:25, 26.
2. Smith, *Church History and Modern Revelation*, 1:480.
3. Ludlow, ed., *Encyclopedia of Mormonism*, 2:586–87.

103

BACKGROUND

Because of their collective failure to become a Zion people, the Latter-day Saints living in Jackson County, Missouri, had been driven from their homes and settlements during November and December 1833, and their properties and possessions had been pillaged and confiscated illegally by mobs.[1] From adjoining counties in Missouri, primarily Clay County, the Saints had tried without success through their lawyers to seek relief through local courts.

Nonetheless, in November 1833, Governor Daniel Dunklin of Missouri led the Saints to believe that the state of Missouri would support them in returning to their homes if they could raise and arm a force sufficiently large to protect themselves from the mobs after their escort of state troops left.[2] He would do this, he later stated, by temporarily making the Mormon volunteers a company of the state militia.[3] The Mormons would have to defend themselves. Consequently, on 12 February 1834, Lyman Wight and Parley P. Pratt left Clay County, Missouri, for Kirtland to explain the situation to the Prophet. They arrived in Kirtland on 22 February and two days later met with Joseph and the high council there, on 24 February.

Two months earlier, on 16 December 1833, the Lord had already let the Prophet Joseph know that an armed force from the eastern churches, "the strength of mine house" (D&C 101:55), would be called upon to go to Zion and redeem the land.[4] Sometime before the Kirtland high council met on 24 February, Joseph received the revelation now known as Doctrine and Covenants 103, which gave specific instructions and authorization for gathering that aforementioned force, which would come to be known as Zion's Camp.[5]

However, before this military campaign could begin, men were sent to the four points of the compass as far away as New England, Canada, Michigan, and the Southern states to collect volunteers, arms, money, and supplies both for Zion's Camp and for the dispossessed Saints in Missouri. Also, this was no vigilante movement. It was Joseph's clear intention to work within the law and in cooperation with the state of Missouri in returning the Jackson County Saints to their homes under guard and in protecting them once they were there. On 1 May 1834, the advanced guard of Zion's Camp set out from Kirtland to await the main body at New Portage, Ohio, which had been designated as the rallying point for the Camp. The main body, led by Joseph Smith, left Kirtland on 5 May, and several other groups met up with the Camp at New Portage or along the course of the nine-hundred-mile march. By the time Zion's Camp reached the Salt River in Missouri, it numbered more than two hundred persons.[6]

COMMENTARY

1. Concerning the salvation and redemption of your brethren. Doctrine and Covenants 103 contains the clear and specific instructions for instituting what was given to the Kirtland Saints earlier only in parable form in Doctrine and Covenants 101.[7]

2. On whom I will pour out my wrath. This has both a specific and a general fulfillment. Specifically, it refers to the coming Civil War and other calamities when the very individuals who drove out the Saints would personally feel the wrath of God in that same generation. More generally, it also refers to the tribulations at the second coming of Christ when all the wicked will feel his wrath "without measure" (see D&C 87:6).

3. That their cup might be full. See Commentary on Doctrine and Covenants 101:93.

4. They did not hearken. See Commentary on Doctrine and Covenants 101:7–8.

5–8. Inasmuch as they hearken. . . . But inasmuch as they keep not my commandments. It is critical to recognize the two contrasting conditions whose opposite consequences are emphasized in these verses. "Inasmuch as" means "if." So, the Lord has decreed *two* possible outcomes, depending upon whether or not his people obey his voice. *If* his people obey (see v. 5), then they shall prevail against their enemies starting immediately (see v. 6), but the decree is *conditioned* upon the Saints' obedience. Of course, the Saints are warned of the other possibility in verse 8. *If* they do *not* obey, then the world will prevail against them. Unfortunately, the Saints at that time collectively chose to meet the second of these two conditions and received the terrible consequences decreed to accompany that choice (see v. 8).

9. They were set to be . . . saviors of men. Jesus Christ is the Savior of all mankind. However, the Savior in his mercy often allows his Saints the opportunity and joy—and therefore the responsibility and obligation—of sharing in his redemptive work and becoming with him "saviours . . . upon mount Zion" (Obadiah 1:21). Although this phrase includes our obligation to perform temple work, nothing in scripture limits it to this application alone. Missionaries who preach the gospel to the living, parents who lovingly raise and teach their children, Saints who serve in the Church, members who light the path and ease the burdens of their neighbors—all these in some degree serve their Lord and are, therefore, his agents as saviors on mount Zion.

10. Salt that has lost its savor. See Commentary on Doctrine and Covenants 101:39–40.

11–14. I have decreed that your brethren . . . shall return. Once again, the promise contained in these verses must be recognized as conditioned upon the obedience of the Saints just as it was in verses 5–8. If the Saints purify themselves, they will establish Zion after much tribulation (see v. 12). If they become polluted, they will be thrown down once again (see v. 14).

11. The waste places of Zion. See Commentary on Doctrine and Covenants 101:18.

12. In a former commandment. The reference is to Doctrine and Covenants 58:4.

15. The redemption of Zion must needs come by power. See Commentary on Doctrine and Covenants 85:7. This prophecy could have either an immediate or a long-term fulfillment. The immediate fulfillment would be the reinstatement of the Missouri Saints upon their lands in Jackson County through the efforts of the armed forces of Zion's Camp in conjunction with the state of Missouri, providing the Saints of that generation hearkened to the voice and commandments of the Lord (see vv. 6, 13). The long-term fulfillment would be the final establishment of Zion when the Lord himself, the "one mighty and strong" (D&C 85:7), would assign the inheritances of the faithful Saints by lot (see v. 20 and Commentary on D&C 85:7).

16. A man . . . like as Moses. Joseph Smith is the latter-day prophet like Moses (see 2 Nephi 3:15, 18–21).[8]

17. The children of Israel, and of the seed of Abraham. Note that here and in the verses following, the emphasis is on the Church's descent from Abraham and Jacob (Israel) rather than from Israel after its fall at Sinai (see vv. 19–20; see also D&C 84:23–27 and Commentary). The restored gospel is not a restoration of Old Testament Israel with its lesser law after its sin at Sinai. Rather, it is a restoration of the Abrahamic covenant as it was handed down to Moses anciently before Israel rejected the higher law and also of its continuation in New Testament Christianity in the meridian of time. Between Moses and Jesus was a period when the fulness of the gospel was available to very few in Israel.

18. Your fathers. This phrase apparently refers to the Patriarchs, as it does in Doctrine and Covenants 2:2, and also to the generation led out of Egypt by the power of God.

19. Mine angel shall go . . . but not my presence. Despite popular belief and Hollywood's representations, the presence of the Lord did not travel with the children of Israel in the wilderness under the banner of the lesser law after their great sin at Sinai (see Exodus 23:20; 33:3). The apostle Paul, relying upon the Greek Septuagint text of Deuteronomy 33:2, plainly states that the law of Moses was delivered to Israel after their sin, not by God but by angels (see Galatians 3:19).

20. And also my presence. Unlike the twelve tribes during their forty years in the wilderness, the Lord promises that his very presence will accompany the Saints of Zion's Camp who go up to redeem Zion *if* they hearken unto his counsel (see v. 5).

21. The man . . . in the parable. That is, Doctrine and Covenants 101:55.

21–22. Send up wise men with their moneys. These two verses specifically command the eastern churches to send men and money to Missouri to purchase and hold on to more land in and around Zion.

24–27. It is clearly the intention of the Lord to act within the law and to purchase any lands upon which the Saints will dwell in Missouri. Also, the Saints will use force of arms only in restoring their brethren to lands which are legally and lawfully their own, bought and paid for with the consecrated funds of the Church. Zion's Camp will be no conquest of other people's lands. Nevertheless, with the approval of the state of Missouri and with state law and the Constitution of the United States on their side, the Saints intended, with the Lord's approval given here, to fight for their God-given rights against mob rule.

25. Ye shall avenge me of mine enemies. The mobs in Missouri had not merely fought against the Saints, they had fought directly against the establishment of Zion and against properties and possessions consecrated to the Lord for the holiest of purposes. In addition, it should be noted that by this time the enemies of the Saints in Missouri had come against them more than three times. Assuming that the approach of Zion's Camp would constitute a warning to the mobs in Missouri, any further attack upon the Saints in that state would, according to Doctrine and Covenants 98:28, justify retaliation according to the principles given the Saints by the Lord.

26. Unto the third and fourth generation. See Commentary on Doctrine and Covenants 98:46.

29–34. Five hundred . . . three hundred . . . one hundred. Parley P. Pratt and Lyman Wight were assigned, with Sidney Rigdon and others, to raise volunteers for Zion's Camp. The goal was five hundred; the minimum, one hundred. Eventually, two hundred people made the march.

37–40. These pairings were for the purpose of recruiting volunteers and funds for Zion's Camp. Sidney Rigdon, for example, participated in the recruitment (see v. 38) but did not make the journey to Missouri.[9]

---

1. See Background to D&C 101 and Commentary on D&C 101:2–8.
2. See Smith, *History of the Church,* 1:444–45.
3. See Parkin, "Latter-day Saint Conflict in Clay County," 244.
4. See Commentary on D&C 101:55–62.
5. See Smith, *History of the Church,* 2:36–39; Kirtland Revelation Book, 108–11.
6. See Ludlow, ed., *Encyclopedia of Mormonism,* 4:1627–29.
7. See Commentary on D&C 101:55–62.
8. See Commentary on D&C 28:2–3.
9. See Smith, *History of the Church,* 2:64.

104

BACKGROUND

Before the Saints from Kirtland and the East could hope to go to the aid of the Missouri Saints in the spring of 1834, the Prophet Joseph Smith had to solve crushing financial problems in the Church. As Joseph wrote to Orson Hyde on 7 April, "[U]nless we can obtain [financial] help, I myself cannot go to Zion, and if I do not go, it will be impossible to get my brethren in Kirtland, any of them, to go; and if we do not go, it is in vain for our eastern brethren to think of going."[1]

Two years earlier, in April 1832, the united order (or united firm) had secured a five-year loan for $15,000, an immense sum at the time, primarily for purchasing goods and property in Missouri.[2] When the Saints were driven out of Jackson County, not only did they suffer staggering financial losses and abject poverty, but the united order also lost its collateral on this loan and its primary means of paying it back. Added to this were other debts incurred by the order on behalf of the Church in Missouri and in Kirtland. The provisioning of Zion's Camp also would require a great outlay of funds, as did continuing construction on the Kirtland Temple. Further, an apostate named Philastus Hurlburt was trying to acquire property owned by the united order by suing Church leaders, and defending themselves in court was causing escalating legal fees. And, as always, the needs of

Kirtland's poor Saints also had to be met. For all of these reasons, the Church in the spring of 1834 was deeply in debt.

At a conference in Avon, New York, on 17 March 1834, Joseph Smith proposed, besides raising volunteers and contributions for Zion's Camp, also raising two thousand dollars to pay the debts of the Church in Kirtland.[3] On 7 April 1834, Joseph wrote in Kirtland, "Bishop Whitney, Elder Frederick G. Williams, Oliver Cowdery, Heber C. Kimball, and myself, met in the council room, and bowed down before the Lord, and prayed that He would furnish the means to deliver the Firm [the united order] from debt, that they might be set at liberty; also, that I might prevail against that wicked man, Hurlburt, and that he might be put to shame."[4] Two days later, Hurlburt lost his lawsuit, was put under bond to keep the peace, and was forced to pay court costs.[5]

The next day, 10 April, a meeting of members of the united order in Kirtland agreed that the order should be dissolved and that each member of the order should have his stewardship allotted to him individually as private property.[6] In this way, creditors who might have had a claim against assets of the order could not collect by seizing property allotted to its individual members. This was not an attempt to avoid paying the debts of the Church (see v. 78), but was done to protect Church property while gaining time to raise additional funds. Even so, actual dissolution of the order was postponed for two weeks, apparently in the hope that funds could be raised in time and dissolution could be avoided. On 23 April 1834, Joseph met in council with members of the order and received from the Lord Doctrine and Covenants 104. The Lord instructed that the order was to be dissolved and reorganized into two separate orders, one in Kirtland and one in Missouri, though members of the order were still to receive individual stewardships. In a separate, unpublished revelation received the same day, members of the order in Kirtland were instructed to forgive each other their personal debts to one another and their debts to the order.[7] All of these developments, together with the Lord's financial instructions contained in Doctrine and Covenants 104, allowed the Prophet Joseph to meet the Church's most challenging financial problems and, thus, to begin preparing for Zion's Camp.

COMMENTARY

1. The order which I commanded. That is, Doctrine and Covenants 78:3–14.

1. An everlasting order. See Doctrine and Covenants 78:4. It was not the united order in its original form that God made everlasting, but the covenants of consecration of those who entered into it. It was this broken commandment and covenant obligation that caused such serious consequences for the transgressors as described in verses 5–9.

4. Some of my servants have not kept the commandment. Remember that at this time the united order consisted of about a dozen members in both Kirtland and Missouri and that the Lord had previously expressed his displeasure with some Saints in both locations (see D&C 95:2–6; 98:19–21; 101:2, 6–8, 50).

4. With feigned words. "Feigned words" are words that misrepresent or conceal one's true intent or meaning. The speaker has a hidden agenda or hidden purpose. In this case, the hidden purpose of the guilty parties is covetousness, or the desire to get personal gain.

5. He shall be cursed in his life. Why should covetousness, or the desire for personal gain, be so seriously punished by the Lord in this case? The answer lies in the terms of the covenant made by those who entered the united order. Doctrine and Covenants 78:5–7 specifically requires members of the order to be *equal* in earthly things that they might be equal in heavenly things and to be equal temporally if they hope for a place in the celestial world. The desire by members of the order to benefit personally and get unshared gains *breaks this most solemn covenant.*

6. I, the Lord, am not to be mocked. All agreements with God are strictly voluntary. He forces no one to heaven. One of the most basic principles of eternity is the law of agency. Nevertheless, once we choose to enter a covenant with God of our own free will, he will keep his word—and he expects us to keep ours. Those who know God's commandments, have made covenants with him, and then of their own accord choose to break those covenants face consequences far more stringent than those who have sinned without the knowledge of God's law or without having made covenants with the Lord (that is, without the ordinances of baptism and the temple).

7. That the innocent among you may not be condemned. This refers in part to the reorganization of the order into personal stewardships of private property as commanded in verses 11–13. By making each member accountable for his own stewardship, the common property of the order could not be liable to seizure through the actions of any single member. It is possible that the unsuccessful lawsuit of Philastus Hurlburt illustrated the hazards of collective ownership and therefore of collective legal liability. Further, individual accountability over stewardships within the Church makes financial mismanagement easier to detect and assess than does collective accountability.

9. Ye cannot escape the buffetings of Satan. See Commentary on Doctrine and Covenants 78:12. To be "cut off," of course, is to be excommunicated and therefore to be denied the shield of the gospel covenant, the Atonement, and the priesthood—to be turned over to the hideous abuse of Satan and his minions between that day and the day of redemption.[8]

11. Appoint unto every man his stewardship. The corporate holdings of the order were to be divided up into individual parcels of private property. In most cases, these allotments reflected the informal division of property already in existence between the brethren at the time this revelation was received. Until 1981 public versions of Doctrine and Covenants 104 contained coded names in place of (or along with) the names of the stewards and the properties listed here. This was originally necessary to protect these individuals from enemies seeking to attach their assets by lawsuits.

12–13. The importance of Doctrine and Covenants 104 goes far beyond the division of property in Kirtland, Ohio, in 1834. Here the Lord elaborates upon the principles of individual stewardship and accountability in the Church and kingdom of God already laid down in the law of the Church (see D&C 42:59).[9] Every man and woman in the kingdom is a steward to whom the Master has given talents many or few, as it has pleased him, and each of us will be required—individually—to account to the Master for our use of that stewardship.

15. All things are mine. Even the very air we breathe belongs to God (see Mosiah 4:19–29). God is the Creator, and therefore the owner, of the physical universe and all it contains. In reality we own nothing, not even our time, our talents, or even our lives. This fact is foundational to the laws of consecration and stewardship.

15. It is my purpose to provide for my saints. Note that one of the purposes of creation—to provide for the Saints of God—is entirely consistent with the work and glory of God—"to bring to pass the immortality and eternal life of man" (Moses 1:39).

16. The poor shall be exalted. See Commentary on Doctrine and Covenants 42:30–34, 39. The primary meaning of "exalted" here is economic. The poor will be lifted up out of their poverty by drawing the rich back down to the middle class. In a Zion society, everyone will be middle class, economically speaking (that is, there will be no rich or poor among them; 4 Nephi 1:3; Moses 7:18).

17. The earth is full. Compare verses 11–27; Psalm 104:24. The earth brings forth sufficient abundance to feed all the creatures that live upon it. Even today, if the resources of the earth were stewarded in righteousness, there would be enough of everything to last until the Savior comes. All shortages are greed-based, artificial, man-made, or otherwise part of the Babylon system of world economics.

17. To be agents unto themselves. To human beings alone is given the ability, with informed disregard of the consequences to others, to take more than their allotted share of the earth's bounty. Before there could be enough for all, there would have to be an end to the excesses of Babylon—sin, crime, war, greed, and unconsecrated wealth.

18. If any man shall take . . . and impart not. This is the Babylon choice: to take and keep what does not belong to you—the abundance of the earth—and thus deny it to others, who depend upon it for their living—and thus for their lives.

18. According to the law of my gospel. The law of the gospel in its most basic form is the new commandment given by the Savior to his disciples anciently (see John 13:34–35; 15:12–13, 17) and repeated to his modern disciples (see D&C 88:123; see also 42:45; 59:6; Moses 7:33), that we love one another. This love inspires obedience (see John 14:15, 21) and selflessness, which is the opposite of covetousness. Thus, when we obey the law of the gospel, we "cease to be covetous" and impart "as the gospel requires" (D&C 88:123; compare 3 Nephi 27:19; Acts 4:34–35). James, the brother of Jesus, called this "the royal law" (James 2:8). Observing it brings obedience to the other commandments (compare Romans 13:8–10).

18. Lift up his eyes in hell. The allusion is to the parable of the rich man and Lazarus found in Luke 16:19–31, especially v. 23. Those who insist on taking and keeping more than their portion of the earth's bounty in this life will suffer the pains of hell in the life to come, like the rich man in Jesus' parable.[10]

19–46. Concerning the properties of the order. This section of the revelation is devoted to dividing the Kirtland holdings of the united order into individual parcels of private property. Though these will still be managed as stewardships for the Lord, they will legally be recognized as private property. This arrangement gave the Church holdings at that time more legal protection and provided for more individual accountability on the part of stewards.

20. The place where he now resides. The descriptions in the revelation were not meant to be legally precise, nor did they need to be. In most cases, it will be seen that the individuals named were already living on the premises described. The only thing that changed was the legal ownership—from the order to the individuals.

47–50. No longer be bound . . . to your brethren of Zion. Until this time, the united order, or united firm, both in Kirtland and Missouri, had been a single common entity. The Lord here directs the united order in Kirtland to be separated from the united order in Missouri.

51. For your salvation. It is likely the salvation meant here is primarily the financial salvation of the Church. One reason the separation of the orders was necessary was so that the debts incurred by the Missouri order and losses suffered through subsequent persecution would not bankrupt the entire Church. The Lord intended the Saints to pay all their debts (see v. 78), and this legal separation gave the Kirtland leadership additional time in which to raise the necessary funds (see vv. 84–85).

51. And that which is to come. The Missouri persecutions were not over in April 1834, nor would they be for years to come. Moreover, there would also come a time, in 1838–39, when the Saints in Kirtland would seek their own refuge in Missouri.[11]

52. By covetousness and feigned words. The Lord repeats the substance of verse 4 but in a context that points more directly at the Missouri members as the original transgressors of the order.

53. By loan. The Kirtland order could make future loans to its sister order in Missouri if conditions warranted.

55. All these properties are mine. The Lord reminds the brethren that regardless of who holds *legal* title to the properties described in this revelation, they are all, in fact, both by right of creation and by covenant obligation—*his*. For a steward to accept legal title out of the Church's necessity but then take personal control and ownership away from the Church would be hypocrisy at least and breaking of the covenant at worst.

58. To print my words, the fulness of my scriptures. In the strictest sense, "the fulness of my scriptures" refers to Joseph Smith's translation of the Bible. Grammatically, however, the entire verse may also be understood to include all of God's revelations both past and future, as God's words and as the fulness of his scriptures. Moreover, the copy of Doctrine and Covenants 104 found in the Kirtland Revelation Book and dated 18 August 1834 contains some extra lines at this point, directing the brethren to secure copyrights for the Book of Mormon, "the articles and covenants," "all my commandments," "and *also* the copyright of the New translation of the Scriptures."[12] This would seem to support identifying the Joseph Smith Translation as *part* of "my words, the fulness of my scriptures" along with the other revelations specified in the Kirtland Revelation Book.

60–66. A treasury. The Lord now directs the first of two treasuries, to be called the "sacred treasury" (v. 66), to be established exclusively for the sacred work of publishing the scriptures. Even the profits, or "avails" (v. 65), of these funds are to be kept sacred.

67–78. Another treasury. A second treasury is to be established for all other Church purposes. This general treasury will receive all Church revenues besides those derived from the sale of scriptures. Even though the property of the order is now legally private property, the Lord still expects it to be managed for the benefit of the Church, and any profit generated is to be placed into the general treasury. It is not to be considered personal income (see v. 70). On the other hand, disbursements for the improvement of these properties and for other Church purposes may be made from this general treasury (see v. 73).

78. Pay all your debts. Again, it must be emphasized that the purpose of these reorganizations was *never* to avoid paying their debts or the debts of the Church but to allow Church leaders the additional time necessary to raise the needed funds and avoid bankruptcy.

81. Write speedily to New York. The Church's unsecured loans were held by New York banks. Here the Lord promises, if Joseph is diligent and humble, to soften the hearts of the lenders to allow him to renegotiate the loans.

83–84. This once . . . a chance to loan money. In other words, this one time, the Lord will permit Joseph to *borrow* additional funds to renegotiate the debt of the Church.

85–86. And pledge the properties. Not only will the Lord allow Joseph to borrow money for the needs of the Church, but he will allow the Prophet to put up the properties of the Church, including even the Kirtland Temple, as collateral on the loans. Eventually, as much as $14,000 had to be borrowed to complete construction of the Kirtland Temple.[13]

1. Smith, *History of the Church,* 2:48.
2. See Cannon and Cook, *Far West Record,* 48.
3. See Smith, *History of the Church,* 2:44.
4. Smith, *History of the Church,* 2:47–48.
5. See Smith, *History of the Church,* 2:49.
6. See Smith, *History of the Church,* 2:49.
7. See Frederick G. Williams Papers, as cited in Cook, *Revelations of the Prophet Joseph Smith,* 211.
8. See Lee, *Teachings of Harold B. Lee,* 58.
9. See Commentary on D&C 42:30–42.
10. See Commentary on D&C 76:84–85.
11. See Anderson, *Joseph Smith's Kirtland,* 235–41.
12. Kirtland Revelation Book, 105; emphasis added; see also Woodford, "Historical Development," 2:1351–53, 1366.
13. See Anderson, *Joseph Smith's Kirtland,* 164.

105

BACKGROUND

By the spring of 1834, the first high council of the Church had been organized (see D&C 102), the united order of the Church had been dissolved and had been reorganized as the united order in Kirtland, and the financial affairs of the Church had been temporarily stabilized (see D&C 104). These measures made it possible for the Prophet Joseph Smith to turn his entire attention to the problems of the dispossessed Saints in Missouri.

Several reports had reached Joseph that Missouri governor Daniel Dunklin was willing to arm the Saints and return them to their lands under military escort, if the Saints could somehow provide sufficient forces to retain their lands after the troops were gone. Thus, since February, volunteers and donations had been solicited from Kirtland and the eastern churches for the purpose of providing an armed force, with the aid and consent of the governor, to install and maintain the Missouri Saints on their former properties.[1]

On 1 May 1834, an advance party of the expedition known as Zion's Camp left Kirtland. They were followed four days later by the main body of eighty-five volunteers led by the Prophet Joseph Smith. Another group of about twenty Saints, gathered between Michigan and Missouri by Hyrum Smith, met Joseph and the main column by the Salt River in Missouri early in June. By that time, Zion's Camp numbered approximately 207 men, 11 women, and 11 children, additional members having been gathered from branches and settlements along the way.[2]

On their overland march of nine hundred miles or more from Kirtland to western Missouri, Zion's Camp suffered from some internal grumbling and dissension. In consequence, Joseph prophesied in early June that the Lord would scourge the camp.[3] It was no surprise, then, to Heber C. Kimball and others when, on June 24, at the end of their march, on Rush Creek east of Liberty in Clay County, Missouri, cholera struck the camp, eventually sickening sixty-eight persons and killing thirteen.[4] Perhaps an even greater blow to the faith of some in Zion's Camp had occurred on 15 June when Orson Hyde and Parley P. Pratt returned from Governor Dunklin in Jefferson City, where they had been sent by Joseph Smith "to ascertain if he was ready to fulfill the proposition which he had previously made to the brethren to reinstate them on their lands in Jackson county, and leave them there to defend themselves."[5] In short, the governor was no longer ready to do so. While he freely admitted that the rights of the Saints were being violated, Governor Dunklin declared that the use of force to secure those rights was impractical, and he feared it would lead to civil war. On 22 June 1834, while still at Fishing River, east of Liberty, Missouri, Joseph Smith received Doctrine and Covenants 105. This revelation explained the reasons behind the successes and failures of Zion's Camp and gave directions to the Prophet for the future of Zion.[6]

Because it had never been Joseph's intention to go to war contrary to the laws of the state and of the nation, the governor's change of policy effectively changed the mission of Zion's Camp. Joseph used the donated funds and supplies to aid the Missouri Saints in Clay County. He reorganized the leadership of the Missouri Saints and disbanded the volunteers of Zion's Camp. Many of them chose to stay in Missouri, but most of them returned to their homes in Ohio and the East.

COMMENTARY

1. Mine afflicted people. The Missouri Saints.

2. The transgressions of my people. This should not be limited to the Missouri Saints alone. The Lord had originally requested five hundred volunteers from Kirtland and the East, and Joseph had set out originally with barely one hundred. There had been complaining and contentions among members of Zion's Camp along the way, leading eventually to the scourge of cholera as punishment. Both the Missouri and the Kirtland churches had been warned in previous revelations about their sins (see D&C 95:2–6; 98:19–21; 101:2, 6–8, 50).

2. Speaking concerning the church and not individuals. Every individual will be held accountable for his or her own sins, which is fair. However, the Church collectively makes progress or is retarded in its progress according to the *collective* faithfulness of its members, and the transgressions of some members can bring down afflictions upon the whole Church as the Church seeks its collective goals.

3. And do not impart of their substance. The primary transgression which has prevented the Saints from redeeming Zion is their failure to live the celestial law of consecration by giving of their substance for the benefit of the poor among them.[7] Because this is a basic requirement for establishing Zion, the Missouri properties cannot be "redeemed" (v. 2) on any other principles.

4. And are not united. Compare Doctrine and Covenants 38:27: "And if ye are not one ye are not mine."

6. My people must needs be chastened. See Commentary on Doctrine and Covenants 95:1–2; 101:2–8.

7. The first elders. Joseph Smith and Oliver Cowdery are not among the transgressors (see D&C 20:2).

8. Churches abroad. This is the usual designation for congregations outside of Kirtland, Ohio.

8. Where is their God? The Lord addresses the skepticism of those Latter-day Saints who are waiting to see whether or not God will redeem Zion *before* they will commit their money to Zion's

Camp or to the larger interests of establishing Zion at all. This, of course, is backwards. While it might make good sense in the logic of Babylon, in the Lord's economy the blessings only come *after* the trial of one's faith or after much tribulation (see D&C 58:4).

10. That my people may be taught more perfectly. The Lord was ready for the redemption of Zion, but the Church was inadequately prepared.

11–13. Until mine elders are endowed with power. Besides their collective unfaithfulness, the greatest difficulty facing the elders in redeeming Zion was their lack of knowledge of the type of power to be received in the house of the Lord. The Kirtland Temple would be dedicated in March 1836, at which time some of the ordinances of the temple would be available to these elders and Church leaders. Thus, the "little season" (v. 13) was originally a two-year period during which the elders would wait for certain ordinances in the Kirtland Temple before Zion could be redeemed.[8] However, further transgressions caused that little season to be extended until "after many days," when the Lord will accomplish all things pertaining to Zion (v. 37).

14. I will fight your battles. The Lord had promised the Saints ten months earlier in Doctrine and Covenants 98:37 that he would fight their battles. Most of Zion's Camp were grateful that the Lord had accepted their offering, but a few, caught up in the spirit of war and bloodshed, were disappointed, and some even apostatized when the Camp was disbanded without fighting.[9]

15. The destroyer I have sent forth. The Lord had already set in motion the historical events that would lead to the destructions prophesied upon his enemies. There would still be a process of "many years" during which the Saints would seek out and exhaust in vain all the legal remedies of the nation (see D&C 101:85–89; see also the Background to D&C 87). Nevertheless, the eventual outcome of the struggle is sure when the Lord fights one's battles.

16. I have commanded my servant Joseph Smith, Jun. The reference is to Doctrine and Covenants 101:55–57.

17. Have not hearkened unto my words. Taken all together, the Church had not obeyed sufficiently to redeem Zion at that time. When the Lord requested five hundred men, he eventually got two hundred, but only one hundred and five set out from Kirtland in early May. Many in the Church were waiting to see how Zion's Camp turned out before contributing their money (see v. 8), and even if the governor had supported the Saints in returning to Jackson County, the Lord would not allow Zion to be redeemed until the Saints learned to impart of their substance to the poor and afflicted among them (see vv. 3, 5).

18–19. There are those who have hearkened. Nevertheless, there were a sufficient number of faithful Saints for the Lord to accept their offering as part for the whole. Zion might not be redeemed at this time, but the endowment of power from on high might still be given—if they continued faithful. These faithful Saints, like the patriarchs of old, had been tested with a trial of their faith. Among the blessings that followed the suffering of Zion's Camp were the preparatory ordinances of the Kirtland Temple. Also, nine of the original Quorum of the Twelve and all of the First Quorum of the Seventy would be called from those who volunteered for Zion's Camp. A further blessing that is sometimes overlooked is that the elders were not required to fight any battles or to shed blood.

20. A commandment . . . let them stay. It should perhaps be noted that even though the Kirtland Temple was yet to be finished and the Church would yet receive important ordinances there, the geographical center of the Church had clearly shifted to the west.

23. And reveal not the things which I have revealed unto them. The Church in Jackson County had made some rather foolish public relations errors which contributed to their being driven out of that place. Here the Lord counsels the Saints in Clay

County and elsewhere in Missouri to be more wise in what they say to the "old settlers" about the future of Zion.

24. Talk not of judgments. The Saints should practice good public relations and avoid arousing negative feelings among the people of the region. Certainly, few things would be more frightening to the old settlers than talk of "judgments" or "mighty works" misinterpreted as threats from the Saints aimed at the non–Latter-day Saint population of Missouri. Here the Lord instructs his Saints to be nonthreatening—even unintentionally—in their conversation and behavior toward those not of their faith.

25–28. I will give unto you favor and grace in their eyes. If the Saints will only be wise and prudent in their public relations, the Lord will bless them with peace and safety. This policy will also allow Joseph and the Church time to prosper and accomplish the purposes of Zion by peaceful means, while at the same time collecting the strength to provide security for the Church in the exercise of its rights. The army of Israel is not for conquest, for the Lord fights Israel's battles (see D&C 98:37; 105:14); the army is only for security in the exercise of Israel's rights (see v. 30).

29. These lands should be purchased. Even after the Saints had been driven from Jackson County by mobs, and even after Zion's Camp had marched to Clay County under arms, the Lord still insists that the only way property shall be acquired for Zion is by legal purchase. This restates his instructions to the Saints first delivered in July 1831 in Doctrine and Covenants 57:4 and often repeated (see, for example, D&C 58:37, 49–52; 63:27–30; 101:70–71).

29. The laws of consecration. See Commentary on verses 3–5 and on Doctrine and Covenants 104:18.

30–32. These verses express long-term, millennial goals of the Church and kingdom of God upon the earth.

33. Should receive their endowment. See Commentary on verse 11; Doctrine and Covenants 38:32; Background to Doctrine and Covenants 110.

35. A day of calling . . . a day of choosing. See Commentary on Doctrine and Covenants 121:34.

36. It shall be manifest unto my servant. On 23 June 1834, the day after Doctrine and Covenants 105 was received, Joseph Smith assembled a council of Missouri high priests and selected fifteen to travel to Kirtland to receive ordinances when the temple was completed there. They were Edward Partridge, William W. Phelps, Isaac Morley, John Corrill, John Whitmer, David Whitmer, A. Sidney Gilbert, Peter Whitmer Jr., Simeon Carter, Newel Knight, Parley P. Pratt, Christian Whitmer, Solomon Hancock, Thomas B. Marsh, and Lyman Wight.[10]

37. After many days. Even when faithful Saints have been endowed with power from on high, the Lord reveals that it will still be after many days that all things pertaining to Zion will be accomplished.

39–40. Lift up an ensign of peace. See Commentary on Doctrine and Covenants 45:9. Note the irony in closing this revelation to Zion's Camp, a force that left Kirtland armed for war, with a four-fold commandment from God to seek and proclaim peace.

1. See Background to D&C 103.
2. Backman, *Heavens Resound*, 185.
3. See Smith, *History of the Church*, 2:80, 114–20.
4. Backman, *Heavens Resound*, 187–88.
5. Smith, *History of the Church*, 2:88–89.
6. Smith, *History of the Church*, 2:108–11.
7. See Commentary on D&C 42:30–45; 104:18.
8. Smith, *History of the Church*, 2:145.
9. See Backman, *Heavens Resound*, 192–94.
10. Smith, *History of the Church*, 2:112–13.

DOCTRINE AND COVENANTS

SOURCES

⌒

Alexander of Aphrodisias. *Quaestiones*. Translated by R. W. Sharples. 2 vols. Ithaca, N.Y.: Cornell University Press, 1992–94.

Anderson, Karl Ricks. *Joseph Smith's Kirtland: Eyewitness Accounts*. Salt Lake City: Deseret Book, 1989.

Backman, Milton V., Jr. *The Heavens Resound: A History of the Latter-day Saints in Ohio, 1830–1838*. Salt Lake City: Deseret Book, 1983.

Backman, Milton V., Jr., and Richard O. Cowan. *Joseph Smith and the Doctrine and Covenants*. Salt Lake City: Deseret Book, 1983.

Bauer, Walter, William F. Arndt, and F. Wilbur Gingrich. *A Greek-English Lexicon of the New Testament and Other Early Christian Literature*. 2d ed., rev. and augmented by F. Wilbur Gingrich and Frederick W. Danker from Walter Bauer's 5th ed., 1958. Chicago: University of Chicago Press, 1979.

Benson, Ezra Taft. "Prepare Yourselves for the Great Day of the Lord." *Brigham Young University 1981 Fireside and Devotional Speeches*. Provo, Utah: Brigham Young University, 1981, 64–69.

———. *The Teachings of Ezra Taft Benson*. Salt Lake City: Bookcraft, 1988.

Black, Susan Easton. *Who's Who in the Doctrine and Covenants*. Salt Lake City: Bookcraft, 1997.

Cannon, Donald Q., and Lyndon W. Cook, eds. *Far West Record: Minutes of The Church of Jesus Christ of Latter-day Saints, 1830–1844*. Salt Lake City: Deseret Book, 1983.

Church News. A weekly supplement to the Deseret News. Salt Lake City, 1931–.

Clark, James R., comp. *Messages of the First Presidency of The Church of Jesus Christ of Latter-day Saints.* 6 vols. Salt Lake City: Bookcraft, 1965–75.

Collier, Fred C., and William S. Harwell, eds. *Kirtland Council Minute Book.* Salt Lake City: Collier's, 1996.

Conference Report of The Church of Jesus Christ of Latter-day Saints. Salt Lake City: The Church of Jesus Christ of Latter-day Saints, 1900–.

Cook, Lyndon W. *Joseph Smith and the Law of Consecration.* Provo, Utah: Grandin Book, 1985.

———. *The Revelations of the Prophet Joseph Smith: A Historical and Biographical Commentary of the Doctrine and Covenants.* Provo, Utah: Seventy's Mission Bookstore, 1981.

Dahl, Larry E., and Donald Q. Cannon, eds. *Encyclopedia of Joseph Smith's Teachings.* Salt Lake City: Deseret Book, 2000.

Dahl, Larry E., and Charles D. Tate, Jr., eds. *The Lectures on Faith in Historical Perspective.* Provo, Utah: Brigham Young University Religious Studies Center, 1990.

Deseret News. Salt Lake City, The Church of Jesus Christ of Latter-day Saints, 1850–88.

The Doctrine and Covenants Student Manual. Church Educational System Religion 324–325 student manual, 1981.

Ehat, Andrew F., and Lyndon W. Cook, comps. *The Words of Joseph Smith: The Contemporary Accounts of the Nauvoo Discourses of the Prophet Joseph.* Provo, Utah: Brigham Young University Religious Studies Center, 1980.

The Evening and the Morning Star. Independence, Mo.: W. W. Phelps & Co., June 1830–July 1833.

Dodds, E. R. *The Greeks and the Irrational.* Berkeley: University of California Press, 1951.

Ensign. Salt Lake City: The Church of Jesus Christ of Latter-day Saints, 1971–.

First Presidency and Council of the Twelve Apostles. "The Family: A Proclamation to the World." *Ensign,* November 1995, 102.

General Handbook of Instructions: Instructions to Presidents of Stakes, Bishops and Clerks. Salt Lake City: The Church of Jesus Christ of Latter-day Saints, 2001.

Ginzberg, Louis. *The Legends of the Jews.* 7 vols. Translated from the German manuscript by Henrietta Szold. Philadelphia: Jewish Publication Society, 1909–1938.

Grey, Matthew J. "Joseph Smith and the Civil War: Prophecies of America's War by an American Prophet." In *Selections from BYU Religious Education 2nd Student Symposium.* Provo, Utah: Brigham Young University Religious Education Student Symposium, 2000, 1–22, esp. 12–13.

Hinckley, Gordon B. *Teachings of Gordon B. Hinckley.* Salt Lake City: Deseret Book, 1997.

Howard, Robert P. *Illinois: A History of the Prairie State.* Grand Rapids, Mich.: Eerdmans, 1972.

Improvement Era. Salt Lake City: Young Men's and Young Women's Mutual Improvement Associations, 1897–1970.

Jenson, Andrew. *Latter-day Saint Biographical Encyclopedia: A Compilation of Biographical Sketches of Prominent Men and Women in The Church of Jesus Christ of Latter-day Saints.* 4 vols. 1901–36. Reprint, Salt Lake City: Western Epics, 1971.

Jessee, Dean C., ed. *The Papers of Joseph Smith.* 2 vols. Salt Lake City: Deseret Book, 1989–92.

———. *The Personal Writings of Joseph Smith.* Salt Lake City: Deseret Book, 2002.

Johnson, Clark V., ed. *Mormon Redress Petitions: Documents of the 1833–1838 Missouri Conflict.* Provo, Utah: Brigham Young University Religious Studies Center, 1992.

Johnson, Joel H. *A Voice from the Mountains: Life and Works of Joel Hills Johnson.* Mesa, Ariz.: Lofgreen's, 1982.

Journal of Discourses. 26 vols. London: Latter-day Saints' Book Depot, 1854–86.

Kirtland Revelation Book [ca. 1831–34]. Transcribed by Barbara J. Faulring, 1981. LDS Church Archives, Salt Lake City, Utah.

Lee, Harold B. *Teachings of Harold B. Lee.* Edited by Clyde J. Williams. Salt Lake City: Bookcraft, 1996.

Ludlow, Daniel H., ed. *Encyclopedia of Mormonism.* 5 vols. New York: Macmillan, 1992.

SOURCES

Madsen, Truman G. "The Meaning of Christ—The Truth, the Way, the Life: An Analysis of B.H. Roberts' Unpublished Masterwork." *Brigham Young University Studies* 15 (Spring 1975): 259–92.

Matthews, Robert J. *"Plainer Translation": Joseph Smith's Translation of the Bible, a History and Commentary.* Provo, Utah: Brigham Young University Press, 1975.

McConkie, Bruce R. *Doctrinal New Testament Commentary.* 3 vols. Salt Lake City: Bookcraft, 1965–73.

———. *The Millennial Messiah: The Second Coming of the Son of Man.* Salt Lake City: Deseret Book, 1982.

———. *Mormon Doctrine.* 2d ed. Salt Lake City: Bookcraft, 1979.

Millennial Star. Liverpool, England, 1840–1970.

Millet, Robert L., and Kent P. Jackson, eds. *Studies in Scripture.* 8 vols. Salt Lake City: Deseret Book, 1984–89.

"A Mormon Prophecy." *Philadelphia Sunday Mercury.* 5 May 1861. LDS Church History Library broadside, Salt Lake City, Utah.

Murdock, John. Journal [ca. 1830–1859]. LDS Church Archives, Salt Lake City, Utah.

Murdock, S. Reed. *John Murdock: His Life and His Legacy.* Layton, Utah: Summerwood Publishers, 2000.

Nibley, Preston, ed. *History of Joseph Smith By His Mother, Lucy Mack Smith.* Salt Lake City: Bookcraft, 1958.

Painesville Telegraph. Painesville, Ohio: Charles B. Smythe and J. Hanna, 1828–46.

Parkin, Max. "Latter-day Saint Conflict in Clay County." In *Missouri,* a volume in *Regional Studies in Latter-day Saint Church History* series. Edited by Arnold K. Garr and Clark V. Johnson. Provo, Utah: Brigham Young University Department of Church History and Doctrine, 1994.

Peterson, Paul H. *"An Historical Analysis of the Word of Wisdom."* M.A. thesis, Brigham Young University, 1972.

Pratt, Parley P. *Autobiography of Parley P. Pratt.* Edited by Parley P. Pratt Jr. Classics in Mormon Literature series. Salt Lake City: Deseret Book, 1985.

Price, Lynn F. *Every Person in the Doctrine and Covenants.* Bountiful, Utah: Horizon, 1997.

The Priesthood Bulletin. Salt Lake City: The Church of Jesus Christ of Latter-day Saints, 1965–74.

Proctor, Scot Facer, and Maurine Jensen Proctor, eds. *Revised and Enhanced History of Joseph Smith by His Mother.* Salt Lake City: Bookcraft, 1996.

Roberts, B. H. *A Comprehensive History of The Church of Jesus Christ of Latter-day Saints. Century One.* 6 vols. Salt Lake City: The Church of Jesus Christ of Latter-day Saints, 1930.

———. *New Witnesses for God.* 3 vols. Salt Lake City: Deseret News, 1911–51.

Robinson, Stephen E. "The Apocryphal Story of Melchizedek." In *Journal for the Study of Judaism in the Persian, Hellenistic, and Roman Period* 18 (1987): 26–39.

———. *Are Mormons Christians?* Salt Lake City: Bookcraft, 1991.

———. *Following Christ: The Parable of the Divers and More Good News.* Salt Lake City: Deseret Book, 1995.

Robison, Elwin C. *The First Mormon Temple: Design, Construction and Historic Context of the Kirtland Temple.* Provo, Utah: Brigham Young University Press and BYU Studies, 1997.

Rubenstein, Richard L. *The Cunning of History: The Holocaust and the American Future.* Reprint, New York: Perennial, 2001.

Shipps, Jan, and John W. Welch, eds. *The Journals of William E. McLellin, 1831–1836.* Urbana, Ill.: University of Illinois Press in cooperation with BYU Studies, 1994.

Smith, Hyrum M., and Janne M. Sjodahl. *The Doctrine and Covenants Commentary.* Salt Lake City: Deseret Book, 1951.

Smith, Joseph. *History of The Church of Jesus Christ of Latter-day Saints.* Edited by B. H. Roberts. 2d ed. rev. 7 vols. Salt Lake City: The Church of Jesus Christ of Latter-day Saints, 1932–51.

———. Letter to "Beloved Brethren." 6 Aug 1833. Joseph Smith Collection, LDS Church Archives, Salt Lake City, Utah.

———. *Teachings of the Prophet Joseph Smith.* Selected by Joseph Fielding Smith. Salt Lake City: Deseret Book, 1976.

Smith, Joseph Fielding. *Answers to Gospel Questions.* Compiled by Joseph Fielding Smith Jr. 5 vols. Salt Lake City: Deseret Book, 1957–66.

————. *Church History and Modern Revelation.* 2 vols. Salt Lake City: Deseret Book in association with The Council of the Twelve Apostles of The Church of Jesus Christ of Latter-day Saints, 1953.

————. *Doctrines of Salvation.* 3 vols. Compiled by Bruce R. McConkie. Salt Lake City: Bookcraft, 1954–56.

Smith, L. M. *Biographical Sketches of Joseph Smith and His Progenitors for Many Generations.* 1853. Reprint. Provo, Utah: Grandin Books, 1995.

Snow, Lorenzo. *The Teachings of Lorenzo Snow.* Edited by Clyde J. Williams. Salt Lake City: Bookcraft, 1996.

Sperry, Sidney B. *Doctrine and Covenants Compendium.* Salt Lake City: Bookcraft, 1960.

Talmage, James E. *Articles of Faith.* 12th ed. Salt Lake City: The Church of Jesus Christ of Latter-day Saints, 1924.

Taylor, John. *The Mediation and Atonement.* 1882. Reprint, Salt Lake City: Deseret News, 1975.

Times and Seasons. Nauvoo, Ill.: Taylor and Woodruff, 1839–46. Reprint. 6 vols. Independence, Mo.: Independence Press, 1986.

Van Wagoner, Richard S. *Sidney Rigdon: A Portrait of Religious Excess.* Salt Lake City: Signature Books, 1994.

Webb, W. L. *Battles and Biographies of Missourians; or, The Civil War Period of Our State.* Kansas City, Mo.: Hudson-Kimberly Publishing, 1900.

Webster, Noah. *American Dictionary of the English Language.* 1828. Reprint, San Francisco: Foundation for American Christian Education, 1980.

Whitmer, John. *An Early Latter Day Saint History: The Book of John Whitmer, Kept by Commandment.* Edited by F. Mark McKiernan and Roger D. Launius. Independence, Mo.: Herald Publishing House, 1980.

Widtsoe, John A. *Evidences and Reconciliations.* 3 vols. in 1. Arranged by G. Homer Durham. Salt Lake City: Bookcraft, 1960.

————. *Joseph Smith: Seeker After Truth, Prophet of God.* Salt Lake City: Bookcraft, 1951.

Woodford, Robert J. 1974. "The Historical Development of the Doctrine and Covenants." 2 vols. Ph.D. dissertation, Brigham Young University.

Woodward, Robert J. "Jesse Gause, Counselor to the Prophet." *Brigham Young University Studies* 15 (Spring 1975): 362–64.

Woodruff, Wilford. *The Discourses of Wilford Woodruff.* Edited by G. Homer Durham. Salt Lake City: Bookcraft, 1969.

INDEX

---

spiritual laziness, 2:155; of Saints
for refusing whole doctrine of
Christ, 3:51–52; Church under,
of God, 3:52–53; of man, 3:190
Condescension of God, 3:180
Conference, 1:174, 192, 211, 253;
priesthood, 2:44, 117; in
Missouri, 2:160, 161
Confession, 2:157
Confidentiality, 2:32
Confirmation: ordinance of, 1:228;
meetings, 2:74
Confusion, spiritual, 2:36
Consecration, 1:120–21, 262; 2:8;
3:19; celestial law of, 1:264; 2:4,
21–22, 97–98, 352, 354; 3:127,
306; law of, in Ohio and
Missouri, 2:111–12; 3:214, 223;
principles of, 2:112–13, 257,
351; 3:15, 72; failed attempt at,
2:127–29; administering law of,
2:254; law of, in eternity, 2:324;
storehouse kept by, 3:20–21; and
stewardship, 3:265, 299;
everlasting covenants of, 3:297
Consequences: of rejecting the
gospel, 1:19–20; political and
social, 1:212
Conspiracies, rise of, 3:92
Conspiracy, lost manuscript pages
and, 1:72
Constitution of the Restored Church,
1:128
Constitution of the United States,
3:235, 280
Contention, 1:76–77, 107, 217; in
Thompson Branch, 2:129; over
building Zion, 2:152; among
disciples, 2:211–12; over law of
Moses, 2:276–77
Contrition, 1:139
Conversion, 1:123, 233; need for,
1:272; of Gentile nations, 2:41
Converts, Lord to care for, 3:117
Convictions, religious, 1:212–13

Cook, Lyndon W., 2:283
Copley, Leman, 2:90–93, 115;
excommunication of, 2:92;
mission of, to Shakers, 2:92–93;
Saints evicted by, 2:127–28
Copyright, 1:6; infringement of,
1:110–11
Corporations, Church-owned,
2:351–52
Corrill, John, 2:108; selected to
receive ordinances, 3:310
Council: premortal, 1:38; of high
priests, 3:141
Councils: Church disciplinary, 2:31,
213–14; kingdom governed by,
3:4
Counselors, role of, 3:4
Courts, civil, 2:31
Covenant: everlasting, 1:22;
Abrahamic, 1:32; 2:51, 54; gifts
and, 1:81; entering the, 1:119,
137; sacramental, 1:143; of
baptism, 1:155; old, 1:155–56;
2:312; new and everlasting,
1:156, 272; 2:312; 3:36, 45–46;
responsibility for, 1:276; as
contract, 2:305; relationship,
3:45; new, 3:53–54; ark of the,
3:76; immutable, 3:232–33
Covenants: keeping, 1:216; 2:106;
faith to accept, 2:11; meaning of
term, 2:13; promises and
blessings attached to, 2:14, 54;
Church, 2:30; breaking of,
2:205–6, 355; 3:12; obligation
of, 3:10; binding nature of, 3:13;
temple, 3:32; keeping financial,
3:76; of baptism and of the
temple, 3:98; remaining faithful
to, 3:239; everlasting, of
consecration, 3:297
Coveting, 1:120–21
Covetousness, 3:64, 202, 297, 301
Covill, James, 1:269–70, 275–76
Cowan, Horace, 2:363

2:42, 203; of Jesus Christ, gift of, 2:224; death of, 3:128; escaping spiritual, 3:152

Debt, 1:124; 2:217; 3:302

Deceivers, to be cut off from Church, 2:104

Deception, guarding against, 2:75; spiritual, 2:103–4

Decisions, 2:171

Declarations, Official, 1:13

Defense, 3:243; family, 3:241

Deification, 3:32, 44

Deity, sons and daughters of, 1:134

Delaware Indians, 1:192, 220; 2:144

Dependents, rights of, 3:19

Desires, unrighteous, 2:76

Desolation, 1:197; meaning of term, 2:56; of abomination, 3:65

Despair, 2:61

Destroyer, Lord sends forth, 3:307

Destruction, of unrepentant, 1:48

Devil, 1:206; Church of the, 1:107; 3:80; children of the, 1:117; Greek meaning of term, 2:295; forsaking the, 3:194. *See also* Satan

Devils, doctrines of, 2:74–75

Dibble, Philo, on D&C 76, 2:286–87

Disasters: natural, 2:61; 3:62, 64–65, 90; man-made, 3:90

Discernment, spiritual, 1:191; 2:120; gift of, 2:79–80, 81

Disciples of Christ, 1:235

Discipleship, determined by actions, not beliefs, 2:4

Disciplinary council, 3:286–87; right to appeal decision of, 3:287–88

Discipline, Church, 2:31–32

Discord, in last days, 2:59–60

Discussions, missionary, 1:142

Disease, desolation by, 2:59–60

Dishonesty, 2:21; intentional, 2:193

Disobedience, consequences of, 3:108–10

Disputes, settling of, 2:31–32

Dissension: over Church indebtedness, 2:217; among elders at Hiram, Ohio, 2:233

Diversity, 2:5; of gifts of the Spirit, 2:76–77

Divisiveness, 2:324–25

Divorce, 2:30, 96

Doctrine, 2:277–78; interpretation of, 1:x; false, 1:226; of Jesus Christ, 3:54; new, 3:158

Doctrine and Covenants: as capstone of Restoration, 1:1–2; funds for printing, 1:8; as title of revelations, 1:8; contents of, 1:10–11; as missionary tool, 1:12; editions of, 1:12–13; acceptance of, 1:13; chronological order of, 1:36, 69, 81; study of revelations in, 1:83–84; preface to, 2:252; influence of Joseph Smith Translation on, 2:272–73

Doctrines, influence of Joseph Smith Translation on, 2:272

Dogberry, O., 1:110

Doubts, of Hiram Saints, 2:233

Drinks: hot, 3:146; nonalcoholic, 3:150

Drugs: industry in, 1:240; 3:145; harmful, 3:140, 146

Dunklin, Daniel, 3:258, 280, 304; promises assistance to Saints, 289; refuses assistance, 3:305

Dust, casting off, 1:166

Duty, of priesthood holders, 2:273

Dyer, Alvin R., 1:189

Eames, Ruggles, 2:363

Earth, 1:21, 23; wasting of the, 1:32–33; cleansing of, 1:185; 2:42, 301, 358; ripe in iniquity of inhabitants of, 1:198; renewal of, 1:203; celestialized, 1:263; 3:105–6, 272; righteous to

Heart, 1:43, 62–63; hardening of the, 1:73; broken, 1:138–39; 3:221; symbolism of, 1:184; pure in, 2:139–40; 3:225, 227; turning, of children to fathers, 3:240

Heathen nations, 2:282, 314

Heathens, wicked, 2:314

Heaven: hosts of, 1:256; kingdom of, 1:273; 2:224; obtaining powers of, 3:41; unfolding of curtain of, 123–24

Heavens: plural, Joseph Smith asks Lord about, 2:286; governance of, 2:321

Hedrick, Granville, 3:25

Heirs, rightful, 3:82

Hell, 2:315, 319–20; meaning of, 1:78; nature of, 1:111–12; suffering of wicked in, 1:115, 206, 225, 259; 2:26–27; 3:108, 280–81, 300; gates of, 1:151–52; spiritual, 1:198; false beliefs about, 2:287–88; consignment to, 3:57. *See also* Telestial

Herbs, 3:147

High council: revelation on organization of first, 3:283; Prophet organizes, 3:284; purpose of, 3:285; local, 3:287

High Priesthood: Joseph Smith sustained and set apart as president of, 2:279–80; Jesse Gause ordained counselor in Presidency of, 3:1–3

High priests: office of, 1:128; 2:243; first, 2:117–18; millennial duties of, 2:344–45; council of, 3:95–96, 141

Hinckley, Gordon B.: on serving the Lord, 3:115; on Constitution of United States, 3:280

Hiram, Ohio, 2:201, 232, 242

Historian, Church, duties of, 2:254

Historical records, importance of keeping, 2:85

Holiness, 3:32; walking in, 1:151

Holland, American South appeals to, 3:88–89

Holy Ghost: gift of the, 1:24, 47–48, 81–82, 90, 130, 133; 2:105–6; 3:31–32, 39; 3:193; as revelator, 1:62–63; as spirit of prophecy, 1:84; as witness, 1:95; 3:254–55; sinning against the, 1:115–16; 2:17, 77, 211, 297, 319; 3:46; repentance and, 1:119; companionship of, 1:137; whisperings of the, 1:196; confirmation of, 1:228; 2:14–15, 206; inspiration of the, 1:271; 2:74, 244; power of the, 1:272; 2:290, 364; 3:63; missionaries to teach through, 2:12, 119; losing gift of, 2:20–21, 192–93; recognizing promptings of, 2:104–5; as Holy Spirit of Promise, 2:305; 3:98–99; ministrations of, to telestial beings, 2:320–21; exaltation of, 2:321; and transfiguration, 3:33; John the Baptist filled with, 3:38

Holy land, 3:55

Holy Spirit, 3:39, 180; sanctification through, 3:42; of Promise, 3:98–99, 184; bears witness of truth, 3:168; gospel and gifts and power of, 3:249; seeds planted by, 3:253

Homes, as holy places, 2:61

Homosexuality, 2:164

Honesty, of Edward Partridge, 2:6

Hope, 1:43–44, 106

Hopelessness, in last days, 2:59

Hosanna, 1:124

House, Saints at Kirtland commanded to establish a, 3:129

House of Israel: adoption into, 2:219; 3:43; restoration of, 3:24

House of Joseph, 3:159

Hubble, Mrs., 2:34

Humility, 1:87; leadership and, 2:107; of Newel K. Whitney, 2:266

Hurlburt, Philastus, 3:295–96, 298

Husbands, claim on, 3:19

Hyde, Orson, 1:12; 2:242–43; 3:85; missions of, 2:243; letter from, 3:57; records revelation, 2:213; 3:284; sent to Independence, 3:252, 256–57, 258; returns to Kirtland, 3:259; on waste places of Zion, 3:269; letter of Joseph to, 3:295; returns from meeting with Governor Dunklin, 3:305

Hymns, 2:131; selection of, 1:172

Hypocrisy, 1:224–25; 2:73; spiritual, 3:265

Hypocrite, meaning of term, 2:103

Idleness, forbidden, 2:25, 283

Idol, false, 3:66

Idolatry, 1:22; 3:65

Idumea, meaning of term, 1:27

Ignorance: of heathen nations, 2:282; condemnation of Saints for preferring, 3:53; freedom from slavery of, 3:102; sinning in, 3:209

Illness, 2:26

Immaturity, spiritual, 3:37

Immortality, 1:94

Improvement, 3:113

Incorporation of Religious Societies, 1:129

Independence, Missouri, 1:3; 2:129; purchase of land in, 2:198; as center stake of Zion, 2:143, 217; 3:268; temple cornerstone laid in, 2:148; construction of temple in, 3:25, 265

Indian: Removal Bill, 1:191–92; Territory, commerce with, 2:144

Indians, relationship of Church members with, 1:6. *See also* Lamanites

Indignation, cup of, 1:201; 3:255

Influences, negative, 2:105

Inheritance: faithful Saints to obtain, 2:217; 3:122, 261; laws of, 3:20; arranging, by lot, 3:75

Iniquity, 1:241; 3:266; ripe in, 2:56–57

Injury, disputes involving, 2:31–32

Innocence, declaration of, 3:11–12

Innocent blood, 2:18

Inspiration: worthiness to receive, 2:15; seeking, 2:74, 353; false, 2:74–75; true, 2:75; attempt to write revelation without, 2:234–35; speaking with, 2:244–45; regarding Church calling, 2:266

Intellect, faith and, 2:190–91; revelation and, 2:234–35

Intelligence, 3:50; and truth, 3:102; energy as form of, 3:103; premortal existence of, 3:184–85, 188; spiritual quality of, 3:188–89; through gift and grace of God, 3:189; definition of true, 3:194

Intemperance, 1:88

Internet, 3:239

Interpolations, 3:168

Interpretation of tongues, gift of, 2:80

Investigators, 2:73–74

Isaac, 1:32

Isaiah, 3:28; book of, 1:132–33; on riches of Gentiles, 2:24

Islands of the sea, 1:19

Israel: gathering of, 1:42, 60–61, 77, 217, 227, 255; 2:56, 344; 3:81, 281; children of, 1:89, 121; 3:34, 292; member of the house of, 1:122; salvation of, 1:243–44; gospel to be taken to, 2:40; blood of, 2:58; state of, as fulfillment of

2:340; receiving fulness of,
3:191–92, 273
Judah, tribe of, 1:122, 181; 2:51
Judge in Israel, 2:153, 219, 267
Judges, self-appointed, 3:76
Judgment: unbelieving are sealed to,
1:20; eternal, 1:112; day of,
1:114, 117; 2:50; 3:58; after
Second Resurrection, 1:204;
final, 1:297, 259; 2:40; 3:48; of
wicked, 1:272; 2:62; of heathen
nations, 2:65–66; of those who
reject gospel, 2:282; after
probationary state, 2:315–16;
Joseph Fielding Smith on,
3:16–17; scourge and, 3:54–55;
Father has committed all, to the
Son, 3:118; by the Lord, 3:122;
at end of this dispensation, 3:227
Judgments, escaping, 2:200
Just, resurrection of the, 2:291,
303–13; 3:274
Justice: law of, 1:20–21, 114;
3:11–12, 242; demands of,
1:201, 240, 259, 272; satisfied by
Atonement, 2:50; civil, 2:31,
213; of the Lord, 2:140, 151–52;
forgiveness and, 2:214; mercy
and, 3:61, 92; infinite, 3:63;
spiritual principle of, 3:103
Justification, 1:133, 136, 173, 196;
by works, 1:225; by faith, 1:243;
in civil law, 3:235

Kaw Township, Missouri, 2:148;
3:18
Keys: to mysteries of kingdom, 1:1,
242; 2:210; priesthood, 1:25,
30–31, 61, 91, 244, 266; of
sealing power, 1:31, 262;
apostolic, 1:129–30; authority
and, 1:183–84; of kingdom,
2:223; 3:3–4; 158; and
ordinances, 3:116, 205
Killing, of animals, 2:97, 98

Kimball, Heber C., 3:71, 296, 305
Kimball, Spencer W., 1:129; and the
Doctrine and Covenants, 1:1; on
deception, 1:193; on Lamanites,
1:221; on commitment in
marriage, 2:19–20; on parable of
ten virgins, 2:67; on
responsibility to serve missions,
2:245–46; on sin against Holy
Ghost, 2:298; on final judgment
at resurrection, 2:329; on
selfishness, 3:16; on power to
pierce the veil, 3:175–76
Kindliness, 1:229; 3:32
King Herod, 3:40
Kingdom: millennial, 1:42; 3:59–60;
mysteries of the, 2:198, 210,
289; advancement from one to
another, 2:329
Kingdom of God, 1:244, 261;
possession of, 2:210; 3:17; keys
of, 2:223; preservation of, 3:91
Kingdoms: governance of, 2:321;
glory of, 2:322; succession of,
3:37; and laws, 3:110
Kirtland, Ohio: Church to move to,
1:250–51; Sidney Rigdon's sect
in, 2:1–2; erroneous practices in,
2:8; rapid Church growth in,
2:45–46, 86; as temporary
gathering place, 2:141, 216;
persecution in, 2:209; D&C 72
received in, 2:264; consecration
of, 3:14; as city of stake of Zion,
3:198; warning to Saints in,
3:231; sins of Saints in, 3:241
Kirtland Council Minute Book,
3:95–96, 170
Kirtland Revelation Book, 1:98, 220;
parts of D&C 42 recorded in,
2:10; mentions origin of D&C
77, 2:337; records origin of D&C
81, 3:1; and D&C 88, 3:96;
records ordination of First
Presidency, 3:155; records origin

nature of, 3:38; gospel of Jesus Christ renders obsolete the, 3:120

Law of the Church, 2:29; 3:19; compared to law of Moses, 2:16–17; power to implement, 2:46

Law of the land, obedience to, 2:31, 153; 3:20, 234

Laziness, 2:250–51; spiritual, 2:154, 167

Leaders, Church: self-appointed, 1:193; sustaining, 2:39; gift of discernment given to, 2:81, 106–7; as instruments, 2:107; temporal needs of, 2:114–15; instructions for, 2:265

Leadership: prerogative of priesthood, 1:175; false claims of, 2:37; differing styles of, 2:78; members' need for, 2:181, 187–88; financial principles of, 2:268

Learning, leaders of the Church seek, 3:129

Lectures on Faith, 1:10, 12–13; 3:132

Lee, Ann, 2:90–91

Lee, Harold B., 1:127, 129; on Lord reigning in Zion, 1:27; on discerning imposters, 2:13; on priorities, 2:283; on role of counselors, 3:5; on keeping Word of Wisdom, 3:151

Legal system, corruption of, 3:92

Lehi: sons of, 1:91; descendants of, 1:39–40

Liahona, 1:39, 99

Liberties, political, 3:236

Life: waters of, 1:77; eternal, 1:94; 2:43; 3:31; light and, 1:269; God's power over, and death, 2:189; span of, during Millennium, 2:203; sealed up to

eternal, 3:98, 209; staff of, 3:148–50

Light: loss of, 1:26; Christ as, 1:269; 3:50; of the Spirit, 2:105

Light of Christ, 1:271; 2:199–200, 204–5, 237; among heathen nations, 2:66; order imposed by, 2:293, 301; role of, 3:111; sinning against, 3:190, 209

Lineage, 1:159

List, scriptural meaning of term, 2:94

Literary Firm, 1:4–5, 7; 2:256, 269–70, 350; 3:15, 18, 214

Loans, 3:303

Loins, girding up, 1:184

Lord: great and dreadful day of the, 1:32; service to, 1:42–43; tempting, 1:72; words of, 1:96; arrival of, 1:124; listening to voice of, 2:49; power of, to be manifest in Zion, 2:69; word of, is truth, 3:50; face of, revealed, 3:123. *See also* Jesus Christ

Lord's Preface, the, 1:18; 2:252

Lots, casting, 3:286

Love, 1:24–25, 43; 3:103, 300; charity synonymous with, 1:106; falling out of, 2:19; 2:19–20; decline of, in last days, 2:59–60

Loyalty, to spouse, 2:19–20

Lucifer, 2:294

Lund, Anthon H., 3:143

Lust, 2:20

Lying, 2:193

Magic, 2:107, 194

Malachi, 1:3

Man: nature of, 1:134; measure of, 2:96–97; fear of, 2:170; creation of, 2:346; as spirit, 3:190

Manasseh, Ephraim and, 3:159–60

Manifestations, contrary to Church authorities, 1:190

Mansions, heavenly, 2:266

Manuscript, lost pages of, 1:72–73

return of Zion of Enoch at beginning of, 1:258; 2:53; mortal life during, 2:67, 202–3; roles of old and new Jerusalem during, 2:69; births during, 2:96–97; lack of telestial elements during, 2:204; four trumpets to sound in, 2:303; as Sabbath of earth, 2:344; wicked to be in Satan's power for, 3:61; time and, 3:62; wicked redeemed at end of, 3:105; Christ to visit earth during, 3:113; unjust judged at end of, 3:125; no death during, 3:273–74

Mind, 1:43, 62–63; natural, 2:239; premortal existence of, 3:184–85

Minister, self-appointment as, 1:82

Ministry of salvation, 3:159

Miracles, 1:165, 239; power to perform, 2:106; seeking, 2:188; faith followed by, 2:191; working of signs and, 3:56

Missionaries, 2:245; and D&C 1:12; and those who reject gospel, 1:20; 2:61; and D&C 4, 1:42; preparation of, 1:82; and gospel of repentance, 1:97; and gospel basics, 1:120; 2:14; and arguing, 1:123; first full-time, 1:160; support of, 1:164; 2:282; to Lamanites, 1:192, 219–20, 235–36, 245; voice of, 1:196; into every corner of earth, 1:227; and scriptures, 1:228; non-LDS, 1:238; testimony of, 1:241; calling to be, 1:247–48; 3:23–24; power of, 2:106; to travel in pairs, 2:119; characteristics of, 2:120; commanded not to be idle, 2:173; commanded to preach while traveling, 2:176; water travel by, 2:177; responsibility of, 2:181; support of, 3:58; and possessions, 3:63; Lord to care for converts of,

3:117; and obedience to Word of Wisdom, 3:143; seek remnants of house of Joseph, 3:160; instruction of, in temple, 3:224; merciful treatment of, 3:249–50; promise given to, 3:254–55

Missionary: discussions, 1:142; funds, use of, 2:186

Missionary work: basic principles of, 2:12, 93, 363; obstacles to, 2:48; fear of, 2:125, 170; of traveling Saints, 2:279, 281; compared to harvest, 2:280–81; obligation to Saints of, 3:57–58, 118; support of, 3:58

Missions: full-time, 2:245; preparation of brethren to serve foreign, 3:119. See also Missionaries

Missouri: designated as "regions westward," 2:12; Church purchase of land in, 2:143, 159; early missionaries in, 2:169; 3:8; missionaries commended for work in, 2:184–85; conference, 3:8; Saints called to, 3:72; Lord to chasten Saints in, 3:163

Missouri River, W. W. Phelps's vision at, 2:174–75; curse upon, 2:177

Mob: manifesto of, 1:7; destroys printing press, 1:18; 3:217; activities of, 3:230, 252, 293–94

Moderation, 1:70–71, 87; in spiritual matters, 2:104

Moon, as symbol of terrestrial glory, 2:318

Morley, Isaac, 2:201; 3:205; farm of, sold to finance Zion, 2:215; receives Lord's forgiveness, 2:215; selected to receive ordinances, 3:310

Mormon Creed, 1:128

Moroni, 1:29–30, 39, 102, 130; 3:122, 125–16; and keys, 1:181

Mortality: performance during,

Power: of Latter-day Saint
community, 2:46–47;
supernatural, false claims of,
2:19; priesthood, 2:361; 3:56

Pratt, Orson: and revelation
manuscripts, 1:2; chairs
publication committee, 1:13; and
D&C 2, 1:31; and D&C 22,
1:154; baptism of, 1:221;
revelation for, 1:231–34; and gift
of prophecy, 1:234; on wording
of D&C 42, 2:22–23; on Martin
Harris's character, 2:156; on
sustaining and setting Joseph
Smith apart, 2:280; and D&C 85,
3:70–71; and D&C 87, 3:87; on
removal of veil between God and
his people, 3:114; on silence in
heaven, 3:123–24; on John the
Baptist, 3:178

Pratt, Parley P., 1:192, 213, 219;
3:222–23; conversion of, 1:221;
as missionary, 1:223, 231;
mission of, to Shakers, 2:92–93;
on spiritual excesses, 2:101–2;
called as teacher in School of the
Elders, 3:219–20; harvests efforts
of earlier missionaries, 3:253;
meets with Prophet, 3:289;
assigned to raise volunteers for
Zion's Camp, 3:294; returns from
meeting with Governor Dunklin,
3:305; selected to receive temple
ordinances, 3:310

Pray, leaders counseled to, 3:4–5

Prayer, 1:71, 172, 217–18, 222;
2:221; vocal, 1:122, 160;
importance of, 1:229; for further
knowledge, 2:3; for Church
leaders, 2:39; as guard against
deception, 2:75; frequent, 2:206;
for God's kingdom to go forth,
2:224; parental responsibility to
teach, 2:250; private and public,
2:205, 251; alms and, 3:96;

answers to, 3:114; fasting and,
3:118; ancient pattern of Jewish,
3:130; of Manasseh, 3:168;
continual, 3:196; God's seal and
testament on righteous, of Saints,
3:232

Preachers, 1:82–83

Preaching, 1:77–78, 119

Preface, the Lord's, 2:252

Prejudice, against Church, 2:48

Premortal life, 1:206; 3:82, 173,
184–85; choices made during,
2:300–301; existence in, with
God, 3:187

Preparation, 1:265; 2:354; lack of,
2:49; of five wise virgins, 2:67

Preparedness, oil of, 1:229

Presidency, 1:130; keys of the, of the
Church, 1:61; 3:3–4; power of,
in Aaronic Priesthood, 1:90; of
the High Priesthood, 3:156, 170;
Saints instructed to build house
for, 3:201

President, death of, of Church, 3:3

Presiding bishop, 2:152–53, 247;
3:40–41; responsibility of, for
funds, 2:268

Pretenders, spiritual, 2:103–4

Pride, 1:159, 267; 2:32, 308–9; Ezra
Thayre rebuked for, 2:135;
overcoming, 2:323; and
selfishness, 3:108

Priestcraft, 1:76, 202, 226

Priesthood: restoration of, 1:24, 42;
3:82; keys of, 1:25, 30–31, 61,
244; 2:223; duties of, 1:140;
ordination to, 1:140; line of
authority, 1:213; false claims of,
2:13; authority of, 2:35; Satan to
be bound by, 2:42; leaders of, as
instruments, 2:107; quorums,
2:272; eternal nature of, 2:307;
power, 2:343, 361; ordinances,
3:4; and obtaining powers of
heaven, 3:41; and receiving

1:166–67; parable of laborers in, 1:225–26; redemption of the, 3:277–78

Violence, 3:246; to escalate in last days, 2:59

"Vision, the," received as D&C 76, 2:285

Visions, D&C 76 a series of, 2:292

Voice: still, small, 1:265; warning, 1:267

Vote, sustaining, 1:175, 192

W. W. Phelps Printing Company, 1:3, 7

Wakefield, Joseph, 2:107–8

War, 3:300; civil, 3:85–88; first "modern," 3:88; worldwide, 3:88–89; Satan's love for, 3:90; renouncing, 3:239

War in heaven, 2:295

Warning, voice of, 1:19

Wars, 1:264–65; 2:59, 68; 3: 92; killing in, 2:18; of last days, 2:29; D&C 87 and, 3:78

Washing: and anointing, 3:117; ordinance of, the feet, 3:134–35

Wastefulness, 2:98

Wasting of the earth, 1:32–33

Watch-tower, 3:267

Water, 1:143; symbolic meaning of, 2:178

Waters: Satan's power over, 2:176–77; blessed at time of Creation, 2:178; curse upon, in last days, 2:178; Saints not prohibited to travel upon, 2:180

Waters of life, 1:77

Wayne County Sentinel, 1:110

Weaknesses, 1:24–25; human, 2:94; faith to be saved from, 2:304

Wealth, 1:267; 2:139; 3:17; unconsecrated, 3:300

Welfare program, Church, 2:26, 267

"Western countries," Saints to travel to, 2:68

Wheat, 3:150

Wheat and tares, 2:342–43; 3:78–80

Whitmer, Christian, 3:310

Whitmer, David, 1:94, 195, 212; as witness, 1:47, 95, 98–99, 101; revelation to, 1:53; and Oliver Cowdery, 1:56, 93; and organization of Church of Christ, 1:127; selected to receive temple ordinances, 3:310

Whitmer, John:

Callings and missionary labors of: copying of revelations by, 1:2, 5; appointed editor of *Messenger and Advocate,* 1:9; takes copy to Independence, 1:18; as missionary, 1:213; to preside over Church in Kirtland, 1:236; as Church historian, 2:83, 254; to travel to Missouri with Oliver Cowdery, 2:253

Life of: revelation for, 1:96–97, 174; meets with Joseph Smith in Harmony, Pa., 1:178; is present when D&C 29 is received, 1:195; D&C 47 directed to, 2:83; excommunication of, 2:84; instructions given to, 3:71; letter to, 3:75; selected to receive temple ordinances, 3:310

Teachings of: on D&C as scripture, 1:12; on D&C 38, 1:254; on communal practices of Kirtland members, 2:2; on receiving law of the Church, 2:9–10; on false prophetess, 2:34; on effects of D&C 43, 2:35; on date of first general conference, 2:44; on D&C 46, 2:71; on D&C 47, 2:84; on unrighteous Shaker traditions, 2:93

Whitmer, Peter, Jr., 1:94, 96–97, 195; and organization of the

Church of Christ, 1:127; as
missionary, 1:213, 219; as special
witness, 1:222; selected to
receive temple ordinances, 3:310
Whitmer, Peter, Sr., 1:93–94, 153,
187; revelation received at home
of, 1:104, 195; and organization
of Church of Christ, 1:127, 147
Whitney, Elizabeth Ann, 1:171, 193
Whitney, Newel K., 2:124; 3:7, 296;
appointed as agent, 2:159; store
of, 2:201–2; to maintain Kirtland
store, 2:217; called as bishop,
2:266, 213; appointed as agent
for united order, 3:18; breaks leg,
3:22; mission of, 3:64–65;
houses Smiths above store, 3:70;
and School of the Prophets,
3:133; instructed to employ
agent, 3:161; shares resources
with Prophet, 3:162; assigned
control of Church-owned
property, 3:213
Whitney, Orson F., 1:122
Wicked: destruction of the, 1:20–21,
48–49, 197–98, 200; 2:67, 70;
3:92, 273; and day of the Lord,
1:32; suffering of the, 1:114–15,
206, 225, 259; 2:64; vengeance
upon, 1:201; unrepentant, 1:204;
2:314–15; and degree of glory,
1:237; residue of the, 1:259; to
be separated from righteous,
2:204; and telestial glory, 3:109,
125; rule by the, 3:237; Lord's
punishment of the, 3:243; and
cup of iniquity, 3:266; and wrath
of God, 3:291
Wickedness, 1:73; 3:10, 92
Widows: stewardships and, 3:20;
claims of, 3:21
Widtsoe, John A., 3:103, 3:148
Wife, 2:19–20
Wight, Lyman, 1:236; 2:117–18;
3:289; to raise volunteers for

Zion's Camp, 3:294; to receive
temple ordinances, 3:310
Wilderness, Missouri as, 2:142
Will of God, 1:70; 3:233; disobedience to, 2:201; willingness to
obey the, 3:145
Williams, Frederick G., 1:220;
2:134; 3;296; farm of, deeded to
Church, 2:216; 3:2, 161, 205;
called as counselor, 3:1–3, 155,
170; serves as scribe, 3:2;
3:23–24, 78, 247; blessing to,
3:4; copy of letter by Joseph
Smith: 3:70; washes feet of
Joesph Smith, 3:135; rebuked for
neglecting instruction of
children, 3:195; describes vision
of temple, 3:205–6
Wine, 1:178–79; dregs of, 2:151;
prohibition against, and strong
drink, 3:146
Winepress, symbolism of, 2:326–27
Wings, symbolism of, 2:340–41
Wisdom: as gift of Spirit, 2:78–79;
in use of natural resources,
2:167; spiritual blessing of,
3:151; of Solomon, 3:168
Witness, 1:133; spiritual, 1:47;
2:192; receiving a, 1:50; Holy
Ghost as, 1:95; responsibility to
bear, 1:99; of Quorum of the
Twelve, 1:108; for Christ, 1:140;
of sacrament, 1:144
Witnesses: law of, 2:12; 3:243; two,
2:348; special, 3:56
Women, claim of, on husbands, 3:19
Wonders, 1:239
Wood, Reese, Doniphan and
Atchison, 3:259
Woodford, Robert J., 1:128, 188–89
Woodruff, Wilford, 1:1; on value of
D&C 76, 2:288–89; on work of
angels, 2:342; on destruction of
cities, 3:64; on prophecy on war,
3:86